Onto-Cartography

Speculative Realism

Series Editor: Graham Harman

Since its first appearance at a London colloquium in 2007, the Speculative Realism movement has taken continental philosophy by storm. Opposing the formerly ubiquitous modern dogma that philosophy can speak only of the human-world relation rather than the world itself, Speculative Realism defends the autonomy of the world from human access, but in a spirit of imaginative audacity.

Editorial Advisory Board

Jane Bennett
Nathan Brown
Levi Bryant
Patricia Clough
Mark Fisher
Iain Hamilton Grant
Myra Hird
Adrian Johnston
Eileen A. Joy

Books available

Quentin Meillassoux: Philosophy in the Making by Graham Harman
Onto-Cartography: An Ontology of Machines and Media by Levi R. Bryant

Forthcoming series titles

Adventures in Transcendental Materialism: Dialogues with Contemporary Thinkers by Adrian Johnston
Form and Object: A Treatise on Things by Tristan Garcia, translated by Mark Allan Ohm and Jon Cogburn
The End of Phenomenology: Metaphysics and the New Realism by Tom Sparrow
Fields of Sense: A New Realist Ontology by Markus Gabriel
Romantic Realities: Speculative Realism and British Romanticism by Evan Gottlieb
After Quietism: Analytic Philosophies of Immanence and the New Metaphysics by Jon Cogburn

Visit the Speculative Realism website at
www.euppublishing.com/series/specr

Onto-Cartography

An Ontology of Machines and Media

Levi R. Bryant

EDINBURGH
University Press

Edinburgh University Press Ltd
The Tun – Holyrood Road
12 (2f) Jackson's Entry
Edinburgh EH8 8PJ
www.euppublishing.com

Typeset in 11/13 Adobe Sabon by
Servis Filmsetting Ltd, Stockport, Cheshire,
and printed and bound in the United States of America

Reprinted 2014

A CIP record for this book is available from the British Library

ISBN 978 0 7486 7996 6 (hardback)
ISBN 978 0 7486 7997 3 (paperback)
ISBN 978 0 7486 7998 0 (webready PDF)
ISBN 978 0 7486 7999 7 (epub)

Contents

Acknowledgments

Onto-Cartography would not have been possible without the helpful comments and assistance of many other people. During the Fall of 2012, Collin College granted me a sabbatical that allowed me to complete the composition of this work. While developing the concepts and arguments found in what follows, I benefited enormously from the insights of Melanie Doherty, her criticisms, her encouragement, and her comments on various chapters and lines of thought. Without her it is unlikely that this book would have ever been completed. Similarly, Carl Clark engaged in numerous discussions with me as I developed my arguments, graciously listening to my ramblings and offering insights and criticisms as I worked through these ideas. Nathan Gale, Karl Steel, and Joe Hughes provided invaluable insight on issues pertaining to time, agency, and events. Daniel Sacilotto provided me with valuable insights regarding normativity, materialism, and epistemology. In the digital world, Jeremy Trombley, Michael of the brilliant blog *Archive Fire*, and Alex Reid have provided endless inspiration from the worlds of ethnography, their meditations on objects and matter, and their work in rhetoric. In developing my ecological ontology, I also benefited deeply from the criticisms of Jeffrey Jerome Cohen. Although his work doesn't appear in the pages that follow, there is not a page of the present text that hasn't been deeply inspired and influenced by John Protevi's work on Deleuze and Guattari, autopoietic theory, developmental systems theory, and evolutionary and developmental biology. I sometimes think that my work is just a poor man's version of his extraordinary and wide ranging thought. Similarly, this book would not have been possible without the encouragement and inspiration of Ian Bogost, Graham Harman, and Timothy Morton. Finally Michael Flower composed the diagrams for the text that follows and provided helpful comments as it was composed.

During the year of 2012, I was fortunate to give a number of talks allowing me to test-run ideas developed here. Stacy Alaimo and Kenneth Williford kindly invited me to give a talk at the University of Texas, Arlington where I explored post-human ethics and ethical machines. Rory Rowan hosted me at the Space Art Studio in London where I presented my ideas about society as an ecology that is continuous with nature. Cary Wolfe kindly hosted me at Rice University where I was given the opportunity to present my claims about the ontology of machines. James Williams invited me to talk at Edinburgh University where I discussed the being of machines and flat ontology. I was also fortunate to give a keynote address at Liverpool Hope University where I presented my views on ecology. The input I received from these audiences has been invaluable and made this a much better book than it would have otherwise been. All that is good in the book that follows is due to the criticism, insight, and support of those listed here and many others besides.

Series Editor's Preface

Levi Bryant's *Onto-Cartography: An Ontology of Machines and Media* is the second book in the Speculative Realism series at Edinburgh University Press. It is a remarkable effort by an author who has established himself as an irreplaceable figure in contemporary philosophy. Bryant's early work was strongly influenced by Gilles Deleuze and the psychoanalysis of Jacques Lacan, and the lessons learned from these figures still animate Bryant's thinking today. In an age when better and worse philosophy blogs proliferate, Bryant's widely read "Larval Subjects" blog remains the most formidable gathering-point for younger philosophers in the Continental tradition. Every post on the blog reflects Bryant's omnivorous reading, his willingness to let his position evolve in the face of new evidence, his boundless appetite for dialogue with readers, and even his colorful autobiography, rare among academic authors. One of the most exceptional (and amusing) features of Bryant's life history, as lucidly retold on his blog, is the fact that he wrote his PhD dissertation *before* his MA thesis – since his advisors at Loyola University in Chicago felt that the MA was too substantial a piece of work to be wasted on a non-terminal degree, and thus asked him to write a shorter work before resubmitting the initial thesis for his doctorate. Bryant's candor and his lively style have led to famous polemical disputes with detractors, but have also earned him thousands of admirers across the globe. He is also an active international lecturer, increasingly influential in fields well beyond the discipline of philosophy.

Bryant has published two books prior to this one. The first was his highly regarded book on Deleuze, *Difference and Givenness: Deleuze's Transcendental Empiricism and the Ontology of Immanence* (2008). Many readers regard this as the best available work on Deleuze's masterpiece *Difference and Repetition*, despite the crowd of worthy contenders for that honor. It was shortly after the publication of his debut book that I became personally acquainted with Bryant, an intellectual friendship that had profound consequences for both of us. He quickly became a key figure in the movement known as "Object-Oriented Ontology" (or "OOO"), a term that Bryant coined himself in 2009. His involvement with the object-oriented paradigm and the work of Bruno Latour led to his second book, *The Democracy of Objects* (2011). It is a book of numerous merits, but is perhaps most noteworthy for its synthesis of an astonishing range of thinkers: from established continental notables such as Badiou and Deleuze to still-underutilized authors including Francisco Varela, Humberto Maturana, and the German systems theorist Niklas Luhmann. Beyond its many intriguing references, the book is characterized by a freshness and lucidity that make it likely to be read for decades to come.

Given Bryant's unusual capacity for intellectual growth, the reader will rightly expect yet another new turn in his latest book. The rallying point of *Onto-Cartography* is the word "materialism," which Bryant wants to defend from its admirers and its opponents alike. Though he is an ardent materialist opposed to any appeals to immaterial reality, it is Bryant's other critique that will hit closer to home: his impatience with so-called materialists who become lost in the forest of text-based cultural studies. As he wonderfully puts it:

> Having brought about the dissipation of the material in the fog of the diactrical differences of the signifier, there was no longer a place for thinking the real physical efficacy of fossil fuels, pollutants, automobiles, sunlight interacting with the albedo of the earth, and so on. Even among the ecotheorists in the humanities we find a preference for discussing portrayals of the environment in *literature* and *film*, rather than the role that bees play in agriculture and the system of relations upon which they depend.

Although Bryant expresses some embarrassment in having been converted to his robust materialism by the videogame *SimCity*, in which the placement of non-discursive entities such as power lines, factories, museums, and sports arenas has tangible effects on the populace, his embarrassment is already obsolete – note the recent surge in serious attention to videogames (by thinkers such as Ian Bogost) as a profound political tool and a form of high art in waiting.

Bryant's conclusion that the world is made up entirely of material rather than purely signifying or discursive realities amounts to a vision of "units or individual entities existing at a variety of different levels of scale . . . that are themselves composed of other entities." This leads him to formulate a *machine-oriented ontology* that forms the backbone of the book now before you. Entities are machines because they "dynamically *operate* on inputs producing outputs." Further, this theory becomes a cartography insofar as it develops "a map of relations between machines that analyzes how these assemblages organize the movements, development, and becoming other machines in a world." Ultimately, Bryant's recent work aims at a new form of political philosophy: "The aim of onto-cartography is not to close off styles of inquiry, but to expand our possibilities for intervening in the world to produce change so as to better understand how power functions and devise strategies so as to overcome various forms of oppression."

Onto-Cartography is not only a thought-provoking and erudite book, but also a thoroughly enjoyable one. It will prove immediately accessible even to those who are unfamiliar with Bryant's previous work. Much like the powerful blog posts for which he is famous, this book offers another path into the coming years of philosophy.

Graham Harman
Cairo, June 2013

For the banyan trees, sequoias, cephalopods, capybara, tanukis, tardigrades, microbes, viruses, Amazonian rain forests, coral reefs, and hitherto yet unimagined technologies.

Introduction: For a Renewal of Materialism

This books attempts a defense and renewal of materialism. This is a defense and renewal needed in the face of critics and *defenders* alike. On the side of the critics, materialism must be defended against obscurantists that seek to argue that materialism is reductive, mechanistic, and that there is something about human beings, culture, thought, and society that somehow is other than the material. However, it is perhaps the defenders of materialism that are today the greater threat. Among Continental critical and social and political theorists, we are again and again told that their positions are "materialist," only to see the materiality of matter up and disappear in their analyses. In these discourses and theoretical orientations, the term "materialism" has become so watered down that it's come to denote little more than "history" and "practice." It is certainly true that matter evolves and develops and therefore has a history, and practices such as building houses engage with matter. Unfortunately, under the contemporary materialism, following from a highly selective reading of Marx, "history" has largely come to mean *discursive* history, and practice has come to mean *discursive* practices. History became a history of discourses, how we talk about the world, the norms and laws by which societies are organized, and practices came to signify the discursive practices – through the agency of the signifier, performance, narrative, and ideology – that form subjectivities. Such a theory of society was, of course, convenient for humanities scholars who wanted to believe that the things they work with – texts – make up the most fundamental fabric of worlds and who wanted to believe that what they do and investigate is the most important of all things. Material factors such as the amount of calories a person gets a day, their geographical location (e.g., whether or not they're located in a remote region of Alaska), the rate at which information can be transferred through a particular medium, the effects of doing data entry for twelve hours a day, whether or not people have children, the waste output of travel, computing, how homes are heated, the way in which roads are laid out, whether or not roads are even present, the morphogenetic effects of particular diets, and many things besides completely fell off the radar. With the "materialist" turn in theory, matter somehow completely evaporated and we were instead left with nothing but language, culture, and discursivity.

The term materialism became so empty that Žižek could write, "[m]aterialism means that the reality I see is never 'whole' – not because a large part of it eludes me, but because it contains a stain, a blind spot, which indicates my inclusion in it" (Žižek 2006: 17). This is a peculiar proposition indeed. What need does matter have to be witnessed by anyone? What does a blind spot have to do with matter? Why is there no talk here of "stuff", "physicality", or material agencies? It would seem that among the defenders, materialism has become a *terme d'art* which has little to do with anything material. Materialism has come to mean simply that something is historical, socially constructed, involves cultural practices, and is contingent. It has nothing to do with processes that take place in the heart of stars, suffering from cancer, or transforming fossil fuels into greenhouse gases. We wonder where the materialism in materialism is.

We might attribute this to a mere difference in intellectual historical lineages – those descended from the Greek atomist Democritus on the one side and the critical theorists hailing from historical materialism on the other – but unfortunately, this perversion of materialism, this reduction to the cultural and discursive, has very real analytic and political effects. At the analytic level, it has had the effect of rendering *physical* agencies *invisible*. This arose, in part, from the influence of Marx's analysis – who was not himself guilty of what is today called "historical materialism" – of commodity fetishism, which showed how we relate to things under capitalism is, in *reality*, a relation between people (Marx 1990: 165). Marx was *right*. When a person buys a shirt, they are not merely buying a *thing*, but are rather participating in an entire network of social relations involving production, distribution, and consumption. However, somehow – contrary to Marx's own views – this thesis became the claim that things aren't *real*, or that they are merely crystallizations (Marx 1990: 128) of the *social* and *cultural*. Based on this elementary schema of critical theory, the critical gesture became the demonstration that what we take to be a power of things is, in reality, a disguised instance of the economic, linguistic, or cultural. Everything became an alienated mirror of humans and the task became demonstrating that what we found in things was something that *we* put there. To speak of the powers of *things* themselves, to speak of them as producing effects beyond their status as vehicles for social relations, became the height of naïveté.

This placed us materialists in an uncomfortable position. On the one hand, we were supposed to be "hard-nosed materialists," believing that everything is physical, that the idea or concept doesn't determine the being of being as in the case of Hegel or Plato. Weren't we supposed to turn Hegel on his head? Didn't turning Hegel on his head entail showing that ideas issue from material relations, rather than material things issuing from ideas? On the other hand, our theorizations somehow led us to see discursivity, the concept, the social, the cultural, the ideological, text, and meaning – the *ideal* – as being the stuff that forms being. How had this happened? We went so far in our "historical material-ism" that we even came to denounce all the findings of science and medicine as discursive social constructions (which isn't to say these practices shouldn't be subjected to ideological critique).

The analytic and political consequences of this were disastrous. Analytically we could only understand one half of how power and domination function. The historical materialists, critical theorists, structuralists, and post-structuralists taught us to discern how fashion exercises power and reinforces certain odious social rela-tions by functioning as a vehicle for certain meanings, symbolic capital, and so on. Yet this is only part of the story. As Jane Bennett puts it, things have their power as well (see Bennett 2010). Unfortunately, discursivist orientations of social and political theory could not explain how things like turnstiles in subways, mountain ranges, and ocean currents also organize social relations and perpetuate forms of domination because they had already decided that things are only vehicles or carriers of social significa-tions and relations. Because things had been erased, it became nearly impossible to investigate the efficacy of things in contribut-ing to the form social relations take. An entire domain of power became invisible, and as a result we lost all sorts of opportunities for strategic intervention in producing emancipatory change. The sole strategy for producing change became first revealing how we had discursively constructed some phenomenon, then revealing how it was contingent, and then showing why it was untenable. The idea of removing "turnstiles" as one way of producing change and emancipation wasn't even on the radar. This was a curious anti-dialectical gesture that somehow failed to simultaneously recognize the way in which non-human, non-signifying agencies, structure social relations as much as the discursive.

On the other hand, the shift from materialism to the discursivism of variants of historical materialism rendered it impossible to address one of the central political issues of our time: climate change. Thinking climate change requires thinking ecologically and thinking ecologically requires us to think how we are both embedded in a broader natural world and how non-human things have power and efficacy of their own. However, because we had either implicitly or explicitly chosen to reduce things to vehicles for human discursivity, it became impossible to theorize something like climate change because we only had culture as a category to work with. Having brought about the dissipation of the material in the fog of binary oppositions introduced by signs, there was no longer a place for thinking the real physical efficacy of fossil fuels, pollutants, automobiles, sunlight interacting with the albedo of the earth, and so on. Even among the ecotheorists in the humanities we find a preference for discussing portrayals of the environment in *literature* and *film*, rather than the role that bees play in agriculture and the system of relations upon which they depend.

I write these things with the fervor of the converted who was once himself in the historical materialist camp. Prior to 2006, before I had heard anything of speculative realism or object-oriented ontology, I was firmly entrenched in discursivism. Heavily entrenched in the work of Žižek, Lacan, Derrida, Adorno, and the structuralists and post-structuralists, I was entirely convinced that social relations are structured by language and culture, that the diacritical differences introduced by signs carve up the world, and that change was effected by debunking these signifying assemblages. I had read my Hjelmslev.

I was awoken from my dogmatic slumbers by, of all things – and I'm embarrassed to say – a computer game I played to gain some respite from the drudgery of marking in November of 2006: *SimCity 4*. This game shook my commitments to their core. For those not familiar, *SimCity* is a simulation game where you build and design a city and watch it grow. However, it would be a mistake to conclude from the term "design" that you have complete control over how your city evolves. You make decisions as to how to zone different areas (residential, commercial, industrial, and so on), where to lay roads and power lines, where to place factories and power plants, whether or not to build museums and sports arenas, and so on. But the city grows of its own accord, attracting residents or not attracting residents, attracting businesses or not attracting businesses. If you lay out your roads wrong, traffic congestion occurs, your citizens get angry, and you lose the tax base that allows you to invest in other things. If you place your energy plant in the wrong place, pollution occurs, your citizens get angry and sick, and begin to leave and suffer health issues preventing them from working. If you forget to properly connect and add power lines, the business and industrial regions of your city fail to grow, and you're unable to attract new people to move into the residential districts because there are no jobs. You might choose to build a sports arena to make your citizens happy, but then they get angry about the increase in taxes and the congestion of traffic. On top of all this, there are periodic natural disasters to which you must respond.

What *SimCity* taught me is that the signifier, meaning, belief, and so on are not the sole agencies structuring social relations. Whether or not a commercial district grows as a function of the amount of energy available to that zone from the power plant is not a *signifying* or *cultural* difference. Whether or not people begin to die or move away as a result of pollution produced by garbage, coal-burning power plants, and industrial waste is not a signifying difference. Whether or not people vote you out of office because they're angry about traffic congestion is not the result of a signifier. To be sure, there are social relations here insofar as it is people that produce all these things and people that are flocking to this city, moving away, or voting you out of office, but the point is that the form the city takes is not, in these instances, the result of a signifier, a text, a belief, or narrative alone. It is the result of the real properties of roads, power lines, pollution, and so on.

As mundane and ridiculous as it sounds, I was startled by this encounter. My entire theory of social relations, power, and domination was threatened. Despite being mediated through something as apparently immaterial – in both senses of the term – as a computer game, I had had an encounter with real materiality, with physical stuff, with things, and encountered the differences they make. This would be the seed that eventually led me to object-oriented ontology, the writing of *The Democracy of Objects* (Bryant 2011), and the idea of onto-cartography. The materialism that I defend in the pages that follow is unabashedly naïve. I do not seek to determine what matter in-itself might be. On the one hand, I believe this is a fool's errand insofar as philosophy, which works with concepts, does not have the tools to answer such questions. This is a question best left to physics and chemistry, and if history has been any indicator, whenever philosophers believe that they can provide a concept of the essence of matter, they have later been proven wrong. On the other hand, I am not convinced that matter is *one* type of thing. Rather, everything seems to point to the conclusion that there are many different types of matter. Similarly, I do not try to resolve esoteric questions such as the relationship between the qualitative and the quantitative. These abstractions, I believe, contribute to leading us to ignore matter, transforming it into a concept rather than recognizing it as a thing.

Rather, by "matter," all I mean is "stuff" and "things." The world, I contend, is composed entirely of "stuff" and "stuff" comes in a variety of different forms. Even ideas and concepts have their materiality. What this stuff might turn out to be is an open question. It might turn out to be various forms of energy, strings, fundamental particles, and so on. In describing my position as unabashedly naïve, I only mean to say that the world is composed of physical things such as trees, rocks, planets, stars, wombats, and automobiles, that thought and concepts only exist in brains, on paper, and in computer data banks, and that ideas can only be transmitted through physical media such as fiber optic cables, smoke signals, oxygen-rich atmospheres, and so on. I have given arguments elsewhere as to why I believe the only coherent ontology is one that recognizes the existence of discrete, emergent entities (see Bryant 2011: ch. 1), so I will not rehearse these demonstrations here. Rather, what follows begins with the premise that worlds are composed of units or individual entities existing at a variety of different levels of scale, and that are themselves composed of other entities. I call these entities "machines" to emphasize the manner in which entities dynamically *operate* on inputs producing outputs.

While a number of ontological and epistemological issues are discussed, the main aim of what follows is social, political, and ethical. What *Onto-Cartography* attempts to analyze is the way in which relations between machines – at both the discursive and physical level – organize social or ecological relations. I say "social *or* ecological" because onto-cartography argues that societies are both particular types of ecologies and that they always open onto broader ecological relations with the natural world in which they're embedded. "Onto-cartography" – from "onto" meaning "thing" and "cartography" meaning "map" – is my name for a map of relations between machines that analyzes how these assemblages organize the movement, development, and becoming other machines in a world. In other words, onto-cartography attempts to account for why power functions as it does, why forms of social organization persist as they do and are resistant to change, why societies simply don't disintegrate as a result of entropy, and to devise strategies for changing oppressive social systems. The thesis of *Onto-Cartography* is that social relations or ecologies take the form they take due to the gravity – my term for "power" – physical and discursive machines exercise on elements that inhabit assemblages, worlds, or ecologies.

While onto-cartography overlaps with many issues and themes dealt with in geographical cartography, it differs from the latter in that geography, in one of its branches, maps geographical space, whereas onto-cartography maps relations or interactions between machines or entities and how they structure the movements and becomings of one another. With that said, onto-cartography does contend that geography is the queen of the social sciences as it is that branch of social theory that least dematerializes the world and social relations, avoiding the transformation of social ecologies into discursivity. If this is so, then it is because geography recognizes the manner in which social relations are always embedded in a particular space or place, that communication takes time to travel through space and requires media to travel, and that geographical features of the material world play an important role in the form that social relations take. Social and political philosophy needs to become more geographical.

While onto-cartography is critical of the tendency in social and political thought to reduce social relations to the discursive or semiotic, it does not proceed from the premise that these theories are mistaken or false when their scope is properly clarified. As Whitehead observes, philosophies seldom fail as a result of poor reasoning or outright falsehood, but rather ". . . the chief error in philosophy is overstatement" (Whitehead 1978: 7). The problem with the thesis common among the critical theories that discursivity contributes to the structuration of reality in a variety of ways is not that it is false but that it is overstated. In light of this, in what follows I have attempted to develop a framework robust enough to integrate the discoveries of the critical theories, while also making room for a non-reductive account of the role played by physical media in the structuration of social relations.

While the aims of onto-cartography are political and ethical in nature, I do not advocate for any particular ethical or political paradigm in what follows. In other words, the work that follows can be described as a work of meta-politics and meta-ethics. It does not stipulate what political issues we should be concerned with, what we ought to do, or what ethics we ought to advocate, but rather attempts to outline the ontological framework within which political and ethical questions should be thought. Recently Adam Miller has proposed the concept of "porting" to describe this sort of theorizing (Miller 2013: 4–5). In computer programming, porting consists in reworking a program so it is able to function in a foreign software environment. It is my hope that a variety of political preoccupations – Marxist critiques of capitalism, anarchist critiques of authority and power, feminist critiques of patriarchy, deconstructive critiques of essences, critiques of ideology, queer theory critiques of heteronormativity, ecological critiques of environmental practices, post-humanist critiques of human exceptionalism, post-colonial critiques of racism, and so on – can be fruitfully ported into the framework of onto-cartography, assisting in the development of new avenues of inquiry and political practice, revealing blind-spots in other theoretical frameworks, and helping to render certain concepts and claims more precise and rigorous. The aim of onto-cartography is not to close off styles of inquiry, but to expand our possibilities for intervening in the world to produce change so as to better understand how power functions and devise strategies so as to overcome various forms of oppression.

Chapter Outline

Chapter 1 argues that worlds are composed entirely of machines, and broadly outlines the different types of machines that exist (discursive, physical, organic, technological, and inorganic). Here I attempt to address criticisms likely to arise in response to the claim "that the world is composed entirely of machines" and I propose a post-human media ecology in which a medium is understood as any entity that contributes to the becoming of another entity affording and constraining possibilities of movement and interaction with other entities in the world. Chapter 2 develops the general ontology of machines. I argue that machines ought to be understood in terms of their operations, transforming inputs that flow through them, producing a variety of different types of outputs. Insofar as machines operate on flows, they are to be understood as "trans-corporeal" or interactively related to other machines through flows of information, matter, and material that they receive from other entities. In Chapter 3, I argue that we must engage in "alien phenomenology" to understand how machines interact with other entities in the world about them. As articulated by Ian Bogost (see Bogost 2012), an alien phenomenology is an observation of how another entity observes or interacts with the world about it. Finally, Chapter 4 argues that machines are assemblages of other machines, and argues that every machine faces the problem of entropy or potential disintegration. I argue that in order for machines to persist across time, they must engage in perpetual operations that allow them to maintain their organization.

Chapter 5 explores the structure of worlds. I argue that a number of different worlds exist and that worlds are ecologies of machines. Here I also investigate the relationship between expression (the realm of discursive or semiotic-machines) and the world of content (the realm of physical machines) and how they influence one another. The concepts of content and expression, drawn from Deleuze and Guattari, allows onto-cartography to retain the findings of the semiotically inclined critical theorists, while also remaining attentive to the power exercised by physical things. In Chapter 6, I explore the structure of time and space as understood within an onto-cartographical framework. I reject the Newtonian conception of space as an empty milieu containing entities where motion is possible in all directions, instead arguing for a topological conception of space composed of paths – themselves composed of machines – between machines determine what is related to what and the vector along which an entity must move to reach a particular destination. I argue that the topological structure of paths plays a key role in how power is organized within assemblages.

Similarly, I argue for a pluralistic concept of time where time is understood as the rate at which a machine can receive inputs from other machines and carry out operations. Here I explore issues that arise when machines with different temporal structures interact with one another, complicate notions of historicity common among historical materialists and new historicists, and explore energy-related themes such as fatigue and information saturation. I attempt to demonstrate that thermodynamic and temporal issues play an important role in how power is structured and why certain oppressive social ecologies persist. I conclude this chapter by arguing that the form most social relations take result from a variety of different causes or overdetermination and that we need to be attentive to this distributed causality to properly understand social assemblages.

In Chapter 7 I address questions of agency and structure in social assemblages. Drawing, by analogy and metaphor, on Einstein's theory of relativity, I argue that social assemblages are held together not by "social forces," but by the manner in which machines structure the spatio-temporal paths along which other entities move, become, and develop. I refer to the way in which semiotic and physical machines curve the space-time of other entities as "gravity," my proposed replacement term for the concept of "power" common in social and political theory. The advantage of the term "gravity" is that it helps us to overcome the anthropocentric connotations of "power," drawing attention to the way in which non-human machines such as plants, animals, bacteria, technologies, infrastructure, and geographical features also contribute to the form that social assemblages take. Here I distinguish between the different types of objects that "gravitationally" structure ecologies – dark objects, bright objects, satellites, dim objects, rogue objects, and black holes – and distinguish between subjects and agents. I argue that agency comes in a variety of degrees ranging from that found in the humble bacteria all the way up to the sort of agency exercised by institutions and states, and argue that "subject" ought to be understood as a *functional* term that can be transitorily occupied by humans and non-humans alike, living and non-living beings alike. Drawing on Serres's concept of "quasi-objects," a subject, I argue, is an operator that *subjects* or that quilts or draws other machines together in an assemblage.

Chapter 8 outlines a geophilosophical framework for social and political thought. Geophilosophy argues that only the material and natural world exists, that societies and cultures are assemblages within the natural and material world, that the broader natural world plays a key role in how social assemblages come to be organized, that there is no social assemblage that doesn't draw on material flows for energy to resist entropy, and that causally the form socially assemblages take is overdetermined by a variety of different machines. Drawing on the resources of developmental systems theory (DST), I argue for a model of development that investigates the form entities take in terms of bidirectional causality involving genes, environment, and the active participation of the organism itself in the construction of itself. Not only does DST provide us with a nice example of analysis sensitive to overdetermination, but it also reflects a path beyond problems we encounter in sociology and critical theory. Gene-centric biologists tend to treat the organism as a mere *effect* of unilateral causality through genes or to treat the organism as an effect of a combination of the genes and the environment. The organism itself is here reduced to an effect and doesn't play an active role in its own formation or construction. A similar framework is reflected in critical theories – especially of the Marxist variety – where agents are often treated as a mere effect of conditions and relations of production. DST argues that the organism plays a role in its own formation, development, or construction through the selective relations it entertains to its environment and the way in which it constructs its own niches. As such, it provides fruitful paths for thinking beyond the crisis of agency that arises from a tendency to reduce agents to effects of "scene" or environment.

The chapter closes with a discussion of the three dimensions of geophilosophy: cartography, deconstruction, and terraformation. Cartography is the mapping of interactions and relations between machines composing assemblages or ecologies. Here I propose four types of maps – cartographical maps, genetic maps, vector maps, and modal maps – and argue that political practice requires good maps of assemblages in order to effectively intervene in worlds to produce more just, equitable, sustainable, and satisfying assemblages or ecologies. Deconstruction consists in the traditional deconstructions we find in the various critical theories, as well as the active severing of oppressive relations in the material world. I argue that in order to change the world it is often necessary to deconstruct relations between machines at the level of expression and content. Finally, terraformation consists in the construction or building of alternatives that would allow people to escape the oppressive circumstances in which they live. Here I argue that while critical theory has done a good job at deconstructing oppressive machines at the level of the plane of expression or semiotic-machines, many oppressive relations result not from people having mistaken ideological beliefs, but from living in material circumstances that provide no alternative. We need to do a better job, I believe, at actively constructing alternatives allowing people to escape circumstances. For example, people might readily recognize that dominant agricultural practices contribute greatly to the destruction of the environment and climate change, but lack alternatives for food. Terraformation here would consist in building assemblages of locally grown food in environmentally friendly ways that would provide people with alternatives.

Part 1

Machines

1

Towards a Post-Human Media Ecology

We didn't have to await Archimedes for the invention of the machine, for being has never consisted of anything but machines. Nature or being consists of nothing but factories, micro- and macro-machines – often wrapped within one another – drawing on flows of material from other machines and producing flows with new forms as their products in the course of their operations. In short, being is an ensemble or assemblage of machines. As the *Oxford English Dictionary* puts it, machines consist of "... material or immaterial structure[s] [composing] the fabric of the world or of the universe." "Machine" is thus our name for any entity, material or immaterial, corporeal or incorporeal, that exists. "Entity," "object," "existent," "substance," "body," and "thing," are all synonyms of "machine."[1] If we are partial to the term "machine" to denote the elementary units of being, then this is for two reasons. First, the concept of machine admirably captures the essence of entities as beings that function or operate. To be is to do, to operate, to act. Second, where "object" evokes connotations of a being opposed to or posited by a subject, "machine" avoids these associations, allowing us to step outside a four hundred year old philosophical obsession with interrogating the relationship between subjects and objects. As the *OED* observes, a machine is "a body regarded as functioning as an independent body . . ."

Common Prejudices About Machines

All Machines Are Rigid Machines

However, if we are to develop a machine-oriented ontology (MOO), it is first necessary to clear away some prejudices or assumptions we have regarding the nature of machines. The first of these prejudices is the view that "rigid machines" are exhaustive of the being of machines as such. A rigid machine is a machine composed of fixed material parts, characterized by routinized functioning, and is incapable of learning, growth, and development. Examples of rigid machines would be automobiles, primitive computers, cell phones, and lamps, but also rocks, dead planets and comets, atomic particles, and so on. Rigid machines are unable to undergo changes in their operations and their only destiny is entropy or eventual dissolution. However, if it is true that all beings that exist are machines, it is clear that rigid machines can only form a sub-species of the machines that are. Unlike automobiles, plants grow and develop. Many insects like butterflies live significant portions of their existence as very different organisms like caterpillars. Living planets go through very distinct climatic phases where their operations differ from epoch to epoch. Children, otters, organizations, etc., are capable of learning and changing their behavior and operations as a consequence of what they have learned.

Moreover, not all machines are material in nature. While all linguistic entities require a material body in the form of speech or writing to exist, they nonetheless possess an incorporeal dimension that allows them to remain dormant for long periods of time, only to begin acting on other beings at another time. A national constitution is not a being composed of fixed material parts like a cell phone, but is nonetheless a machine. A recipe does not itself have any ingredients, but is still a machine for operating on ingredients. A novel does not itself contain any people, rocks, heaths, animals, bombs, or airborne toxic events but nonetheless acts on other machines such as people, institutions, economies, etc., in all sorts of ways. Debt is nothing that we could identify as a material thing in the world, but is a machine that organizes the lives of billions of people.

A tree is no less a machine than an airplane, and a constitution is no less a machine than a VCR. If it is granted that all of these beings are machines, then it follows that rigid machines are only one *type* of machine among many other types of machines. We require a much broader concept of the machinic than that of an entity composed of fixed, material parts operating on flows of matter in a routine fashion. It also requires a substantial revision of our conception of mechanism and the mechanical. Where familiar conceptions of mechanism inherited from the sixteenth century treat that which is mechanistic as opposed to the creative and as characterized by routinized activity, examples such as trees, works of art, and humans and animals capable of learning suggest a theory of creative mechanism, where, for many types of machines, we do not yet know what a machine can do. And indeed, when we look around at the various sciences such as biology, complex systems theory, chaos theory, etc., we everywhere see that old characterizations of materialism as incapable of accounting for creativity because it characterizes being as "mechanistic" are everywhere coming up short. Instead, in the last one hundred years, materialism seems to everywhere show that matter, without need of spiritual or supernatural supplement, is profoundly creative. At any rate, machine-oriented ontology is in need of both a concept of machine broad enough to capture that shared nature of these different types of machines, and a field we might call "mechanology," not unlike zoology and botany, that investigates the essential features of different types of machines such as living machines, incorporeal machines, artistic machines, political machines, etc. As of now, we are not even certain of what different genera and species of machines exist.

All Machines Are Designed

The second great prejudice is that machines are designed. The designer of machines is conceived either as an intelligent rational being such as humans or as some sort of divinity, like the God of the monotheistic traditions or the demiurge in Plato's *Timaeus*. We might think, for example, of William Paley's famous argument for design, where we are to infer the existence of a divine designer from the presence of order and teleology in nature. In the wake of the Darwinian revolution, there are few who continue to be persuaded by the teleological argument for the existence of God, yet when we hear the term "machine," it is difficult to escape associations to *human* designers. Here we encounter an anthropomorphic peril similar to that which arises with reference to the term "object." Just as the term "object" immediately leads us to think of a subject that grasps, posits, intends, or encounters that object, the term "machine" leads us to think of that person, rational being, or people that designed and fabricated the machine. We encounter a Dutch windmill and are led to think of those that conceived and built the windmill. We encounter the windmill as a trace of the designs and work of these people.

The term "machine" allowed us to escape the anthropocentric associations of the term "object" by drawing our attention to beings that operate as independent bodies, thereby avoiding focus on objects as what are regarded or intended by subjects. Yet the term "machine" carries its own peril in that it arouses associations to people who conceived and fabricated the machine. It would seem that we still face the danger of anthropocentrism in replacing the concept of objects with machines. Yet if all beings are machines and we can safely say that teleological arguments for the existence of God have collapsed in the wake of Darwin,[2] then it follows that only a small subset of machines is designed by humans or other intelligent beings that might exist elsewhere in the universe. Within this ontology trees, living planets, and copper atoms would all be instances of machines, yet none of these machines were *designed* by anyone. Rather, as Manuel DeLanda would have it, these machines *emerged* from out of other machines without any intentionality guiding this emergence.[3]

Indeed, even in the case of machines fabricated by humans such as refrigerators and works of art, reflection raises serious doubt that these machines are simple products of human models and intentions. Under traditional accounts of *techne*, artifacts are conceived as arising from a model that is first conceived in the mind of the artisan and then imposed on passive matter through his agency. Such is the hylomorphic account of creation that has tended to dominate discussions of art and technology throughout the history of philosophy. The term "hylomorphism" comes from the Greek *hyle* signifying "matter" and *morphe* denoting "form." Under this model of fabrication, the artisan *first* has a sort of blueprint of what he wants to produce in his mind (the form), and *then* imposes that model on matter giving it form.[4] I first have a mental model of the knife I wish to produce in my mind and then set about fashioning the materials of the world about me into that form.

Yet when we look more closely at the actual *activity* of fabricating a work of art, tool, or technology, we see that something very different takes place. To be sure, the artist has some sort of intention to produce something like shelter from the elements, and this intention can involve a more or less elaborated model as in the case of an architect's blueprint, but this is where the similarities to the hylomorphic model end. The problem with hylomorphic models of how artifacts are produced is that they forget both the time of production and engagement with the materials of the world. What attentiveness to the time of production and engagement with matter reveals is that the production of any artifact is much closer to a *negotiation* than the simple imposition of a form upon a passive matter. And as is the case with all negotiations, the final outcome or product of the negotiation cannot be said to be the result of a pre-existent and well-defined plan.

In his discussions of matter in the *Critique of Dialectical Reason*, Sartre provides suggestive examples to illustrate this point. Following Lewis Mumford, Sartre points out that because steam engines required constant care on the part of stokers and engineers, they encouraged a tendency towards large industrial plants (Sartre 2004: 159). This is because a large industrial plant would be more efficient and cost-effective than small ones due to the labor-intensive characteristics of maintaining steam engines. The point here is simple. The intention behind fabricating a steam engine was to, for example, create energy to run a saw for cutting wood. That's it. Nothing about this purpose or aim itself implies the aim of producing a large industrial factory. Yet certain exigencies of the steam engine, its labor-intensive nature requiring a great deal of work to be maintained, encouraged the creation of large factories where they might be implemented so as to function at maximum economic and material efficiency. This, of course, would also entail the production of larger steam engines to run a variety of saws. Here we have an example of the *machine itself* issuing certain imperatives on its designer that run away from the intentions of the designer. The machine itself ends up contributing to the design in a way not intended by the designer.

What Sartre says here about the steam engine encouraging large factories holds for matter in general. Matter imposes imperatives on designers at all levels. Keeping with the example of the steam engine, take the invention of trains. The size of the train, the nature of its wheels, its speed, etc., is, in part, going to be a function of the materials available. Can the steels and metals we've produced up to this time withstand this weight of the engine when used as rails? How will those metals fare when encountering significant changes in temperature such as those found in the Sahara, Alaska, or Siberia? What temperatures can the steel of the boiler withstand? What sources of energy are available – wood, coal, gasoline, electricity, etc. – to run the engine and how do these different sources of energy contribute to the configuration of the engine and its capacities? The designer of the train might very well have an ideal blueprint in her mind, but as she begins to engage with the material features of both the environment in which the train will operate, existing technologies, and available fabricated materials such as those found in metallurgy, imperatives are imposed on her design that transform what she initially intended. Indeed, these considerations don't even begin to approach issues of economic feasibility and availability of materials, all of which similarly contribute to the form the train will finally take. The designer of the train is no less designed by the train than she designs the train. For this reason, Sartre will argue that there is a sort of "technical intentionality" that arises not from the intellect and aims of designers, but from the things themselves. It's as if we're caught in a drama, a struggle of intentions, between what matter and existing technologies "will" or are aiming at as a result of their properties and tendencies, and what we aim at.

In a similar vein, Sartre will later say that wherever humans live, tools impose their techniques upon us (Sartre 2004: 197). What Sartre says here of tools is no less true of environments. Both tools and environments issue certain problems as imperatives to be solved. These imperatives, of course, can be responded to in a variety of ways, but they are no less insistent for all that. There is a variety of ways in which this takes place. First, a tool or environment comes to habitually structure the body. The ink pen calls for certain ways of being grasped. Not only does it likely have an effect on the form that muscle and bone morphology take over the course of repeated and continuous use, but it also generates various neurological schema or tendencies to grasp that, in their turn, close off other ways of grasping. This is no less true of natural environmental factors. My grandfather who spent his life at sea building bridges for the state of New Jersey walks with a curious gait, his legs slightly apart, his shoulders slightly hunched over. It is likely that he walks in this way because he is a sort of embodied wave that has formed this schema of movement as a result of the rolling surface of the barges and tugboats upon which he worked. Just like the orchid and the wasp spoken of by Deleuze and Guattari, our bodies internalize the features of other machines in their own way.

Second, the tools that we use also generate *social* exigencies to which we must respond. Social imperatives begin to issue from the world of things that we've produced. The most striking example here might be the invention of the clock and, especially, the personal clock. With the invention of the clock and timepieces, all of social life begins to change. Where before, time told by light and dark as well as the position of the sun entailed a certain looseness as to when people would meet. With the invention of precise time-telling devices available to all, life and labor comes to be striated in a new way. Gradually, as timepieces become available to all, it becomes an *imperative* for people to structure their labor, their days, their encounters with one another according to chronological time. "You will be here at this particular time." "This meeting will have this particular duration." "You will work for this amount of time." "Your meals will be taken at this time and you will wake at that time." To be sure, it is possible to opt out of the tyranny of the chronometer, but this only comes at great social cost. Insofar as everyone else falls under the thrall of the chronometer, a whole set of social obligations and expectations arise out of this technology, a whole way of living. Similar points could be made about electric lighting, the invention of newspapers, television, automobiles, and increasingly, the invention of cell phones. All of these technologies generate sets of norms pertaining to the nature of our social relations.

The point here is that the production of any artifact is never simply a matter of envisioning some model in thought and then fashioning matter according to that form. While the craftsman's intentions and map play a role in the production of the artifact, the things themselves, the matter used, the circumstances under which they're produced, all contribute to the final product in ways not anticipated by the craftsman. What is produced is every bit as much the result of the exigencies of matter as the intentions of the craftsman. In this connection, we can only half agree with Hegel's analysis of "objective spirit" in the *Phenomenology of Spirit*. As Hegel remarks:

> . . . in fashioning the thing, the bondsman's own negativity, his being-for-self, becomes an object for him only through his setting at nought the existing *shape* confronting him. But this objective *negative* moment is none other than the alien being before which it has trembled. Now, however, he destroys this alien negative moment, posits *himself* as a negative in the permanent order of things, and thereby becomes *for himself*, someone existing on his own account. (Hegel 1977: 118)

Hegel's point is that in fashioning the alien matter of the world into the form he desires, the bondsman's spirit both takes on an objective permanence insofar as the artifacts he fashions will endure in material things, and the world comes to reflect his own spirit, being, or consciousness. In other words, in fashioning matter, the world about the bondsman comes to reflect his own consciousness (negativity).

However, based on the foregoing, we can now see that matters are quite different. Matter, far from being a passive stuff awaiting our formation or inscriptions, instead modifies our designs in all sorts of unexpected ways. The designer of the train did not intend for the train to have precisely this shape, but rather the exigencies of matter drew the final design of the train to this particular shape and configuration. The inventor of the clock did not intend for it to striate every aspect of life, yet when the clock came into existence and became widely available, daily routines and social relations took on a very different structure. Non-human machines or materials contribute to design as much as our own intentions and plans. And, as the example of the clock suggests, it is not simply that these matters issue imperatives that place constraints on the form the design takes, but it is also that these matters design *us* to the same degree that we form them. The nature of my life, goals, and intentions change with the invention of something like a clock.

It is this, no doubt, that McLuhan had in mind when he famously observed that "the medium is the message." As McLuhan writes:

> Whether . . . light is being used for brain surgery or night baseball is a matter of indifference. It could be argued that these activities are in some way the "content" of the electric light, since they could not exist without the electric light. This fact merely underlines the point that "the medium is the message" because it is the medium that shapes and controls the scale and form of human association and action. (McLuhan 1994: 8–9)

Media – what I am here calling "machines" – are formative of human action, social relations, and designs in a variety of ways that don't simply issue from humans themselves. As a result, it is misleading to talk of design at all insofar as the production of any artifact results both from human intentions and the features of non-humans. Here we encounter a prime example of what I referred to as "gravity" in the Introduction. The features of the machines of the world exercise a certain gravity over us that draws our action and aims in directions we did not ourselves intend. We become caught, for example, in the gravitational pull of the clock despite our own wishes and aims, such that our life increasingly becomes structured around the clock.

Machines Have a Purpose or a Use

The third great prejudice about machines is that they *have* a purpose or a use. This assumption arises from treating rigid machines such as electric knives and power shavers as the paradigm of what constitutes a machine. We say that the purpose of the electric knife is to cut turkey or bread and that the power shaver is used to shave whiskers, and treat these uses and purposes as if they were *intrinsic* features of the machine. However, if it is true that all entities, things, or objects are machines, then clearly this is not the case. Entities as diverse as neutrinos, black holes, seeds, shrubberies, and rabbits are all machines, yet clearly these machines do not have purposes in the sense that electric knives have a purpose or use. A black hole is not *for-the-sake-of* anything. It is indeed a machine in that it operates or functions in a particular way, but it does not have any particular goal, aim, or use beyond itself. While Amazonian capybara certainly have goals and aims for themselves, they do not have an *intrinsic* purpose that lies *beyond* themselves such as serving as food for crocodiles and leopards or breaking down plant life through digesting it for the sake of creating fertile soil for other plants. Capybaras can be *put to* these uses by other machines such as crocodiles, leopards, and plants, but these uses are not a part of their being as machines.

What is said here of machines such as black holes and capybaras is true of rigid machines such as ballpoint pens and automobiles as well. Even where designed and fabricated for a particular purpose, these types of rigid machines do not *have* a use as an intrinsic feature of their being, though they can be *put* to a use. The reason for this is that all machines, whether fabricated by humans or not, are *pluripotent*. In biology, a pluripotent cell is a cell such as a stem cell that has the capacity to become a variety of different types of cell such liver cells, muscle cells, or nerve cells. A pluripotent cell is a cell that has multiple powers of becoming, which is to say that it is capable of actualizing itself in a variety of different ways.

While the pluripotency of no entity is unlimited – no entity can become every other type of entity – it is nonetheless the case that all entities are pluripotent or possess a range of possible becomings allowing for the genesis of distinct forms and functions. Let's take the example of a simple rigid machine like a rock. Rocks are pluripotent both in the sense that they can take on many different phases depending on the environmental conditions in which they find themselves – they can become magma when heated, brittle when cooled, etc. – but also in the sense that they can *take on* many different uses. Rocks can be used as paperweights, doorstops, weapons when hurled, devices for boiling when heated and placed in water, stones in a wall, and so on. They don't have *a* use, but rather are *put to* a use.

This is no less true of rocks than ballpoint pens. Clearly the ballpoint pen was designed and fabricated for the sake of writing, but that intention doesn't define the being of the pen nor undermine its pluripotency. Just as rocks can take on many different functions or uses, ballpoint pens can be used as weapons to stab, tubes to shoot spit wads, straws to drink soda, posts to prop up bean plants, air passages for tracheotomies, and so on. The history of the uses of a rigid machine like artifacts made by humans is thus better described in terms of the biological concept of exaptation than design. In biology, the phenomenon of exaptation consists in a trait taking on a different function than the one it originally served. For example, it is often suggested that lungs did not originally serve the function of breathing, but rather served as air filled flotation devices for various organisms. Similarly, black powder transitioned from being used to fire guns and cannons to blasting rocks in mines. We can think of the history of technology as a history of exaptations where the potencies of various technologies are explored and problems that emerge when those technologies are put to new use arise and call for resolutions. The use of black powder in mining, for example, created the problem of how to set off the powder with enough delay to allow those miners who had set the charge to escape from the explosion. This problem was not fully resolved until William Bickford created the safety fuse in 1831. Exaptations generate new problems that themselves lead to the formation of new types of beings.

Machines do not *have* a purpose or use, but rather *take on* a purpose or use when structurally coupled to other machines. The concept of structural coupling was introduced by biologists and autopoietic theorists Maturana and Varela to denote interactive relations between entities that perturb one another and thereby develop in relation to one another.[5] Relations of structural coupling can either be unidirectional or bidirectional. A structural coupling is unidirectional when one entity triggers a response or activity in another entity without that response, in turn, triggering a response in the first entity. Here we might think of the relationship between a flower and the sun. The sun triggers all sorts of responses in the flower ranging from the rate at which it engages in photosynthesis to the direction in which the flowers and leaves of the plant point, but the responses of the flower do not, in their turn, trigger any responses in the sun. In short, not all interactions between entities are reciprocal. Later we will see just why this is so. By contrast, a structural coupling will be bidirectional when an action on the part of a machine A triggers a response on the part of a machine B, and when the response on the part of machine B, in its turn, triggers a response in entity A. Biological evolution seems to function in this way. Through processes of random mutation, natural selection, and heritability, one type of entity develops armor, camouflage, or speed that allows them to evade their predators. The powers of the predator triggered a response in the species through the creation of selection pressures. These selection pressures, in their turn, led the species to evolve or develop along a particular vector. However, these evolutionary adaptations in response to predators themselves create selection pressures for the predators. Those predators that have more discerning vision, that are a bit faster, that have sharper claws and teeth allowing them to pierce the armor of their prey will have a greater likelihood of eating that will, in turn, allow them to live longer, thereby increasing their likelihood of reproducing and passing on their genes. In a bidirectional structural coupling of this sort, we thus get a sort of arms race between predator and prey where both are bound up with one another in such a way as to mutually influence the becomings of the two species.

Varieties of Machines

We saw earlier that rigid machines are not the only type of machine, but rather there is a variety of different types of machine. Before proceeding to give a thumbnail sketch of these different types of machine, it is important to note that often these machines can be mixed in a variety of ways – there can be machines that have both corporeal and incorporeal components, for example – and that these distinctions are not absolute, but admit to a variety of differences in degree. For example, a virus is not quite a rigid, inanimate corporeal machine, nor a fully plastic, animate, corporeal machine. The first great division between types of machine is between corporeal and incorporeal machines. A corporeal machine is any machine that is made of matter, that occupies a discrete time and place, and that exists for a duration. Subatomic particles, rocks, grass, human bodies, institutions, and refrigerators are all corporeal machines. Incorporeal machines, by contrast, are defined by iterability, potential eternity, and the capacity to manifest themselves in a variety of different spatial and temporal locations at once while retaining their identity. Recipes, scores of music, numbers, equations, scientific and philosophical theories, cultural identities, novels, and so on, are all examples of incorporeal machines.

In discussing incorporeal machines we must take care lest we fall into a sort of Platonic dualism where we treat these entities as subsisting ideally in some other realm. All incorporeal machines require a corporeal body in order to exist in the world. Numbers, for example, must occur in brains, computer data banks, graphite, chalk, etc., in order to exist in the world. Why, then, refer to these machines as incorporeal if they always require some sort of corporeal body? The incorporeality of an incorporeal machine consists not in being an immaterial ghost, but rather in the capacity of these machines to be multiply-instantiated, iterated, or copied while retaining their identity. Multiple copies of *The Waves* can be made, while Woolf's novel remains *that* same novel. Moreover, it remains that novel regardless of the corporeal body it has. Its corporeal body can be chalk on a board, paper, the thought of a person who has exceptional memory, a computer data bank, etc. The same is true of incorporeal machines such as the number 5 that can be thought and inscribed at various places in the universe, while remaining itself. It is true of cultural identities as well that can be instantiated in a variety of people.

Incorporeal machines are incorporeal not by virtue of being immaterial, but by virtue of being iterable while retaining their identity. It is this iterability that imbues them with a *potential* eternity. So long as the inscription remains or the incorporeal machine is copied or iterated, it continues to exist. If this eternity is only potential rather than actual, then this is because operations of iteration can always cease leading the incorporeal machine to cease its repetition, or because inscriptions can always be lost or erased, leading them to pass from the world. In any case, incorporeal machines differ markedly from corporeal entities in their temporality because, unlike the tree in my back yard that exists only at this time, in this place, for the duration that it exists, incorporeals can occur as identical again and again. When the tree dies and decays, it will never exist again, whereas a number or equation can be repeated endlessly as the same entity.

Incorporeal machines significantly complicate our understanding of causality. With inanimate, corporeal machines such as rocks, an effect is always the result of the immediately preceding events. Here the preceding event disappears with the occurrence of the new event.

$$E_1 \rightarrow E_2 \rightarrow E_3 \rightarrow E_4 \ldots E_n$$

In the causal sequence above, E_2 is the cause of E_3 and E_2 disappears with the occurrence of E_3. In the case of inanimate, corporeal machines, the cause is the immediately preceding event. Thus we don't get circumstances in which, for example, E_1 directly causes E_4. E_1 has disappeared in the mist of time. With incorporeal machines, by contrast, matters are entirely different. Because incorporeal events are inscribed and preserved in some medium, the remote past can influence the immediate present. The Bible, for example, continues to have a tremendous influence on contemporary culture. A person can elect to organize their ethical life according to the teachings of the Greek Stoic Epictetus. DNA developed in the remote past continues to influence the development of organisms in the present.

Moreover, we can also speak of *sleeping* or *dormant* incorporeal machines. Here I draw on Graham Harman's concept of "dormant objects," though I develop it within a machine-oriented framework (see Harman 2010). These are incorporeal machines that continue to exist through their corporeal bodies, but that are no longer active or are no longer remembered by any sentient machines. Here we might think of forgotten texts or letters that never arrive at their destination, such as the *Dead Sea Scrolls* or Lucretius's *De Rerum Natura*. Like the tick described by Deleuze and Guattari that lays in wait until a warm-blooded entity happens along, it's as if these incorporeal entities exist in a state of hibernation or suspended-animation, awaiting their rediscovery so that they might transform the present. Stephen Greenblat describes precisely such a thing with the rediscovery of Lucretius's *De Rerum Natura* (Greenblatt 2012). *De Rerum Natura* had been lost for centuries as a result of attempts to destroy the book. When it was rediscovered in the fifteenth century it quickly had a decisive impact on European thought, influencing art, science, philosophy, theology, and political thought in all sorts of far reaching and profound ways. Here we encounter the way in which incorporeal machines can disrupt the historical determination of the contemporaneous present, opening new avenues of thought and life for people living in that moment.

Corporeal and incorporeal machines interact in a variety of complicated ways. We must therefore take care not to assume that corporeal machines do not influence incorporeal machines. As theorists such as Walter Ong argue, for example, communications technologies have a tremendous impact on what sorts of incorporeal machines are possible (Ong 2002). It is difficult to imagine geometry, calculus, and other forms of mathematics conducted only in speech or without writing and certain symbols. Now writing-machines are a combination of both incorporeal machines and corporeal machines. The symbols used, their syntax or rules of combination, etc., are all incorporeal machines. However, paper, pencils, and ink and graphite inscriptions are themselves corporeal machines. As cognitive scientist and philosopher Andy Clark notes, these corporeal machines are not without their cognitive contributions (Clark 2003: 7). Due to limitations of short-term memory our minds are generally incapable of carrying out lengthy and complicated chains of reasoning because we can't keep all of the steps of a geometrical proof or calculus problem in our heads. As Clark argues, it is the paper and graphite *itself* that allows us to surmount this problem. Because the paper and graphite remember, as it were, the steps of the proof on our behalf, we're able to ignore earlier steps, concentrating on the operations we're currently carrying out, while still being able to return to these earlier steps later when we need to call on them. The paper remembers on our behalf and allows us to engage in mathematical operations that we would never be able to undertake in speech. Here we have a case where the material medium affects incorporeal machines.

Matters work in reverse as well. Incorporeal machines can significantly impact corporeal machines. Things like dietary codes, recipes, educational curriculums, parenting advice, etc., are all incorporeal machines. When activated, these incorporeal machines act on the development of corporeal bodies. The body of a person raised on a 1950s diet will be different from the body of a person raised on a contemporary diet. While it is certainly the foods themselves that affect how the body develops, it is nonetheless an incorporeal machine that selects these particular foods and excludes others. Likewise, brains taught within this particular educational curriculum will be different from brains raised in another curriculum. As Judith Butler rightly argues, even our sexuality results, in part, from the agency of incorporeal machines acting upon our bodies (Butler 2006). Our sexuality is not something that is biologically given, but rather is something that forms in an interaction of incorporeal social machines and biological corporeal machines.

Like corporeal machines, incorporeal machines range from the absolutely rigid to the plastic. Rigid incorporeal machines are machines that are not susceptible to change and that cannot be modified by the flows that pass through them. Mathematical equations are of this sort. Faced with a function like $f(x) = 2x + x^2$, the input that flows through this machine (whatever value of x we choose) will not modify the basic structure of the function. While the function will produce a variety of different outputs, its functional structure will always remain the same. Like corporeal machines, incorporeal machines have different degrees of rigidity. Mathematical equations are absolutely rigid. Bureaucratic rules and procedures, inflexible moral codes, state constitutions, etc., are rigid but nonetheless admit of modification. Then there are incredibly plastic incorporeal machines such as novels, music, cultural and gender identities, theories, and so on. All of these incorporeal entities are subject to wide variation and modification over the course of time.

In the case of corporeal machines, the three great species are inanimate, animate, and cognitive machines. Inanimate machines are machines that can only undergo change through external causes or internal processes that unfold within them. A rock, for example, does not undergo change unless it encounters another machine such as a change in temperature. Stars undergo changes as a result of the nuclear processes that unfold within them. Inanimate corporeal machines do not attempt to maintain their organization, nor do they grow. Unlike an animate machine, if a rock is chipped it doesn't engage in operations to heal the part of itself that is missing. Unlike inanimate machines, animate machines engage in operations to preserve their organization. If a cat is cut, for example, its wound will heal in more or less the same configuration that its body previously had. Finally, cognitive machines are corporeal machines that are capable of directing their own action. Cats can regulate their temperature by varying their distance from a fire. Birds can engage in activities to distract predators from their chicks. Dogs, dolphins, octopuses, humans, institutions, and certain technologies are capable of learning. Cognitive machines differ from simple animate machines in that they are intentionally goal-directed.

Again, these distinctions can overlap and there are all sorts of differences in degree between these different types of machine. Dolphins, for example, are both cognitive machines and animate machines. They are capable of learning and acting based on goals, and are therefore cognitive machines. Their bodies heal themselves and they are therefore animate machines. Other machines, such as governments, are combinations of incorporeal machines, animate machines, and cognitive machines. They are inhabited by all sorts of incorporeal machines such as laws, directives, and procedures, are goal-directed, are capable of learning, and replenish their elements when people retire. In yet other cases, it is difficult to determine where a particular type of machine falls. Viruses, for example, resemble animate machines in that they reproduce themselves, yet also resemble inanimate machines insofar as they do not heal themselves and seem only to act in response to causes.

Post-human Media Ecology

Machines do not *have* a use or purpose, but only *take on* a use or purpose in being structurally coupled to another machine. The purpose of the capybara is not to serve as food for the leopard, but rather it only takes on this function in relation to or structural coupling with the leopard. In isolation from the leopard, the capybara just is what it is. The purpose of the pen is not to write, but only takes on this function in relation to a person or chimpanzee. In and of itself, the pen is merely a particular configuration of matter. Following McLuhan, we will thus say that when one entity enters into structural coupling with another entity, it functions as a *medium* for that entity. McLuhan argues that every medium is an extension of man, such that it ". . . extends or amplifies some organ or faculty of the user" (McLuhan and McLuhan 1998: viii). For example, writing extends speech and the ear by allowing us to "hear" the words of others when they are no longer present. The automobile extends the foot, allowing for a faster rate of travel. The camera extends vision allowing us to see that which is not present, and so on. A machine functions as a medium for another machine when it is structurally coupled to another machine, extending its powers and capacities in some way.

We can see just how broadly McLuhan expands the concept of media, giving it a much deeper ontological significance than it is often taken to have. Often when we think of media we immediately think of things such as newspapers, television, music, etc. While these are indeed examples of media, McLuhan expands the notion to include everything from forks to seeing eye dogs. McLuhan thus recovers the Latinate sense of media as *medius*, denoting "intermediary." A medium is an intermediary that relates one thing to another. Thus, for McLuhan, a medium does not so much refer to a particular medium of *communication* such as speech, sign-language, radio, television, writing, or smoke-signals – though all of these things are included in his theory of media – but rather places emphasis on both the materiality of media and the specific nature of that materiality, as well as the manner in which these media extend and amplify our sense-organs.

Each medium has its material characteristics that will encourage and diminish certain things. Take the example of the difference between speech and writing with respect to societal laws. As historian and anthropologist Jean-Pierre Vernant observes, "[s]etting [laws] down [in writing] not only ensured their permanence and stability; it also removed them from the private authority of the [ruler], whose function was to 'speak' the law" (Vernant 1982: 52–3). While the imperative *content* expressed in a law in speech or writing might indeed be the same, the materiality of the two media greatly affects how law functions. When expressed in the material medium of speech or soundwaves, laws have a very low coefficient of permanence. Speech disappears nearly as soon as it is articulated, leaving traces only in the memories of those who have heard it. This renders the law especially subject to the whims of the ruler that articulates the law; but also – as in the game of telephone where a message undergoes transformation when it is passed from person to person, becoming, in the end, quite distinct from the original message – transmission of law through speech allows a law to undergo a high degree of transformation as it is passed down through the functionaries of the ruler as well as the inhabitants of the city. Far along in the chain of transmission, the law can come to be articulated in an entirely different way with a very distinct meaning from the one that was initially conveyed by the ruler.

With inscription of the law in writing, this situation changes markedly. First, insofar as the law has been inscribed or written down, it takes on an objective value that rescues it from the whim of the ruler. In being inscribed, the law becomes a thing or machine in its own right rather than a command of the ruler. To be sure, the law written down issued from the ruler, but in its inscription on parchment or the wall of a temple, it now takes on an alien existence, an independent existence, that the ruler himself must contend with. Today he might be inclined to enact a different law, but because his "speech" lingers in the form of the written document, the ruler now finds that he must mesh what he said last year with what he wishes to decree today. Indeed, not only must he contend with what *he* said last year, but he must also contend with what previous rulers inscribed. Writing creates a material-ized memory no longer subject to the decay of brains sodden by alcohol and the forgetfulness of age. Second, in being written down, the articulated is freed from the limitations of speech trave-ling through the air, allowing the inscribed to travel throughout a much greater geographical expanse in time and space. Now laws can travel to remote regions of the kingdom, allowing people who have never met one another nor ever heard the decrees of the ruler to see themselves as subject to the same laws. To be sure, these people will interpret the law differently as people always do, but there will still be this minimal identity of the inscribed produced through writing that unites diverse people as a result of sharing the same body of texts.

The point here is that the materiality of the medium, its material properties and powers, substantially modify human activities and relations in ways that outpace the *content* of the medium. It was not the content or meaning of the law that gave it a permanence and allowed for larger kingdoms and cities by creating an identity people could share who had never met one another, but rather material features of writing itself independent of any meaning that writing might have. This is what McLuhan has in mind when he says that "the medium is the message." He is not inviting us to attend to the *meaning* or *signification* of a message conveyed in a particular medium such as a beer advertisement in neon lights – though that too – but rather to the way in which the material properties of the medium modify our activities and ways of relating to one another. This is the lesson we should draw from his example of electric lights at the beginning of *Understanding Media* (McLuhan 1994: 8–9). If electric lights are the "message" in this particular case, it is not because they convey a particular propositional content or narrative, but rather because they modify our activities and the ways in which we relate to one another. Electric lights open entirely new domains of night-time social relations that weren't there before. Where before the night was a time of terror where we remained indoors because of the menacing darkness and that which is veiled within it, now night becomes a domain for romantic leisurely strolls along the Seine, night-time baseball games, late-night reading, and, of course, all sorts of night-time labor. It becomes far more feasible, for example, for a factory to have multiple shifts increasing productivity exponentially. To "get the message," in this case, is to attend to the way in which this medium has modified our activities and ways of relating to one another for good or for ill.

However, as promising as McLuhan's conception of media is, we believe that it remains too restrictive and needs to be modified in two ways. First, McLuhan restricts media to amplifications and extensions of organs and, in particular, organs of sense. However, while these are indeed instances of machines extending the organs of other machines, it seems to us that the category of media is far broader than simply extending or amplifying sense-organs. *A machine functions as a medium for another machine not only when it amplifies or extends a sense-organ, but also whenever it modifies the activity or becoming of any other machine.* Vitamin B functions as a medium for our bodies when it modifies our moods. Cigarettes function as a medium for lung cells when it modifies how they maintain and reproduce themselves. The temperature of the nest in which a crocodile has laid her eggs functions as a medium for those eggs insofar as it plays a role in the sex of the developing eggs. Smart phones function as a medium for humans insofar as they modify the sorts of activities we engage in. Where before we felt no inclination to text and constantly check our email and Facebook for updates, we now find ourselves compulsively engaging in these activities. A theory functions as a medium when it modifies how we act in the world, as in the case of washing our hands as a consequence of the germ theory of sickness. Investigation of media is not solely concerned with how machines amplify and extend *sense-organs*, but also with how machines modify and extend the activity and becoming of entities.

Second, McLuhan treats media as consisting of extensions of *man*, yet there seems to be no reason to restrict the concept of media to humans.[6] A medium is any machine that modifies the becoming or activity of another machine, or that extends the sense-organs of another machine. This holds no less for non-humans than it does for humans. Electric lights are no less a medium for non-humans than they are for humans. The light on my patio attracts all sorts of insects. The lizard that lives beneath the wooden flag of Texas by this lamp uses this medium to hunt those insects and fatten up. This medium thus changes social relations between insects and lizards, modifying predator–prey relationships. Similarly, not only can humans serve as media for other humans as in the case of a lawyer that extends the speech of the person they represent in the court room, humans can also serve as media for *non-humans*. I am quite literally a medium for my beloved cat Tasha who uses me to extend her claws and hunting prowess, seducing me so that she can live a life of leisure. It is not so much that she is my pet as I am her loyal servant. In a more menacing example, Kafka, in *Amerika*, depicts an example of a human being a medium for the steam engine on the ship that he attends to, condemned to spend his days shoveling coal into the engine to run the ship (Kafka 1974: 3–37). The steam engine is not an extension of the stoker, but rather the stoker is an extension of the steam engine that provides it with flows of energy so that it might continue functioning.

Nor need these media relations involve humans at all. Sharks are media for remora that use the shark to extend their own opportunities to get food. The abandoned shells of snails are media for hermit crabs. Electro-magnetic fields produced by the earth's molten core are media for birds and a variety of ocean-going creatures allowing them to navigate from one place to another. The rotting carcasses of animals are media for the plants, bacteria, and fungi that grow in them. Wind is a medium for sand and pollens, allowing them to travel far from their original location. The same is true of ocean waves and currents.

We are now in a position to see why McLuhan's theory of media is of general *ontological* significance. McLuhan's notion of media explodes its restriction to particular carriers of human communication and meaning, allowing us to think a medium as structural couplings between machines that modify the becoming, movement, activity, or sensing of other machines. In short, the concept of media provides us with the beginnings of a theory of *relations* and *interactions* between machines. To study media is not simply to investigate technologies, tools, artifacts, and forms of communication, but rather the way in which machines are structurally coupled to one another and modify one another regardless of whether or not humans are involved. In this regard, the investigation of media is closer to ecology than to the investigation of what we ordinarily refer to as "mass media." Moreover, insofar as machines can function as media regardless of whether or not humans are involved, this theory of media is *post-human* in the sense that it is not restricted to how various entities function as media for human beings. In addition to attending to how non-human machines function as media for other non-human machines, and how human artifacts or machines function as media for non-humans, it also investigates how humans can function as media for non-humans. As such, it presents an ecological vision of relations between machines that elides any fundamental distinction between the kingdom of the human and the kingdom of the non-human.

Based on the foregoing, we are now in a position to give our first definition of onto-cartography. In its initial formulation, onto-cartography is the investigation of structural couplings between machines and how they modify the becomings, activities, movements, and ways in which the coupled machines relate to the world about them. It is a mapping(cartography) of these couplings between machines (onta) and their vectors of becoming, movement, and activity. This definition of onto-cartography will be modified and enriched in subsequent chapters, but gives us an initial sense of what this strange science of onto-cartography aims to investigate. In what follows, it should be assumed that whenever I speak of one machine modifying the movement or becoming of another machine I am speaking of machines functioning as media for other machines. Let us now investigate what a machine is.

Notes

1. The concept of machine thus replaces that of object that I introduced in *The Democracy of Objects*. This shift, however, is not absolutely new for there I had already distinguished between objects as allopoietic machines and autopoietic machines in the fourth chapter of that text.
2. For an excellent discussion of design without a designer, see Dennett (1995). While having significant reservations about his genecentrism, we largely endorse his ateleological account of emergence.
3. See DeLanda (2011).
4. For an important critique of hylomorphism, see Simondon (1995).
5. See Maturana and Varela (1998: 75–80).
6. This conception of media as extending the sense-organs or modifying the activity and becoming of any other entity and not just humans arose out of discussions between Ian Bogost and myself.

2

What Is a Machine?

Machines Operate

They whir, they buzz, they spin, and rumble. A world is a fabric of machines. Machines are not exhausted by rigid machines, and neither design nor purpose and use are essential features of machines. Quartz crystals, recipes, novels, and South-East Asian tanukis are no less machines than coffee-makers and bulldozers. What, then, is a machine? We have seen that one shortcoming of the term "object" is that it leads us to think of a subject that posits or observes that object. We think of an object as that which is opposed to a subject, and therefore think of objects as necessarily attached to a subject that experiences them. These associations are avoided with the concept of machines. We can easily imagine a machine operating in the world without anyone there to experience it. The concept of machine thus helps us to escape a highly sedimented philosophical tradition surrounding objects and subjects.

However, another drawback of the concept of objects is that it encourages us to think in terms of subjects and predicates. We think of an object as a subject of predication or as a subject that possesses a set of *qualities* or *properties* that make it the subject that it is. Regarded as an object, that tree over there is a subject of predication, possessing qualities like the color of its bark and leaves, its shape, the configuration of its branches, its texture, its smell, and so on. Asked what the tree is, we list these properties or qualities. It is these properties or qualities that make the tree *this* subject. Yet we notice that some of these qualities change, but the tree still remains *that* tree or subject. In the fall, for example, the leaves change color and fall off the tree. How can the tree simultaneously be that tree and change? We now set about distinguishing those *invariant* properties and qualities that constitute the *essence* of the tree, and those changeable properties that constitute *accidents* of the tree. The tree's being is now said to consist of these invariant properties constituting its essence.

A machinic conception of objects leads us to think of entities in a very different way. Confronted with a machine, our first thought is not of its properties or qualities, so much as its *operations*. A machine is something that operates. As articulated by Ian Bogost, ". . . an *operation* is a basic process that takes one or more inputs and performs a transformation on it" (Bogost 2006: 7). To this I add that in performing a transformation on an input, a machine produces an output. The inputs transformed through an operation can originate from either outside the machine or from inside the machine. Thus, for example, an input originates from inside my body when a particular cell releases a chemical that affects other cells. This cell has performed a set of operations that produce the chemicals that are then released as outputs absorbed by other cells, initiating new operations in those cells. Those other cells, in their turn, perform operations on these chemicals. By contrast, the input arises from outside a machine when it comes from elsewhere, as in the case of a flower drawing water from the soil. *A machine is a system of operations that perform transformations on inputs thereby producing outputs.*

Returning to the example of a tree, we see that we regard it very differently when we regard it as a machine. Rather than regarding the tree as a structure of qualities or properties inhering in a subject, we instead approach it as a system of operations performing transformations. We now ask what operations are performed by the tree and attend to the inputs upon which the tree draws, the transformations it performs and how they're structured, and the outputs it produces as a consequence of these transformations. In short, we attend to what the tree *does* rather than the qualities it *has*. We thus attend to flows of water, soil nutrients, light, and carbon dioxide passing through the tree, how it transforms these flows through operations, and the outputs it produces out of these inputs as a result of these transformations. Far from being a static lump that just sits there, machines are processual through and through.

Within a machinic ontology entities are understood as machines. Being is composed of machines all the way down. The first question to ask of any machine is not "what are its properties?", but rather "what does it *do*?" "What operations does this machine perform?" A recipe is a machine that performs operations on a cook, leading that cook, in her turn, to perform certain operations on various cooking utensils and ingredients. Deleuze and Guattari remark that "[a] book itself is a little machine . . ." (Deleuze and Guattari 1987: 6). They advise us to ask not what a book *means*, but rather to attend to how it functions. How does it operate on language? How do the characters operate on one another and on the other machines that populate the world about them? How do events operate on the characters? How does the novel operate on readers? How does it operate on social institutions and practices as in the case of *The Jungle* by Upton Sinclair?

A scientific paper is less a series of truth-functional propositions to be judged as true or false as it is a machine proposing certain operations. In this respect, it is closer to a recipe than those propositions that tie philosophers up in knots such as "the cat is on the mat." It is a machine that first proposes operations of observation, selecting flows of the observable from the chaos of a world and commanding "attend to this!" It is a machine that proposes the construction of fantastic organs of sense such as Geiger counters, orbiting telescopes, particle colliders, and so on. But it is above all a machine that calls upon us to engage in this or that experiment, to act on this or that machine in this or that way, to see what *happens* when things are operated on in this way.

A frog is a machine that engages in all sorts of operations for catching flies and insects. Its body is a machine that engages in operations to deftly traverse river currents and eddies. It is a machine that engages in operations transforming inputs of air into strange songs that attract mates and warn of predators when they suddenly go silent. It is a machine that produces certain outputs such as carbon dioxide and other wastes that are then taken up as inputs for other operations for machines like algae, lily pads, and cattails. And, of course, it is also a machine that produces copies of itself as outputs through reproduction.

Machines are not expressive, they are not representational, but rather are productive. Worlds are everywhere composed of factories where production in an infinite variety of forms ceaselessly takes place. Of the unconscious Deleuze and Guattari write:

The great discovery of psychoanalysis was that of the production of desire, of the productions of the unconscious. But once Oedipus entered the picture, this discovery was soon buried beneath a new brand of idealism: a classical theater was substituted for the unconscious as a factory; representation was substituted for the units of production of the unconscious; and an unconscious that was capable of nothing but expressing itself – in myth, tragedy, dreams – was substituted for the productive unconscious. (Deleuze and Guattari 1983)

Freud's great discovery, they contend, was the productive unconscious or unconscious as a factory. The unconscious does not *represent*, but rather manufactures or produces desires. The formations of the unconscious are not representations of repressed desires, but are instead productions of new desires. All of this is betrayed, they claim, when Freud introduces the Oedipal theory. The unconscious now becomes a theater of representation in which all formations of the unconscious are understood in terms of expression referring back to an Oedipal drama. Theater versus factory. Expression versus production. Representation versus operation. What Deleuze and Guattari here say about the unconscious is true of all machines. Machines do not express, represent, and do not constitute a theater. Rather, all machines are factories producing outputs through their operations.

Machines Are Split Between their Powers and Products

The being of a machine is defined not by its qualities or properties, but rather by the operations of which it is capable. This entails that machines are *split* between their operations and the output or products of their operations. This split, of course, is not of the sort we get when, for example, we cut an orange in half. Rather, the split between operations and products refer to two dimensions of any machine. On the one hand, there are pure operations taken in their formal being. On the other hand, there are the results produced by these operations when they operate. This distinction is important because a machine can possess certain operations without actually exercising those operations.

I refer to these two halves or dimensions of machines as "virtual proper being" and "local manifestation" respectively. The virtual proper being of a machine is the operations of which it is *capable*. These constitute the "proper being" of the machine in that machines are what they are capable of doing. They are "virtual" in the sense that a machine can possess these operations without *exercising* them. Iron is capable of engaging in operations of producing rust, but only engages in these operations under specific conditions. Iron in outer space, for example, would not produce rust as there is no oxygen present to initiate operations of oxidation. Similarly, a sleeping cat does not engage in operations of vision because its eyelids are shut.

Following philosopher George Molnar, we can call this virtual system of operations possessed by any machine "powers." Molnar attributes five features to powers (Molnar 2006: 57–8). First, powers are characterized by *directedness* in that they produce a particular outcome or product when exercised. For example, plants produce oxygen out of carbon dioxide through operations of photosynthesis. In this regard, powers are like mathematical functions. Given a mathematical function $f(x) = x^2 - 3$, this function is directed at a particular product when it operates on a particular input (x). For example, given x = 2, we get the product 1. The product towards which an operation or power is directed is what is called its "manifestation." It is of crucial importance to note that the power of an operation always has a greater range than the manifestations it happens to produce when operating. In this instance, our power produced 1 when x = 2, yet if x = 3 it would produce 6 as its manifestation. This is yet another reason that powers are characterized by virtuality. They are always capable of producing more manifestations than they happen to produce at any particular point in time.

Second, powers are characterized by *independence* from their manifestations. Not only can powers be manifested in a variety of ways such that no one manifestation exhausts the scope or range of a power, powers can also go unmanifested altogether. Matches have the power to burn, but do not need to manifest this power to possess it. Skunks have the power to produce pungent odors, yet do not need to spray in order to possess this power. Thus, while manifestations are always dependent on powers, powers are not dependent on manifestations. Machines possess their powers even when they are dormant or suppressed. I refer to an unexercised power as "virtual." Consequently, third, powers are characterized by *actuality*. Here "actuality" does not refer to the *exercise* of a power in producing a manifestation, but rather refers to features possessed by a machine. Powers are real or actual features of a machine regardless of whether or not it exercises that power. As a result, fourth, powers are *intrinsic* to the machines that possess them. While it is indeed true that the power of a machine can be suppressed as a result of the presence or absence of other machines as in the case of a match in a vacuum, the power to produce flame is nonetheless an intrinsic feature of the match. Thus, fifth, powers are therefore *objective*. The powers that a machine possesses are features of that machine regardless of whether or not anyone knows of them or has observed them. Although the terms "power" and "operation" are synonymous, the term "operation" evokes connotations of the actual *exercise* of a power. For this reason, I will reserve the term "power" for a *capacity* possessed by a machine regardless of whether or not that power is exercised. By contrast, I reserve the term "operation" for the *exercise* of a power in the production of a manifestation.

In light of the foregoing, we are now in a position to better clarify the relationship between powers and manifestations. A manifestation is the product of the operation of a power on a particular input. Once again, these inputs can come either from within the machine or from outside the machine. An excellent example of inputs initiating operations arising from within a machine is radioactive decay. In the case of radioactive decay, it is not inputs coming from outside the atom that generate the decay, but rather operations taking place inside the atom itself. These operations would take place regardless of whether or not the atom came into contact with other machines. The case is similar with many thoughts. The input that generates a subsequent thought can be a preceding thought rather than an experience received through our sense-organs. By contrast, photosynthetic operations in plants are operations that take place in response to inputs that come from outside the machine such as water, sunlight, and various soil nutrients.

The products of an operation are manifestations. Manifestations are not manifestations to or for someone. A manifestation would be manifest regardless of whether or not another being were there to perceive it. Rather, a manifestation is nothing more than the product or output of an operation. The rust of iron resulting from oxidation is a manifestation and exists regardless of whether or not anyone observes this rust. Manifestations, products, or outputs come in one of three forms. On the one hand, the output or product of an operation can be a *qualitative manifestation*. Qualitative manifestations are manifestations that transform some quality of the machine such as its color, shape, texture, and so on.

When a person's skin is exposed to sunlight after a lazy afternoon spent on the beach, they undergo a qualitative manifestation in the form of acquiring a tan. When exposed to frigid air, we undergo a change in shape where our skin tightens and contracts. Likewise, in heat our skin becomes swollen and flushed. Very cold steel becomes brittle and easily susceptible to snapping. We thus see that the qualities or properties of a machine are not so much things that the machine *possesses* or *has* intrinsically, as they are activities resulting from operations that take place within the machine.

The great Roman poet-philosopher Lucretius makes this point beautifully in his masterpiece *De Rerum Natura*. There Lucretius observes that atoms . . .

> . . . have no color,
> But they do differ in shape, and from this cause
> Arise effects of color variation.
> It makes a world of difference in what order
> They form their combinations, how they are held,
> How give, take, interact. For an example,
> Things black a little while ago turn white,
> All shining white, as a dark sea can change
> From sullen black to the shine of dancing marble
> When the great winds go sweeping over the waves.
> You can say that what we often see as black,
> When its matter gets disturbed, or its order shifts
> With something added, something taken away,
> Looks, almost in a moment, white and shining.
> But if the ocean-surface were composed
> Of blue-green atoms, it could never whiten.
>
> (Lucretius 1969: 73)

While I do not endorse Lucretius' particular theory of atoms, we see here the same basic machinic idea at work in his thought. Color is not a property that the water *has*, but is rather the result of operations taking place within the water through wave action and wind. The color of the water is a manifestation that takes place as a result of certain operations. Thus, when the water is black at night, it really *is* black. It is not that the *water* really is blue and we can't *see* this because of the absence of light, but rather that those operations that produce blue as an *effect* are not taking place because wavelengths of light that bounce off the water producing the color blue are not occurring. Were we to get into a debate as to whether the water is black, blue, green, or white – all manifestations that the water can undergo – we would miss the basic point that the qualities of the water, its color, are the result of operations or activities. The water is all these qualities as a function of the operations on inputs taking place in the water as it interacts with particular inputs.

Second, there are what we might call *agentive manifestations*. Agentive manifestations are transformations in the activity or behavior of a machine as a result of inputs from within or without undergoing particular operations. When our bodies shiver in response to cold we have undergone an agentive manifestation. The changes in behavior and priorities a person undergoes when falling in love are an instance of an agentive manifestation. In a Briggs-Rauscher reaction or chemical clock, a mixture of potassium iodate, malonic acid, hydrogen peroxide, and manganese sulphate that is stirred and heated on a hot plate will begin to oscillate between colors of blue and yellow at regular intervals. Without the inputs of heat and the centrifugal motion produced by stirring, these new forms of activity do not emerge.

Finally, third, there are *material manifestations*. A material manifestation is a manifestation produced by an operation that generates an output that departs from the machine in question. A student that gets her diploma is the material manifestation of an educational machine such as a high school or university. She began as an input that underwent certain educational operations, producing a degreed student as an output. The oxygen produced by a tree in the process of photosynthesis is a material manifestation of that machine. An act of speech in response to a question is a material manifestation. A material manifestation is a product produced by a machine that goes on to circulate throughout the world apart from that machine.

If the manifestations of a machine are *local* manifestations, then this is because the way in which a machine manifests properties, activities, and material outputs will be variable as a function of the operations and conditions in which the manifestation takes place. As we saw in the case of Lucretius' ocean, its color will differ depending on wind and lighting conditions. A tree will grow differently depending on the amount of rainfall it gets, the quality of the air, how much sunlight it receives, soil conditions, and the insects that make it their home. Crops of grapes differ wildly from year to year, yielding dramatically different wines; and grapes from one and the same genetic stock produce very different wines when grown in different regions of the world. It is not simply that operations give form in a perfectly replicable fashion to the inputs that pass through them. Rather, the powers of the inputs engage in operations of their own that modify the being of the machine and the manifestations it produces. One of the central aims of onto-cartography is to map fields of coupled machines functioning as media for one another and how these fields preside over particular local manifestations.

It would be a mistake to believe that the powers constituting the virtual proper being of a machine are fixed. To be sure, many machines possess fairly stable systems of powers that endure through time and that thereby generate fairly regular local mani-festations. The shape of a diamond remains relatively stable so long as it isn't subjected to intense heat or pressure. While the color of a diamond dances and scintillates as it interacts with dif-ferent forms of light, these encounters with light do not seem to modify the powers of this machine. Nonetheless, powers can wax and wane, and machines can gain and loose powers with the limit point being destruction. We are all familiar with the waxing and waning of powers in our own bodies. When we suffer from hunger or sleep deprivation our powers of acting, encountering our envi-ronment, and thinking are diminished. The powers of thinking, acting, and experiencing remain, but have a diminished capacity for operating.

However, it is not simply that the powers of a machine wax and wane; machines can also gain and lose powers as a result of the operations that take place within them as well as encounters with other machines. Along these lines, Catherine Malabou writes that, ". . . the brain of a pianist is not strictly identical to that of a math-ematician, a mechanic, or a graphic artist" (Malabou 2008: 7). Very complex machines such as human beings are not, of course, *born* as pianists, mathematicians, or graphic artists, but rather become these types of machine. Becoming these types of machine entails acquiring new powers or the capacity for new operations. Cognitive scientist and philosopher Andy Clark argues that minds are not what exist between our ears, but are a sort of relation between brain, body, and the entities of the external world.[1] He refers to this as the "extended mind hypothesis," arguing that the mind is literally extended out into the world. Thus, for example, in the case of the blind man that uses a cane or a seeing-eye dog, the cane and dog are literally parts of his mind. If this is so, then it is because the powers of a machine change as a result of the couplings it enters into. The mind of a blind man in isolation is different from that of one with a seeing-eye dog. Similarly, in the metamorphosis from a caterpillar to a butterfly, powers are both gained and lost. Finally, in extremely cold temperatures, steel loses its power of malleability and becomes brittle and liable to fracture.

All machines are more or less characterized by *plasticity*. There is no machine so rigid that it is not haunted by a plurality of virtual manifestations and becomings that may or may not become actualized. To be sure, some machines will be more rigid than others as a result of the operations currently unfolding within them and the stability of the conditions in which they are situated, yet they nonetheless possess an intrinsic and objective plasticity. Nor is it here being suggested that machines are infinitely plastic in the sense that they can become anything. Clearly a rock cannot become a butterfly, nor a butterfly an automobile. Rather each machine has a plasticity proper to the sort of machine that it is. This plasticity is first of all attested to by the variety of local manifestations it is capable of producing through operations, and second through the becomings or the production of new powers machines undergo in the adventure of their existence. With Spinoza, we can thus say that we do not know what a machine can do (Spinoza 2002: 280–1). Contrary to that ontological vision that comprehends entities in terms of predicates inhering in a subject, we can only discover the being of a machine, its powers, through acting upon it and varying its relations to other machines to discern what local manifestations and becomings arise as a consequence.

Machines Are Binary Machines: Trans-Corporeality

Manifestations are local manifestations because the manner in which a machine manifests properties, activities, or material outputs will be a function of both the operations performed by the machine as well as the *inputs* that flow through the machine. Given different inputs, the machine will produce different local manifestations. In short, the qualities, activities, and material outputs of a machine will vary depending on the milieu in which it is embedded. It is for this reason that all machines are *binary machines*. As Deleuze and Guattari observe:

... machines are binary machines, obeying a binary law or set of rules governing associations: one machine is always coupled with another. The productive synthesis, the production of production, is inherently connective in nature: "and ..." "and then ..." This is because there is always a flow-producing machine, and another machine connected to it that interrupts or draws off part of this flow ... (Deleuze and Guattari 1983: 5)

One machine is coupled to another machine that provides a flow for that machine and upon which the second machine performs operations producing outputs in the form of qualities, activities, or material products. As we saw above, when one machine provides a flow for a second machine, that machine functions as a *medium* for that second machine. A tree, for example, is coupled to the sun, the soil, rainfall, a variety of microorganisms, other plants, animals that produce carbon dioxide, and so on, all of which provide flows upon which it carries out operations in cellular metabolism. Many of the inputs upon which a machine performs its operations thus arise from other machines. In providing inputs for a machine they function as media for that machine.

However, while Deleuze and Guattari draw attention to an important feature of machines in underlining the manner in which they are binary or coupled to other machines, we believe that their thesis that one machine is *always* coupled to another machine is deeply problematic. In *Anti-Oedipus* they give the example of a mouth-machine coupled to a breast-machine from which flows of milk are drawn. So far, so good. However, problems emerge the moment we say that the mouth-machine is *always* attached to the *breast-machine*. Sometimes the mouth-machine is attached to the breast-machine, and at other times it is not. As psycho-analysis has taught us, this presence and absence, this *variation* in coupling, plays an important role in the development of the subject. At a more material level, the infant, of course, starves when it is not attached to this machine and its flows. Likewise, as new parents often learn, sometimes the infant proves unable to "latch" at all. At other times, the mouth-machine is attached to a bottle, and at yet other times, it is attached to a thumb (what are the flows here?).

The problem with claiming that one machine is *always* coupled to another machine is that it undermines what is most significant in the thesis that machines *can* be coupled to other machines.

The coupling of machines to one another is significant in that it draws attention to the manner in which couplings *modify* the local manifestations and becomings of a machine. However, where one machine is *always* coupled to another machine from which it draws flows, it will not undergo these variations because the relation (coupling) will always be present. It is only where couplings are variable, where they are sometimes present and sometimes absent, where the coupling is sometimes to this machine and sometimes to that machine, that the thesis of coupling becomes significant. Thus it seems to us that Deleuze is more correct when he remarks that, "[r]elation is not a property of objects, it is always external to its terms" (Deleuze 1986: 10). Here the terms, of course, are machines, while the relations are couplings between machines. Emphasis on the fact that relations or couplings are external underlines the way in which couplings can be severed and new couplings can be produced, both of which generate new local manifestations and becomings in entities. An infant decoupled from breast or bottle becomes jaundiced, for example. Moreover, it is not simply the flows *simpliciter* that preside over local manifestations and becomings, but the *nature* of these flows that play a role. In the case of the gender of newborns, recent research suggests that high-energy diets rich in vitamins such as potassium and B12 are significantly more likely to produce male offspring (*Science Daily* 2008). Here we have an example of the flows drawn off from other machines by the mother that are, in their turn, drawn on by the developing fetus, leading to the production of virtual powers associated with sex. This variability, however, would not be possible without variation in couplings and flows between machines.

When the inputs that flow through a machine arise from outside the machine as in the case of the respiration of a Japanese tanuki or raccoon dog, that machine is characterized by what Stacy Alaimo has called "trans-corporeality." As Alaimo articulates it:

Imagining human corporeality [and I would argue, *all* corporeality] as trans-corporeality, in which the human is always intermeshed with the more-than-human world, underlines the extent to which the substance of the human is ultimately inseparable from "the environment." It makes it difficult to pose nature as mere background . . . for the exploits of the human since "nature" is always as close as one's own skin – perhaps even closer. Indeed, thinking across bodies may catalyze the recognition that the environment, which is too often imagined as inert, empty space or as a resource for human use, is, in fact, a world of fleshy beings with their own needs, claims, and actions. By emphasizing the movement across bodies, trans-corporeality reveals the interchanges and interconnections between various bodily natures. But by underscoring that *trans* indicates movement across different sites, trans-corporeality also opens up a mobile space that acknowledges the often unpredictable and unwanted actions of human bodies, nonhuman creatures, ecological systems, chemical agents, and other actors. (Alaimo 2010: 2)

The concept of trans-corporeality, similar to that of structural coupling and binary machines, underscores the way in which bodies are intermeshed with one another, mutually affecting and being affected by each other. Trans-corporeality teaches us of a world where things that seem to be over there and thus apart from us intermesh with us in ways that significantly impact our local manifestations and becomings. For example, we might think of garbage as something that simply disappears when we put it in a dump. Yet when we understand that spillage from that dump enters the water supply, affecting wildlife, and that we eat that wildlife, we come to understand the way in which nothing is ever really thrown away, but rather eventually enters us through other, indirect means. A body, as it were, is *sheathed* in a world. One of the central aims of onto-cartography is the mapping of trans-corporeal relations between machines, how these interactions affect one another, and how they structure the movements and becomings of which a machine is capable in this world.

The prior discussion of operations and inputs or flows might have given the impression that flows are a passive stuff that pass through the operations of a machine taking on a form as an output. In this regard, the flows that pass through a machine would be like cookie dough submitted to the formative activity of a tin cookie cutter. However, we must remember that the flows that pass through a machine are not something *other* than *machines*, but are themselves machines with their own powers that engage in their own operations. Here, contrary to a philosophical tradition that treats matters as the *formless* awaiting form from some formative agency such as the intellect of God, I adopt the axiom that *there is no structureless matter*. There is no such thing, as Graham Harman sometimes puts it, as "unformatted" beings. To be sure, many beings are *formable* in the sense that they can take on new structure through operations being exercised upon them, but there is no matter, nor has there ever been any matter, that is characterized by pure formlessness. Even fluid machines such as highly viscous mud, water, and clouds have molecular structures characterized by their own powers and operations.

The consequence of this is that machines, in performing operations on flows or inputs, will have to contend with the powers characterizing the being of these flows. It is for this reason that machines are not sovereigns of the flows that pass through them. Rather, in many instances, there is a sort of *reciprocal determination* between flows or inputs and machines exercising operations on these flows. In other words, there are many instances in which the machines that flow through a machine modify the machine that operates. We already saw that this might be the case in the sexed development of a fetus as a result of the mother's diet. In a similar vein, in *Vibrant Matter*, Jane Bennett explores, among other things, how ". . . omega-3 fatty acids [might] make prisoners less prone to violent acts, inattentive schoolchildren better able to focus, and bipolar persons less depressed" (Bennett 2010: 41). Here it is not simply that the body digests the omega-3 fatty acids, forming them into various cellular materials through its operations of metabolism, while retaining the same local manifestations. Rather, the acids modify the local manifestations of the body as well. There is thus a reciprocal determination – the very core of Alaimo's concept of trans-corporeality – between the powers of omega-3 fatty acids and the operations they exercise on cells and the cells of a bodily-machine metabolizing these acids and the operations they exercise on the acids. Artists often talk about something similar with respect to the media they work with. Take the sculptor working with marble. They might begin with a vague idea of what they want the marble to become and even select specific pieces of marble to execute this local manifestation, yet as they begin to work the marble, encountering its grain and veins, they'll talk about how the marble "wants" to become something else. What novelist or philosopher hasn't experienced something similar, where their characters and concepts seem to take on a life of their own, leading the novel or argument to go in a very different direction than that first anticipated?

However, it's important to note that there are degrees of plasticity ranging from absolutely rigid machines to absolutely plastic machines. An absolutely rigid machine is a machine that would be so completely impermeable to the operations of other machines functioning as inputs or media that it only operates transformations on these media without being modified in any way by these media. This seems to be a feature of many incorporeal machines such as mathematical equations that are not changed or modified in any way by the inputs that pass through them as they undertake operations. The Pythagorean theorem remains the same regardless of whether or not the right triangle is this or that size, this or that color, or made of this or that material. It is impermeable to the powers of wood, steel, string, pencil lead, and so on. By contrast, an absolutely plastic machine would be a machine so malleable that it becomes absolutely different in its encounter with a medium. It is likely that there are no absolutely plastic machines because there is no such thing as unformatted matter and therefore no such thing as a machine that doesn't exercise operations on the machines that pass through it. Nonetheless, certain subatomic particles approach absolutely plastic machines insofar as they display a tendency to become something else entirely when encountering other particles or to be destroyed altogether.

Between absolutely rigid machines and absolutely plastic machines, there is a whole range of differences in degree. Thus machines such as industrial factories, tin cookie cutters, bureaucracies, dogmatic theologies and political movements, stove tops, compulsive obsessive neuroses, certain fetishes, etc., approach absolutely rigid machines in that they are only marginally transformed by the inputs that flow through them or upon which they exercise their operations, while nonetheless ineluctably exercising their operations on these flows. By contrast, machines such as organic bodies, great works of art, anarchic political movements, subatomic particles, brains, and so on, seem to be highly plastic machines. These are machines that are strongly modified in terms of their local manifestations and becomings as a result of the flows that pass through them. An organic body, for example, will be strongly affected not only by the nutrients that pass through it, the sort of light that it encounters, and the qualities of the air that pass through it as it develops, but also by the cultural milieu and organic ecosystem in which it exists.

Yet why would a great work of art have these characteristics? Given that these machines more or less maintain their identity or structure across time insofar as they persevere in their being as a sculpture, painting, or architectural edifice, or maintain their pattern as they're replicated like songs, novels and poems, why are they nonetheless plastic? We must not forget that works of art are machines. What seems unique to a great work of art is that it is strangely oblivious to the world into which it falls, not in the sense that, as in the case of a rigid machine like a mathematical equation, it always remains the same and engages in one and the same set of operations, but rather in the sense that it is capable of producing effects of a very different nature as a result of the inputs that pass through it in different historical and cultural contexts. A great work of art *resonates*. If we take the concept of resonance seriously, then we understand it as a power capable of producing *novel* local manifestations as a result of the other entities that it encounters. For example, we can think of two strings of a violin resonating with one another.

This is how it is with great works of art. They somehow manage to resonate with the cultural and historical milieus into which they fall or appear, producing something new as a result. It is not that, like a mathematical equation, they produce the *same* operations in all possible couplings, but rather that they are capable of producing *different* operations in different milieus. A great work of art is an infinitely, or at least indefinitely, productive machine. Let us take Kafka's two great novels, *The Trial* and *The Castle*. These novels are machines that can be read psychoanalytically as reflecting the structure of Oedipus, allowing us to shed all sorts of light on our own libidinal relations to others in the world around us. They can be read politically as critiques of fascism and totalitarianism and how they function. They can be read theologically as speaking to the mystery of God. They can be read as a critique of bureaucracy. They can be read as a handbook for resistance to forces of political power. They can be read as an analysis of our alienation from others in the contemporary world. And it is likely that there are countless other possible readings as well.

A great work of art is plastic in the sense that it is *pluripotent*. It is a machine that is capable of resonating in a variety of ways given the historical and cultural milieus that it encounters. It's as if there is a certain vagueness, a certain floating nature, that characterizes these works allowing them to maximally traverse culture and history. With pluripotent works such as this, we get a reciprocal determination. They both act on their historical and cultural milieu and are acted upon by their historical and cultural milieu. The milieu actualizes the work in a particular way, leading it to be interpreted in a certain way. But the work also organizes the historical and cultural milieu in a particular way leading us to attend to certain cultural phenomena as significant while ignoring others.

Note

1. See Clark (2011).

3

Alien Phenomenology

Machines Are Structurally Open and Operationally Closed

While machines draw on inputs or flows upon which to perform their operations, they cannot draw on all the possible inputs available in the world, nor do they relate to the inputs that they draw upon in the way those machines functioning as flows are for themselves. With respect to this first point, machines "specify" the flows or machines to which they are open. It is in this respect that they are "structurally open" to a world beyond themselves (see Maturana and Varela 1998: 79). However, it is not the case that machines are open to *all* flows available in the world. Rather, machines are only open to a small subset of existing flows. This subset will differ from machine to machine. As a consequence, it is not the case that everything can relate to everything else, nor that everything is related to everything else. This is for the simple reason that machines are not structurally open to all possible flows issuing from other machines.

Hopefully a few examples will suffice to illustrate this point. The mantis shrimp has far more advanced vision than humans. This isn't simply because they are able to see things with greater clarity or at greater distances. Rather, they are able to see things that we are not able to see at all. Where humans can only see combinations of three primary colors, mantis shrimp can see eleven or twelve primary colors (Minard 2008). Mantis shrimp are able to see polarized light, including circular polarized light, whereas humans are not. Likewise, mantis shrimps are able to see infrared and ultraviolet light, whereas we are not. In short, mantis shrimp are open to flows of electromagnetism (light) that are all but non-existent to human beings. They are structurally open to flows entirely invisible to us because of how their eyes and nervous system are put together. As a consequence, mantis shrimps are able to relate to other machines populating a world in ways we are not.

We see similar phenomena of selective structural openness in the case of humans and bureaucracies. When we relate to a person that works for a bureaucracy, we think that we are relating to this other person – and, in part, we are – but in reality we are relating to a bureaucracy-machine. Like any other machine, bureaucracy-machines are only open to certain types of flows. Most commonly, the flows to which bureaucracy-machines are open are *forms*. To communicate with a bureaucracy we must fill out paperwork or a form and submit it to the institution. A form is itself a machine that operates on certain inputs – most generally, circumstances of our lives revolving around taxes, medical matters, permits for building, obtaining a license, grants, professional evaluation, and so on – transforming these inputs into certain structured media of communication. In other words, the form is the machinic-mediator between us and the bureaucracy. A form is a machine that distills human communication to a set of pre-defined parameters. Often we will find that the form contains no parameters pertaining to the sort of communication we wish to engage in. We find no place on the form for the sort of being we are. We can thus note that forms also count persons in particular ways, only recognizing certain types of beings as existing. We might, for example, seek disability assistance, only to find that the form does not recognize the existence of the sort of disability from which we suffer. Like the forms of light that the human cannot see, but which the mantis shrimp can perceive, the bureaucracy is *blind* to these types of beings. Forms are also particularly blind to the singularity of circumstances, filtering out detail and reducing circumstances to a set of generic categories. Finally, while the language of the form *seems* to be in our native language, it often seems to be a form of our native language that is in fact foreign. This is because the language of forms is, in fact, a foreign language. It is the language of the bureaucracy, not the language of humans. We experience this acutely with tax forms and contracts, where we perpetually wonder whether we're responding in the right way. This is why we often have to consult translators – known as accountants and lawyers – to prepare the forms for us.

This is why our experience of bureaucratic-machines is often so acutely painful and frustrating. Like the experience of being lost in a foreign country where we don't know the language and desperately need to reach a particular destination at a particular time, we have the strange experience of feeling as if we're talking to another person, conveying our circumstances, only to find that while being communicated, who we are and our circumstances cannot be conveyed to the official because we are only permitted to transmit what is on the form according to pre-delineated criteria. All that can be communicated is what the form allows us to communicate. Our person, our circumstances, our life, is reduced to the categorical grinder, the sieve, pre-delineated by the form. It is this, and not our speech, to which the bureaucratic-machine is structurally open. The rest is filtered out as mere noise. It was this non-communication that Kafka dramatized so brilliantly in *The Trial* and *The Castle*.

Machines, then, are only selectively related to other machines. This is true of everything ranging from the humblest particle to complex entities capable of perception and cognition. The tiny neutrino, for example, is unable to interact with most matter we are familiar with in our day-to-day lives because of its neutral electric charge. It passes through this matter as if it didn't even exist. As a consequence, one of the central aims of onto-cartographical analysis is to determine the flows to which particular machines are open and the manner in which these machines are open to these flows; that is, how it interacts with these flows.

The complement of structural openness is operational closure. Structural openness refers to the flows to which a machine is open, while operational closure refers to the way in which a machine works over a flow as it passes through it. Operational closure means that a machine never relates to a flow *as it is*, but rather always transforms that flow according to its own operations and "processes" those flows in terms of the internal structure of the machine. To see this point, let us take the imaginary example of a person who has lived their *entire* life on a submarine without windows. The flows to which the submarine is structurally open would be various beeps and pings issuing from sonar as it bounces off of other machines in the ocean. Now clearly these sonar pings are nothing *like* underwater mountains, blue whales, sharks, and other entities that populate the ocean. Not only do all of these other machines have an internal structure, an "endo-structure," that fails to register in the sonar pings, but they have all sorts of other qualities that cannot be registered through sound. The only information we get from the sonar ping is the size, shape, and velocity of the other entity. The first point then is that a flow, which is itself a machine, differs from the thing from which it flows.

However, this is not all. Once the sonar is returned, it takes on a different *functional* status within the submarine than it has for the other machine that the sound bounced off. Within the submarine the sonar ping will take on a particular meaning, telling the submariner to turn left, right, up, or down so as to avoid the obstacle. By contrast, the machine that the sonar bounced off – a shark, blue whale, underwater mountain or canyon, other submarine, etc. – is *oblivious* to the meaning the submarine attributes to it. The shark, for example, is just navigating the ocean to find prey or to insure that water continues to flow over its gills so it can continue to breathe. In other words, once a flow enters a machine it takes on a different functional value – causally or in terms of meaning – than it had for the machine from which the flow issued.

This is the meaning of operational closure. On the one hand, operational closure means that when one machine encounters a flow issuing from another machine, it encounters that flow not as it *is*, but rather in terms of how its operations transform it. Such would be the meaning of Kant's observation that:

> Up to now it has been assumed that all our cognition must conform to the objects; but all attempts to find out something about them *a priori* through concept that would extend our cognition have, on this presupposition, come to nothing. Hence let us once try whether we do not get farther with the problem of metaphysics by assuming that the objects must conform to our cognition . . . (Kant 1998: Bxvi)

Kant's thesis is that the mind is not a *mirror* of the world, but that as the world affects the mind, mind restructures these flows in terms of its own internal structure, giving these flows form. The consequence of this is that we can never know whether or not mind represents the world as it is, because we can never get outside of our own operations to determine whether or not the manner in which they have transformed flows map on to things as they are in themselves. What we relate to is not the things themselves, but the things as they have been worked over by the operations of our mind. What Kant says here about cognitive-machines holds for all machines.[1] Rocks, neutrinos, insurance companies, and capybara no more encounter things as they are in themselves, than our own minds, and this because the other machines of the world, through their operations, work over the affectations or flows that pass through them, just as our minds do. As a consequence, all machines only relate to each other behind "firewalls."[2] No entity directly encounters another – though, contra Harman, I do hold that entities can directly affect one another – and for this reason all machines encounter one another behind firewalls. Within the machine-oriented framework proposed here, these firewalls are the operations of each machine.

This phenomenon of operational closure is so ubiquitous that it deserves to be thought as a general ontological feature of all machines. We encounter it in the way in which one atomic element relates to another atomic element when the two bond forming a molecule. We encounter it in the way in which subatomic particles relate to one another. We encounter it in the way in which rocks respond to being heated. We encounter it in the way that animals respond to various stimuli from their environment. And we encounter it, above all, in conversations between people and in our interactions with institutions. Always we find an operation transforming a flow, making that flow something different for the machine that carries out that operation.

On the other hand, operational closure means that once a flow enters a machine, it takes on a different functional value. Let's return to the previous example of a bureaucratic-machine like a private insurance corporation to illustrate this point. The *person* submitting a *form* to a machine like an insurance company does so for the aim or purpose of getting the medical procedures they require covered. By contrast, the insurance company has a very different aim. Because it is a *private* business, its aim is not to provide *coverage*, but to maximize profit for both its shareholders and the corporation itself. Providing coverage is only a *means* to this end. The form that the *person* fills out is a flow that enters the insurance-machine. Once it enters the insurance-machine it will, as a result of operational closure, take on a very different functional value than it had for the person that sent that flow. Where the person that sent that flow will be seeking coverage for matters pertaining to health, the categorical reduction that takes place as a result of the machine's firewalls (operations) will now take up the form in terms of whether or not providing coverage in this circumstance will maximize profit. In other words, the form takes on a different meaning than it had for the person. In some cases, the form will be rejected as an "unnecessary procedure" (translation: as a procedure that is unprofitable). In other cases, coverage will be provided but of a substandard sort. In yet other cases, the insurance-machine will claim that the request for the procedure is, in fact, a fraudulent request or that the patient is suffering from psychosomatic symptoms and therefore in no need of care. In all cases, from the *insurance-machine*'s point of view, the question will be one not of providing care and coverage, but of maximizing profit through the reduction of expenditure. In short, once entering the insurance-machine, the form takes on a very different significance or meaning than it had for the person submitting it, leading to very different outcomes than those intended by the persons that provided the flow initially.

Because of the selectivity of structural openness, as well as the self-referential nature of operational closure, each machine is blind to much of the world. As sociologist Niklas Luhmann puts it, machines ". . . cannot see what [they] cannot see" (Luhmann 2002a: 129). The flows to which one machine is open are invisible to another machine as in the case of the difference between the visual systems of mantis shrimp and humans. When two machines are open to the same type of flow, these flows can nonetheless take on very different types of causal and meaningful roles in the respective machines by virtue of differences in the organization of their operational closure. We saw this in the case of how the form differs in significance for the sick person submitting the form and the insurance-machine receiving the form. For the sick person, the form pertains to their health and ability to afford the care and treatment they need. For the insurance-machine the form is an economic signal to be evaluated in terms of potential for profit or loss. In this regard, there's a very real sense in which Lacan's aphorism that "all communication is miscommunication" holds true for relations between all entities and not just relations between humans. A smile for a person is a gesture of goodwill, while a chimpanzee encounters the smile as an aggressive bearing of the teeth signifying danger.

What holds true of relations of significance between machines also holds true of causal relationships. On the one hand, we've already seen that not all entities are able to causally interact with one another. The neutrino, by virtue of its neutral electric charge, is unable to interact with most other matter, while our visual systems are unable to register ultraviolet and infrared light. The consequence of this is that the environment of a machine is, as Luhmann notes, always more complex than the machine's openness to that environment (Luhmann 1995: 25). For organic and cognitive machines, this entails that openness will always involve risk (ibid.) In a machinic environment that is perpetually changing and more complex than the manner in which an organic or cognitive machine is open, it is always possible that events will take place to which the machine is blind, but which nonetheless destroy the machine. For organic and cognitive machines, the selectivity of structural openness is always a wager. On the other hand, one and the same causal flow can affect machines receiving that flow in very different ways. In the case of iron, for example, oxygen produces rust, while in the case of animals it plays a role in converting nutrients into energy for work or activity. These points are obvious, but it is nonetheless worth noting that that no machine is open to all flows and that each type of machine carries out different operations on the flows that they share in common.

Luhmann remarks that "[r]eality is what one does not perceive when one perceives it" (Luhmann 2002a: 145). We perceive the world, of course, because our perceptions are initiated by flows that affect us. Nonetheless we do not perceive the world because what we experience – and what all sentient beings experience – are these flows transformed through operations. From the standpoint of the subject, its *lived experience* of the world is indistinguishable from the world itself. This is because each machine only has access to operationally transformed flows it encounters in its internal world. This gives rise to the perils of *epistemological closure* and *confirmation bias* that often plague certain political groups and organizations. For example, because a political group only consumes media that reflect its own ideological worldview back to it, it might become blind to the real causes of various economic, national, and international events. As a result, it becomes unable to respond to these events. Such is the nature of epistemological closure. The machine that suffers from epistemological closure is the machine that is only structurally open to informational flows that reflect its operational presuppositions about the world. The complement of this is confirmation bias, where a machine only selects flows of information that reinforce its operational assumptions. These phenomena, of course, place machines at significant risk insofar as they render the machine unable to respond to environmental events that do not fit with the machine's operational vision of the world. In this regard, epistemological closure and confirmation bias can be partially overcome through a machine relating to environmental events that contradict its operational understanding of the world not as mere noise to be filtered out, denounced, or ignored, but rather as indications that the lived world of the machine differs from the world itself.

We must take care, however, not to conclude that structural openness and operational closure are indelibly fixed in all circumstances. Organic and cognitive machines – plastic machines – are capable of multiplying their structural openness or points of contact with their machinic environment, and are also capable of transforming their operational responses to flows from their environment and of introducing new operations. In organic machines, these processes take place through evolution and processes of random variation, natural selection, and heritability. Evolution is not simply an evolution of the bodily form or shape of a species, but is also an evolution of different forms of structural openness and operations on flows. Through evolutionary processes, a machinic lineage can develop new forms of openness to its environment and new ways of operating on flows that pass through it. In the case of cognitive machines such as dolphins, octopuses, dogs, humans, various computers, and social institutions, new forms of structural openness and new operations can be developed through *learning*. Take the example of psychoanalytic listening as opposed to ordinary listening. When the ordinary person hears a slip of the tongue or witnesses a bungled action, they experience it as a mere mistake. By contrast, when a psychoanalyst hears and witnesses these things, they see them as imbued with significance or meaning, expressing the person's unconscious desire. The forgetting of a favorite umbrella at a friend's house, for example, is no longer encountered as a mere mistake or noise to be ignored, but as an index of the person's desire indicating, perhaps, that they did not want to leave or that they would like to return. Learning to hear and witness psychoanalytically consists in an expansion of one's structural openness to the world, and is the production of new types of operations with respect to the flows one encounters. Where before the bungled action was seen as simply an unfortunate incident, it is now seen as pregnant with significance. Where before one would simply engage in operations of condolence – "oh that's too bad!" – one now engages in *interpretive* operations, seeking to decipher what desire this bungled action or slip of the tongue might express.

Alien Phenomenology, Second-Order Observation, and Post-Vitalist Ethology

Because all machines are characterized by selective structural openness and operational closure, alien phenomenology, second-order observation, or ethology are crucial components to the project and practice of onto-cartography. The term "alien phenomenology" was introduced by Ian Bogost to denote a form of phenomenology that examines how *non-human* entities experience the world around them (Bogost 2012). Alien phenomenology includes, as I understand it, traditional phenomenology, but goes beyond it. Where traditional phenomenology investigates *our* lived experience of the world, alien phenomenology seeks to investigate how other entities such as mosquitoes, trees, rocks, computer games, institutions, etc., encounter the world about them. This practice is what Niklas Luhmann has elsewhere called "second-order observation" (Luhmann 2002b). In second-order observation we are not observing how an entity is presented to *us*, but rather are seeking to observe how the world is presented to *another entity*. We ask what the world is like for a cane toad, for example, rather than what cane toads are like for us. We are observing how another entity observes. Elsewhere, the biologist Jakob von Uexküll, has proposed a similar sort of observation that he calls ethology, where we seek to observe what the world is like for other animals (Uexküll 2010).

Alien phenomenology, second-order observation, or ethology seek to determine the flows to which a machine is open, as well as the way that machine operates on these flows as they pass through the machine. It asks "to what flows is the machine structurally open?", "how does the machine structure those flows?", "how does the machine operate on these flows as they pass through it?", "what is the world like for this machine?" and "what local manifestations take place in the machine as they pass through it?" For example, the alien phenomenologist investigating a bat would be interested in how bats operate on sonic flows – insofar as bats largely encounter their world through sonar – and what significance these sonar flows take on for the bat as it hunts and navigates the world. How, we might ask, does the bat use sonar to distinguish between a mere seed or bit of pollen floating through the air and an insect? We have seen a similar thumbnail sketch of an alien phenomenology in the case of insurance company machines, where we saw the structural openness of an insurance company is largely organized around the form as that flow to which it is responsive, and where it operates on forms to determine whether or not granting coverage would entail economic profit or loss.

In all cases, alien phenomenology consists in the attempt to suspend our own human ways of operating and encountering the world so as investigate non-human ways of encountering the world. Now, when presented with the project of alien phenomenology, it is likely that one will object, on grounds similar to those of Thomas Nagel (Nagel 1974), that it is impossible for us to investigate the experience of another machine for the very simple reason that the experience of other beings cannot be observed and we are not these types of beings. However, while it is entirely true that I cannot *experience* the world of a bat, computer chip, or corporation because I am not a bat, computer chip, or corporation, I can nonetheless make all sorts of inferences about what the world is like for these other machines. In *A Foray Into the Worlds of Animals and Humans*, von Uexküll provides scores of examples as to how this is possible, while also providing techniques for how to conduct these investigations. Our knowledge of the sorts of flows that exist in the world – a knowledge that grows daily as we create instruments to detect flows invisible to us such as ultra-violet light and radiation – coupled with our knowledge of things such as optics and physiology, allow us to make inferences about what flows a machine is structurally open to. For example, our knowledge of various forms of electromagnetism, coupled with our knowledge of optics and what types of optic cells are sensitive to what kinds of light, allows us to infer that mantis shrimps are structurally open to a much broader spectrum of electromagnetic waves than humans. Armed with this knowledge of the flows to which the mantis shrimp is open, coupled with our knowledge of biology that tells us that organic machines are built for eating, surviving, and mating, rather than knowing, we can observe how the mantis shrimp responds in the presence of these electromagnetic flows, thereby inferring what functional value these flows have in the various operations of the mantis shrimp. For example, etho-graphers increasingly think that the openness of mantis shrimp to circular polarized light plays a role in their mating rituals, while their ability to perceive light in the ultraviolet electromagnetic spectrum plays a role in their ability to detect predators and prey transparent in our visual spectrum.

While our alien phenomenologies are fallible and certainly do not deliver a first-person experience of what the world is like for a particular machine, we are nonetheless able to make a number of inferences about what flows other machines are able to causally and meaningfully interact with, as well as the sorts of operations they carry out in response to these flows. Our alien phenomenologies will always be imperfect, but as we well see, as imperfect as they are, they are nonetheless preferable to the epistemic closure of humanism that approaches all of being in terms of what it is for us. As an aside, it is important to note that alien phenomenology, unlike the ethology proposed by Uexküll, is "post-vitalistic." A post-vitalistic ethology is not an ethology that *excludes* the living, just as post-humanism does not exclude the human. Rather, alien phenomenology holds that we can also engage in second-order observations of how non-living, non-human machines such as carbon atoms, cameras, computers, rocks, etc., are structurally open and operationally closed to the world about them. In *Alien Phenomenology*, Ian Bogost gives just such an analysis of the camera, showing how cameras are structurally open to light or electromagnetic waves in a fashion different from humans (Bogost 2012: 47–50). Here, at least in the way I'm formulating it, alien phenomenology is not making a panpsychist claim to the effect that all beings, animate and inanimate, possess consciousness, awareness, perception, and cognition. Rather, the claim is that all machines, regardless of whether they're living, are selectively open to particular flows and operate on these flows in ways unique to that type of machine.

The practice of alien phenomenology, above all, requires us to suspend or bracket our own human aims to investigate what aims, if any, the non-human machines that are the object of our inquiry might have. Such a methodological move, of course, is only necessary when investigating goal-directed non-human machines. This bracketing or *epoché* of human goals or aims is a methodological move, not the suggestion that we should adopt a masochistic denial of our own aims or goals. It is a bracketing undertaken for the sake of understanding the operations of non-human machines. Understanding why non-human machines that have goals operate as they do requires us to temporarily suspend or bracket our own goals so as to discern the goals or aims of these goal-directed non-human machines. This move is required because an alien phenomenology attempts to adopt the point of view or perspective of a non-human machine on the world, rather than the perspective of what that machine is for us. For example, rather than asking "what is our goal when submitting a form to an insurance company?" we instead ask, "what is the insurance company's goal when processing our request for coverage?" Alien phenomenology requires us to distinguish our aims from those of other entities.

There are already a number of available post-human phenomenologies of this sort. In *Animals in Translation*, Temple Grandin adopts the perspective of various animals so as to develop more compassionate ways of relating to them (Grandin 2005). She is especially famous for her use of something like alien phenomenology to reform practices in how cows are herded to their slaughter, designing the sluices through which they pass in ways that would be less traumatic for the cows. While we might be troubled that cows are still being slaughtered, this is nonetheless a use of something like second-order observation that led to a somewhat more compassionate treatment of other animals. By attending to how cows experience the world and what their goals or needs are, she was able to make recommendations that allowed us to more compassionately attend to them.

A more radical example of something like an alien phenomenology can be found in *The Botany of Desire*, by Michael Pollan (Pollan 2002). By adopting the point of view of plants such as apples, potatoes, tulips, and marijuana, Pollan shows how these plants have developed strategies to seduce *humans*, so as to maximize their own survival and reproductive fitness. Our initial response to this thesis is that it is completely absurd. After all, plants lack consciousness, so how could they possibly develop strategies using humans to advance their own aims, much less conspiracies? However, if we remember the basics of evolutionary theory, this thesis makes perfect sense. As Dennett has noted, evolutionary language often adopts the language of the design stance and the intentional stance (Dennett 1995); however, this language is a methodological device used to help us think about the functional value of particular adaptations, not something to be taken literally. At the literal level, evolutionary "design" takes place through *blind* processes of random variation, natural selection, and heritability. Certain random mutations confer a survival or reproductive advantage on a particular organism, that organism survives long enough to reproduce, and for this reason its variations are passed on to the next generation. This is the sense in which various plants have seduced us. It is not that they had a particular *conscious* project to seduce humans, but rather that they underwent certain random mutations that produced something pleasurable or valuable to humans such as the sweetness of apples, the pleasurable affects of marijuana, or the nutritional value of potatoes.

As a result, humans selected for these plants, deciding to cultivate them or organize their society around them. Humans have had to develop all sorts of infrastructure and farming practices to cultivate these plants. Moreover, we've gone to great lengths to cultivate these plants. Thus, for example, in response to the American war on drugs, people have developed all sorts of farming practices, shipping practices, etc., to transport marijuana in ways that are probably against their own biological (reproductive/ survival) self-interest. They have become, as it were, the servants of the survival and reproductive aims of marijuana. In the case of the Great Irish Potato Famine of the nineteenth century, we see an even stronger example of plants exercising natural selection on humans. There humans had become so dependent on a particular species of the potato that when a blight occurred, they were faced with starvation. Only those people hardy enough to survive on the inferior available food sources or migrate were able to survive. As a consequence, this particular species of potato exercised tremendous selective pressure on this population, leading to all sorts of social transformations as a consequence.

When we adopt Pollan's plant-perspective, our social world appears in an entirely different way. We begin with the assumption, for example, that we are the ones who have cultivated grass so as to have aesthetically appealing lawns and places for children to play. However, when we adopt the perspective of grass, we might be led to conclude that grass has seduced us to spread itself around America to maximize its reproductive advantages in ways that are contrary to our self-interest. Those lawns that we so carefully cultivate are against our own self-interest in a variety of ways. On the one hand, we of course expend valuable time and resources mowing, watering, and cultivating our lawns. On the other hand, this space would perhaps be better used to cultivate fruits, herbs, and vegetables, decreasing our own economic burden in food shopping. Moreover, the mowing of lawns is an environmental disaster as a consequence of emissions from lawn mowers, the fertilizers we use, and the gases released as grass clippings rot in garbage dumps. By adopting the perspective of grass, we might conclude that we'd be better off releasing ourselves from the seductions of this plant-life and instead planting other machines.

Similarly, when we adopt the perspective of cows within an evolutionary framework, we get a very different view of the relationship between humans and cows. From an evolutionary perspective, the success of a species is not measured by whether or not *individuals* survive, but by how successfully members of a species are able to pass on their genes. In this framework, the survival of the individual is only of importance insofar as it allows the individual to live long enough to reproduce. Take the example of the octopus. Once impregnated, the female octopus finds a cave where she lays thousands of eggs around the opening. For the next few weeks, the octopus does nothing but clean the eggs and jet oxygenated water over them. During this time she doesn't eat at all. By the time the eggs hatch, she is so weakened from lack of food that when she ventures back out into the ocean she's usually quickly eaten by fish, crabs, and other aquatic life. Clearly the survival strategy octopuses have evolved for caring for their young does not benefit the individual octopus, though it does maximize the chances of her genes being carried on by the thousands of eggs.

Viewed through this lens, our relationship to cows and other livestock looks very different. While clearly it is a horrible thing to slaughter cows as we do, from an evolutionary perspective cows, by seducing humans with their flesh and skin, have hit upon a strategy that allows them to maximize their reproductive success. In their ancient war with trees and predators like wolves, these bovine agents have enlisted humans to clear forests for grazing lands, kill wolves and other predators, and fence-in pastures for their benefit. In countries like the United States that are heavily addicted to beef, this has led to both a simplification of human diets – our diets have far less variety than they once did – and to the structuring of the social world in a variety of ways related to beef. We set aside land specifically for the sake of grazing livestock, develop technologies to transport beef to suburban and urban regions, develop technologies to preserve beef, and so on. Moreover, a diet heavy in beef such as the American diet cannot fail to have developmental consequences for humans. On the one hand, we have an evolutionary or biological imperative to gorge on as much fatty meat as possible because, in the case of our remote ancestors, we didn't know when the next meal was coming and therefore had to stock up on calories and fat whenever we could find it. In a society where fatty meat is ubiquitously present on every street corner, coupled with hominids wired to crave fatty foods, we get a perfect storm of obesity and heart disease. On the other hand, and more dramatically, our proximity to various forms of livestock such as cows, pigs, sheep, chickens, turkeys, and so on, has had, as Jared Diamond notes, significant world historical and biological consequences for humans (Diamond 2005). It's not simply that livestock led us to arrange societies in particular ways, develop various technologies, or kick off agricultural and engineering revolutions through the labor and fertilizers they provided. Rather, those geographical regions that had more domesticatable animals, also had higher incidences of infectious diseases. As a consequence, they also built up greater immunities. As Diamond argues, this is part of what allowed these populations to dominate and destroy other populations. It wasn't the superiority of their culture that allowed them to subjugate these other civilizations, but rather they practiced a form of biological warfare on these populations without knowing it.

Viewed through this lens, it is difficult to determine whether it was humans that built civilization and history, or livestock. Are we the agents and lords of cows, or are cows and other livestock the agents and lords of us? This, of course, is hyperbole. Returning to the theme of reciprocal determination discussed earlier, the point is that we can't smoothly separate the world of nature from the world of culture. Humans are as much determined and formed by the world around them, they are as much domesticated by non-humans, as they form and domesticate beings in the world about them. There is never a unilateralism of determination in the relationship of humans to non-humans.

In *What Technology Wants*, Kevin Kelly advances a similar argument with respect to technology (Kelly 2011). According to Kelly, technology unfolds according to certain vectors or tendencies that are irreducible to the purposes for which humans might develop these technologies. In effect, there's a sense in which technologies "want" something. Again, the thesis here is not that technologies have will, consciousness, goals, or intentionality. Rather, Kelly's argument is similar to that of evolutionary logic where we get design without any teleology or designer. The idea is that there are tendencies and tensions within technology arising from the nature of the materials used, economic feasibility, political issues, and the current state of technology that push the development of technology in one direction rather than another. I discussed an example of this earlier in the case of Sartre and Mumford's analysis of the steam engine. Perhaps no one had the inclination or desire to build large steam engines, but certain exigencies of the technology such as its labor-intensive requirements favored the production of large steam engines rather than small ones, paving the way for large factory production. It's as if the steam engine itself wanted something and strongly encouraged people to realize that aim in this particular way. We saw something similar in the case of trains, where the sort of steel available played a role in how heavy the train could be by virtue of the weight the tracks could bear, what size the engine could be by virtue of the heat the steel could withstand, and what places trains could go by virtue of climatic features such as coldness that renders certain types of steel brittle. The properties of existing steel technology perhaps played a central role in the form early trains took. They delimited, as it were, a "possibility space" of what trains could be or how they could be configured. In practicing alien phenomenology and adopting the perspective of technology itself rather than that of human designers and users of technology, we get a very different picture of why technologies develop as they do. There is an entire non-human history of technology waiting to be written.

Alien phenomenology is crucial to the project of onto-cartography for a variety of reasons: analytic, ethical, and political. First, at the analytic level, insofar as onto-cartography is the mapping of relations or interactions between machines, how they influence one another, how they modify one another, and how they're organized in a world, it's necessary to determine what is able to interact with what and how machines are able to respond to the flows that pass through them. Without an attentiveness to the flows to which machines are open, we're unable to get an accurate mapping of relations between machines in a world. Without attentiveness to the manner in which a machine operates on the flows that pass through it, we're unable to determine why it locally manifests itself in this network of interactions in the way it does. Alien phenomenology is thus a necessary component of sound onto-cartography.

At the ethical level, alien phenomenology opens the way towards more compassionate ways of relating to human and non-human others. Drawing on Lacan's concept of the imaginary, we often relate to human and non-human others as reflections of ourselves, as being like ourselves. We think of others as wanting the same things we want, thinking like we think, having the same motives that we have, and so on. With respect to non-human machines, our tendency is to relate to them solely in terms of whether or not they are conducive to our aims. As Spinoza writes:

> Other notions, too, are nothing but modes of imagining whereby the imagination is affected in various ways, and yet the ignorant consider them as important attributes of things because they believe . . . that all things were made on their behalf, and they call a thing's nature good or bad, healthy or rotten and corrupt, according to its effect on them. (Spinoza 2002: 242)

We treat these properties as being properties of the machines themselves, rather than results of how we relate to non-human things in terms of our own bodies and aims. As a consequence, we tend to be blind to what others, human and non-human, need, instead thinking of them solely in terms of our own aims.

This blindness to the alien and narcissistic primacy of the imaginary has massive deleterious ethical and political consequences. Alien phenomenology, by contrast, opens the possibility of more compassionate ways of relating to aliens, helping us to better attend to their needs, thereby creating the possibility of better ways of living together. Let us take the amusing example of Cesar Millan of the television show *The Dog Whisperer*. Millan is famous for his ability to effectively deal with problem dogs, recommending ways of changing their behavior and solving problems such as excessive barking or soiling the house. What is Millan's secret? Millan's secret is that he's an exemplary alien phenomenologist. Millan attempts to think like a *dog* rather than a *human*. When Millan approaches a problem dog, he doesn't approach that dog as a problem for *humans*, but instead approaches the *dog*'s environment and owners as a problem for the *dog*. Based on his knowledge of dog phenomenology, of what it is like to be a dog and how dogs relate to the environment about them as well as their fellow pack members – which, for the dog, includes its owners – Millan explores the way this environment as well as pack relations lead to the problematic behavior of the dog. He then makes suggestions as to how the environment might be changed or pack relations restructured – i.e., how the behavior of the human pack members might be changed – so as to create a more satisfying environment for the dog in which the problematic behavior will change. In this way, Millan is able to produce an ecology or set of social relations that is more satisfying for both the human owners or fellow pack members and the dog. By contrast, we can imagine a dog trainer that only adopts the human point of view, holding that it is the dog alone that is the problem, recommending that the dog be beaten or disciplined with an electric collar, thereby producing a depressed and broken dog that lives a life of submission and bondage.

A great deal of human cruelty arises from the failure to practice alien phenomenology. We can see this in cases of colonial exploitation, oppression, and genocide where colonial invaders are unable to imagine the culture of the others they encounter, instead measuring them by their own culture, values, and concept of the human, thereby justifying the destruction of their culture as inferior and in many instances the genocide of these peoples. We see it in the way that people with disabilities, those who suffer from war trauma, and the mentally ill are measured by an idealized concept of what we believe the *human* ought to be, rather than evaluating people in terms of their own capacities and aims. We see it in phenomena of sexism, where our legal system is constructed around the implicit assumption of men as the default figure of what the human is, ignoring the specificities of what it means to be a woman. Finally, we see it in the way we relate to animals, treating them only in terms of our own use and how they advance our aims or pose problems for us, rather than entering the world of animals as Grandin or Millan do, striving to attend to what animals might need. The point here isn't that we should adopt some sort of moral masochism where we should always bow to the aims of others and deny our own aims. The point is that through the practice of alien phenomenology, we might develop ways of living that are both more compassionate for our others and that might develop more satisfying social assemblages for all machines involved.

Finally, at the political level, alien phenomenology increases the efficacy of our political interventions. If we grant the premise that institutions like insurance companies are alien minds over and above those that work at them, that they have their own structural openness to the world, their own operational closure, and speak their own language, then our political engagement with these entities requires us to be strategically aware of this fact. All too often we confuse larger-scale machines such as institutions with the people that occupy them such as CEOs. As a consequence, we are led to believe that it is enough to persuade these people to produce changes in these machines. Certainly these forms of political intervention cannot hurt, but if it is true that alien cognition is distributed in these larger-scale machines, then the people that work in these machines are more akin to neurons or neuronal clusters than they are to the agencies that control and direct these machines. To be sure, they influence these larger-scale machines, but the machine is itself its own agent.

If we are to change and influence these machines we must interact with them in terms of how they encounter the world so as to devise strategies for getting them to respond. This entails that we practice alien phenomenology. It is necessary to determine the flows to which these machines are open, how they operate on these flows, and what goals or aims animate these machines. Through this knowledge we are able to develop a broader variety of strategies for intervention. If, for example, boycotts are often more effective than protests in compelling corporations to abandon egregious labor, political, and environmental practices, then this is because boycotts are implicitly aware of the flows and operations that animate corporate machines. They are aware that the flows to which corporations are structurally open are those of profit and loss. In staunching a corporation's profits, a boycott movement thus produces an information event for the corporation to which it is operationally sensitive, thereby compelling a response and a correction of action. Strikes have been historically effective for similar reasons. In order to achieve its aims, a corporate-machine must engage in operations of producing goods to sell for the sake of creating surplus value or profit. A strike shuts down these operations, preventing the corporate-machine from operations that produce profit. In this way, workers are able to create leverage on the machine so as to have their demands met.

We can call these forms of engagement *thermodynamic politics*. Thermodynamic politics is a form of political engagement that targets a machine's sources of energy and capacity for work. As we will see in the next chapter, most machines require work and energy to sustain themselves across time. In the case of a corporate-machine, the energy required consists of the resources the machine draws upon to produce and distribute its goods – natural resources, electricity, water, fossil fuels, capital to invest in production, and so on – as well as the labor that allows the machine to engage in its operations of production and distribution. These are the flows to which a corporate-machine is structurally open. Thermodynamic politics targets these flows of energy and work, effectively speaking the "language" of the machine's operational closure, thereby creating leverage conducive to change. I'll leave it to the imagination of my readers to think of other ways in which thermodynamic politics might be practiced.

In light of the concept of thermodynamic politics, we can see the common shortcoming of protest politics or what might be called *semiotic politics*. Semiotic politics is semiotic in the sense that relies on the use of signs, either attempting to change institutions through communicative persuasion or engaging in activities of critique as in the case of hermeneutics of suspicion that, through a critique of ideology, desire, power, and so on, show that relations of domination and oppression are at work in something we hitherto believed to be just. Semiotic politics is confused in that it is premised on producing change through ethical persuasion, and thereby assumes that institutional-machines such as corporations, governments, factories, and so on, are structurally open to the same sorts of communicative flows as humans. It believes that we can persuade these organizations to change their operations on ethical grounds. At best, however, these entities are indifferent to such arguments, while at worst they are completely blind to even the occurrence of such appeals as machines such as corporations are only structurally open to information events of profit and loss. Persuading a corporation through ethical appeals is about as effective as trying to explain calculus to a cat.

This is not to suggest that semiotic politics is entirely useless, it is just confused about what it is doing. Viewed from a machinic perspective, semiotic politics aims not so much to change institutions as to create more powerful collective entities that might come to exert pressure on private and governmental institutions. In its functioning, a protest is not so much addressed to a government or business as it is to onlookers or other people. Likewise, a critical debunking is not so much directed at those engaged in ideological operations of oppression and exploitation as it is aimed at raising awareness among people regarding these mechanisms of power.

Semiotic politics is thus a set of operations that aims to produce a collective machine that might reach a critical mass in which it becomes possible to change large-scale institutional machines or abolish some of these machines altogether. However, that critical mass requires a shift from semiotic politics to thermodynamic politics.

Notes

1. I owe this thesis to Graham Harman. While I do not share all of his claims about the being of objects, for a detailed defense of this claim (see Harman 2002).
2. For a discussion of how objects relate to one another from behind firewalls (see Harman 2005: 95–9).

4

Machinic Assemblages and Entropy

Machinic Assemblages

There is no such thing as a simple machine. Rather, every machine is simultaneously a unit or individual entity in its own right and a complex or assemblage of other machines. In short, machines are composed of machines. As Harman writes, ". . . a universe [is] made up of objects wrapped in objects wrapped in objects wrapped in objects" (Harman 2005: 85). What Harman here says of objects can be said of machines. Here we cannot fail to think of a beautiful passage from Leibniz's *Monadology*, where he writes, "[e]ach portion of matter can be conceived as a garden full of plants, and as a pond full of fish. But each branch of a plant, each limb of an animal, each drop of its humors, is still another such garden or pond" (Leibniz 1991: 78). Matter teems with machines and each machine itself swarms with other machines. My body, for example, is both a machine in its own right, but also an assemblage of machines composed of various organs. Those organs, in their turn, are composed of other machines, or cells. And those cells, in their turn, are composed of yet other machines. Whether or not there are any fundamental or elemental machines – what we would call "atoms" in the Greek sense – is a question I leave open to be decided empirically.

As a consequence, Harman continues, "[e]very object is both a substance and a complex of relations" (Harman 2005: 85). Every machine is both a unit or autonomous entity in its own right, and a complex of relations among the machines that compose its parts. Here we must proceed with care, lest we confuse two different types of relations. Often machines must be coupled to other machines in order to operate or function. A television, for example, must be plugged into an electric socket in order to operate. The socket, in its turn, opens on to other machines such as electric cables, fuse boxes, and dams, windmills, solar panels, or coal-burning power plants. Similarly, in order for frogs to operate, they must be linked into other machines such as flows of oxygen and flies. However, in treating a machine as a complex of relations, it is not these types of relations that are in question. A frog remains a complex of relations or assemblage of machines when a cruel scientist places it in a vacuum chamber and severs it from its relation to oxygen. A television remains a complex of relations or assemblage of machines when it is no longer plugged into a wall socket. Relations of this sort are *exo-relations*, which is to say that they are *external* relations to other discrete or independent machines that can be *severed* while the machine nonetheless remains that machine. A television remains a television even when it is not plugged into the wall. A frog remains a frog even when it has been severed from oxygen – at least for a time.

The claim that a machine is a complex of relations or an assemblage of machines is thus the claim that a machine is constituted by its *endo-relations*. Endo-relations are *internal* relations between machines that constitute or generate a new machine. It is a relationship between the parts of a machine – which are themselves machines – and the emergent whole, which is a distinct machine over and above its parts. A television cannot be the machine that it is without the parts or other machines that compose it, nor can a capybara be the machine that it is without the parts that compose it. Some of a machine's parts, of course, will be unnecessary to the machine. For example, a capybara can lose a leg and still be that capybara. Likewise, a television can lose its plastic casing and remain that television. There is thus a distinction to be made between essential parts and inessential parts. What is important is that machines have an endo-composition consisting of internal relations between machines that compose the being of a machine. This entails that machines emerge from other machines.

How, then, do we distinguish between exo-relations *between* machines where we're in the presence of two machines, and endo-relations where we get the formation or emergence of a new machine? As we saw in Chapter 2, machines are individuated by their powers, not their qualities. Moreover, there we saw that a machine possesses its powers regardless of whether or not it exercises those powers. In this regard, a television possesses its powers to produce images and sounds, to operate, regardless of whether or not it is plugged into an electric socket. Likewise, a fruit bat possesses its powers, at least for a time, regardless of whether or not it has been severed from oxygen. To be sure, in both of these cases, these machines are unable to *exercise* their powers, yet the powers nonetheless remain as capacities possessed by these entities.

Granting this hypothesis, we can thus conclude that whenever new powers emerge from a coupling of machines that cannot be found in the machines coupled, we are in the presence of a new and distinct machine. Put differently, an assemblage constitutes a new machine or unit when it is able to act on other entities in the world in ways that its parts cannot.[1] Let us take the example of H_2O to illustrate this point. Simplifying matters, H_2O or water is a machine composed of three other machines: two hydrogen atoms and one oxygen atom. I caution that I'm simplifying matters here, as these machines are, in their turn, composed of other machines. If a molecule of H_2O constitutes a distinct machine and is not just an aggregate or heap of machines, then this is because the endo-relations formed among these smaller machines generate powers or capacities that cannot be found among its parts. Thus water has the capacity to put out fires, whereas oxygen and hydrogen, taken alone, are highly combustible. Water has greater density than either oxygen or hydrogen. It freezes at different temperatures than either oxygen or hydrogen, and turns into a liquid or gas at different temperatures than hydrogen or oxygen. The list goes on and on.

Whether we're talking about crystals, animal bodies, social institutions, political collectives, or various technologies, we will always find that these machines have powers or capacities that do not exist in their parts. As such, they are capable of acting upon the world or producing differences in other machines of the world in ways that their parts, taken alone, do not possess. Here it is important to proceed with care, for emergence often is conceived as signifying that the whole is greater than the sum of its parts, such that the whole cannot be *explained* by its parts. Here emergence is evoked as a bulwark against "reductivism," arguing that somehow, through the formation of endo-relations, magical properties emerge that share no relation to their parts. This thesis is not advocated here. Clearly H_2O is only able to do what it does, it only takes on the powers it has, by virtue of the powers of its parts. The point is that these parts must be coupled in this way in order for the powers of water to emerge. Without those relations, these powers do not come into being. Nonetheless, there are no violations of the laws of physics and chemistry here. If we wish to understand the powers of water we have to understand the powers of hydrogen and oxygen and what happens when they bond.

When machines are coupled in ways that form new machines, some couplings will be reversible whereas others will be irreversible. Machinic genesis is reversible when the machine composed out of coupled machines can be broken down in such a way that its parts retain their machinic being and powers. This, for example, is the case with many technologies such as automobiles, but also entities like H_2O. We can break an automobile down into its constituent machines, and, through electrolysis, can break H_2O down into its constituent elements. Here the parts and their powers are not destroyed through machinic coupling. By contrast, machinic genesis is irreversible when the machines coupled are destroyed or transformed into something else in the process of machinic genesis. This is the case, for example, with how the body metabolizes foods. As our bodies develop, the foods we eat contribute to the sorts of powers our bodies will have, but these foods are themselves transformed and destroyed in the process of metabolism. You can't break a body down into the corn it has consumed, the meats it has eaten, the liquids it has taken in, and so on. The situation is similar with the nuclear processes that take place in stars. Whether or not a machinic genesis is reversible or irreversible is an empirical question that can only be answered on a case-by-case basis. Further, as is so often the case with these matters, there are often a number of differences in degree between the reversible and the irreversible. For example, a person that goes through education is changed or transformed, developing new capacities or powers, and thus there is a degree of irreversibility to educational processes. However, they certainly aren't destroyed in that they are able to leave educational institutions and enjoy new adventures.

The assemblage theory of machines in which machines are individuated by their powers entails that machines can exist at a variety of different levels of scale. For example, a government agency is no less a machine than the people that compose it, the organs that compose these people, the cells that compose those organs, the atoms that compose those cells, and the particles that compose those atoms. Every type of machine in this chain is as real as the others because each of these machines possesses powers that cannot be found among the parts. A government agency, for example, has powers that are not possessed by the individual people that work at the agency. It is for this reason that we cannot reduce social machines to individual people as neoliberals would like to do. Machinic ontology thus argues that being is composed of a far greater variety of beings than we sometimes suspect.

Because machines are composed of other machines, every machine is haunted by *machinic problems*. While the machines that compose a machine are often destroyed or transformed in the process of machinic genesis, they nonetheless retain, if only for a time, their own structural openness and operational closure. As a consequence, these parts are only selectively open to flows and operate in their own way. Thus the parts of a machine never quite harmonize. Every machine is simultaneously a unit and a crowd or herd of cats. Put differently, no machine ever manages to totalize or master its parts. Rather, parts continue to possess a life of their own. As Latour dramatically puts it, "[n]one of the actants mobilized to secure an alliance stops acting on its own behalf . . . They each carry on fomenting their own plots, forming their own groups, and serving other masters, wills, and functions" (Latour 1988: 197). A government agency both exercises its own operations and must contend with the plots or aims of the civil servants that work within it. A university both engages in its operations and encounters strife from within as students, faculty, and administrators pursue their aims. Our bodies perpetually struggle with the activity of the cells and organs that compose us, as can be seen in both the process of aging and in more dramatic cases such as cancer, where our cells take on a life of their own and refuse to contribute to the aims of the body. Even entities like rocks encounter strife from the molecules that compose them as these molecules enter into couplings with other molecules.

Machinic problems refer to problems that emerge within a machine as a result of striving to form a unified entity or machine. Somehow the emergent machine must find a way to unify the other machines that function as parts of the machine into elements of a single machine. Because these parts are structurally open and operationally closed in their own right, they "wish" to go their own way. There is tension and friction among the parts or other machines that makes every machine a bit of a bricolage perpetually in danger of collapsing or falling apart. Sometimes the parts just don't quite fit together in a neat or smooth way, generating systematic problems for the machine. This, for example, is the case with biological bodies. Evolution is a *bricoleur*, always building on *pre-existent* biological structures that served different functions in the past (exaptation) and that don't perfectly serve the new functions for which they've been enlisted. Thus, for example, the pelvis of *homo sapien* women isn't quite large enough for human childbirth because it originally evolved for previous hominid species whose heads were smaller. As a result, the infant must twist during childbirth to pass through the pelvic bones at great danger to itself (it can come out breach or hang itself on the umbilicus) and the mother. Similarly, we have bodies that tell us to eat as much fat as we can because, in earlier incarnations of our species, we never knew when the next meal would come along. However, we have developed the capacity to overcome scarcity of food through farming techniques, distribution of labor, and techniques for distributing food through transportation and stores. Despite all of our technological, cultural, and intellectual developments, our hominid ancestry has not left us and we now find ourselves continuing to eat as much fatty food as possible and are doing so in ways that are toxic or destructive to our health. There are even situations where we have parts that were of use in prior ancestors, such as the appendix, that serve no function, and that can kill us. Every machine is jerry-rigged by the anonymous Macgyvers of nature and culture.

The failure of machines to fit seamlessly into a unity forming a new machine is what generates machinic problems. Machines must engage in constant operations to unify their parts and ensure that their essential parts continue to hold together in a unity. At every moment, every corporeal machine threatens to disintegrate. It is also for this reason that no machine is ever entirely responsible for what it is. Insofar as the parts themselves contribute their own local manifestations or differences, what a machine becomes isn't entirely a result of its operations. Every general knows this. When he gives orders, these orders are translated or interpreted in a near infinity of unexpected ways by his officers, troops, support corps, the technologies used by the army, the weather, and the surrounding geography. As a consequence, the *results* of any order are never quite the same as what was intended in the order. We can imagine that generals are regularly surprised by the actualization of their orders: "That's what I meant?"

This is why domination is never quite complete. Machines can destroy their parts, but insofar as their parts retain some machinic being of their own, they always retain subterranean powers of their own, threatening to be unleashed at any time, as in the case of revolutions where people throw off the social operations that order them, or introducing a bit of chaos into the larger-scale machine of which they're a part. Many machines – especially those of the social and organic variety – might strive to transform their machinic parts into docile bodies, but this forever remains an *ideal* never fulfilled in practice. There are always subterranean plots, machinic intrigues, tiny acts of treason, and furtive acts of disobedience among parts. Far from being something to be eradicated, these failures of perfect ordering are part of the creativity of machinic being.

Assemblages and Individuals

The thesis that machines are assemblages of machines and that they are individuated by their powers rather than their qualities raises a number of interesting questions about just how we individuate entities. In *A Thousand Plateaus* Deleuze and Guattari write:

> Spinoza asks: what can a body do? We call the *latitude* of a body the affects of which it is capable at a given degree of power, or rather within the limits of that degree. *Latitude is made up of intensive parts falling under a capacity, and longitude of extensive parts falling under a relation.* In the same way that we avoided defining a body by its organs and functions, we will avoid defining it by Species or Genus characteristics: instead we will seek to count its affects. This kind of study is ethology, and this is the sense in which Spinoza wrote a true Ethics. A race-horse is more different from a workhorse than a workhorse from an ox. (Deleuze and Guattari 1987: 256–7)

In Deleuze and Guattari's vocabulary, "affect" refers to the powers or capacities of a machine. There are two types of affects: passive and active affects. Passive affects refer to ways in which a machine is causally and selectively open to the world, such as a shark's ability to sense the world through electromagnetic waves or a bat's ability to sense the world through sonar. Active affects refer to a machine's capacity to engage in particular sorts of operations or actions, such as a can opener's ability to open cans, a knife's ability to cut, or a cane toad's ability to shoot poison from the pores on its back.

Deleuze and Guattari's thesis – a thesis that I share – is that machines should be classified in terms of their powers or capacities, their affects, rather than genus and species. When they reject classification based on genus and species, they're rejecting classification based on *qualitative resemblance*. Under the genus/species model we treat workhorses and racehorses as belonging to the same species or category because they resemble each other. They resemble each other in terms of their anatomy, their shape, and so on. By contrast, Deleuze and Guattari suggest that it is not resemblances that categorize entities, but rather affects or powers. We should classify entities in terms of their active and passive affects – what they can do and how they are capable of being causally influenced by the world (sensibility) – rather than how they resemble one another. If a workhorse is better grouped with an ox than a racehorse, then this is because workhorses share more passive and active affects or powers in common with oxen than they do with racehorses.

This has far reaching consequences as to just when we say we're in the presence of a distinct entity or machine, as well as how we classify machines. Later, in *A Thousand Plateaus*, Deleuze and Guattari observe that:

> The lance and the sword came into being in the Bronze Age only by virtue of the man–horse assemblage, which caused a lengthening of the dagger and pike, and made the first infantry weapons, the morning star and the battle-ax, obsolete. The stirrup, in turn, occasioned a new figure of the man-horse assemblage, entailing a new type of lance and new weapons . . . (Deleuze and Guattari 1987: 399)

The most important reference in this passage is to the humble *stirrup*. With the stirrup, the man–horse assemblage becomes something quite different than it was before. Before the stirrup, the man–horse assemblage might serve as a machine for quick movement, as a platform for shooting arrows, and so on, but it was not yet, perhaps, an ontological transformation or the formation of a new machine. The stirrup changes everything. Prior to the stirrup, the man on horseback could be easily dislodged from his horse and was unable to exercise much force through his weapons as a result of this. As they say, for every action there is an equal and

opposite reaction. In the absence of the stirrup, the soldier swing-
ing at someone else with a sword during a fast gallop was likely
to be thrown off his horse. With the invention of the stirrup, by
contrast, the man–horse assemblage is now able to consolidate
and preserve the force of the horse. Held in place by the stirrup,
the man–horse assemblage is able to transmit the force of the horse
without losing it when encountering another body. We thereby get
the invention of the lance that will enjoy a decisive advantage in
battle for centuries to come. What we have here is the *emergence
of new powers*.

Within the framework proposed here, entities are individuated
not by their qualities, but rather by their powers. Consequently,
where there is an emergence of new powers there is also the
emergence of a new entity or machine. It will be objected that
the soldier, the horse, the stirrup, and the lance are all distinct
machines. This is true insofar as machines are composed of other
machines. All of these machines are capable of enjoying an independent existence. However, when these machines are assembled
together we get the emergence of new affects or powers, thereby
generating a new machine. The fact that this machine is an aggregate of other machines and that these machines are separable from
one another does not undermine its being as a distinct machine.
In other words, "simple" is not a synonym for "substance." Jet
planes are composed of other machines and can be disassembled,
yet they are no less distinct machines for this reason. Organs can
be removed from a body and transplanted to another body, yet
bodies are no less distinct beings for this reason. H_2O molecules
can be disassembled through electrolysis, but are no less distinct
molecules for this reason. If we grant that jet planes, human
bodies, and H_2O molecules are all distinct entities despite being
composed of other entities, why should we not conclude that the
man–horse–stirrup–lance assemblage is a distinct entity?

The strange consequence of this hypothesis is that the man who
rides the horse and the man–horse–stirrup–lance assemblage are
two distinct individuals. It is not that the *man* rides the *horse*,
but rather that the man–horse–stirrup–lance assemblage rides.
Centaurs really do exist, just not in the sense we thought. On the
one hand, it thus turns out that there are many more entities in
the universe than our language recognizes. On the other hand, we
get the strange result that entities can be discontinuous, flickering
in and out of time like slime molds now existing as a plurality of

discrete organisms, and now existing as a unified collective organism. After battle, the man dismounts from his horse, and horse and man go their separate ways as distinct machines. Circumstances of battle arise again, the man mounts the horse, and the man–horse–stirrup–lance machine comes back into being.

Our deep intuition is to think that a machine only counts as a machine, a distinct individual or discrete entity, if it enjoys a continuous duration over time. We are inclined to say that the man is a distinct individual and the horse is a distinct individual because they maintain their identity as themselves across time. By contrast, we are inclined to reject the hypothesis that the man–horse–stirrup–lance assemblage is a distinct individual, instead treating it as a plurality of individuals, because it pops into existence and then passes out of existence. Yet if entities are assemblages of entities, and assemblages can often be disassembled and reassembled in such a way as to generate the same powers when reassembled, then there's no reason to accept the temporal continuity thesis. A college course, for example, might only exist on Mondays, Wednesdays, and Fridays, but is nonetheless the same course on each of these days.

Extended Minds and Bodies

Cognitive scientist and philosopher of mind, Andy Clark, develops this hypothesis with unparalleled clarity with respect to the human mind (Clark and Chalmers 2011). Under the title of the "extended mind hypothesis," Clark challenges the hypothesis that mind is primarily representational and a set of functions that take place solely in the brain. The representational theory of mind begins with the premise that cognition consists of the manipulation of symbols or representations in thoughts that take place in the brain.

Beginning from a naturalistic perspective that situates human beings as biological beings that exist in a physical environment to which we must respond in real time, Clark argues that representational models of mind are poorly suited to responding in real time to the exigencies of the environment (Clark 1998: 21–3). Imagine, for example, a representational mind cognizing how to leap away from a falling board on a construction site. Such a mind would first have to engage in all sorts of symbolic or representational operations to classify the board or piece of wood flying towards our body. The challenge of this representational cognition would be enhanced because the board is moving through space, thereby presenting itself to the worker from a variety of different perspectives. The mind would thus have to find a way to unify these perspectives and identify them as being phases of the same type of entity under the category of "board." Having successfully identified this entity whose appearance is constantly changing as it falls through space, the representational mind would then have to engage in a series of symbolic manipulations to determine how to move the body to avoid the board. Not only are these symbolic manipulations time-consuming, artificial intelligences that have been modeled on the assumption that the mind is a centralized manipulator of representations in the world have performed very poorly in navigating their environment. As Clark recounts, these artificial intelligences do poorly at identifying entities from varying perspectives, recognizing context and responding appropriately to shifting contexts, and responding in real time. Clearly entities such as this wouldn't survive very long in an environment that is constantly changing such as our own and where we have to respond very quickly. Observations such as this lead Clark to reject the notion that mind is a centralized agency that primarily manipulates representations, instead adopting a distributed conception of mind where a number of non-conscious operations respond to events in the environment without consciously manipulating representations. To be sure, there are instances where centralized symbol manipulation takes place, but this is the exception rather than the rule.

However, this is not where Clark's real originality lies. In recognizing the problem of real-time response, Clark wonders how machines such as ourselves solve this problem. Clearly we require brains to respond as we do, but brains alone will not do the job because of the timely expenditure involved in manipulating representations. Clark thus proposes that mind is not brain alone, but rather that mind is a *relation* between brain, body, and the physical world. In short, what Clark contests is the thesis that mind is something strictly *inside* the head. Rather, according to Clark, mind *offloads* a number of cognitive problems onto the physical world, allowing the world to do the work for it, which, in turn, allows it to respond more quickly in real time. In other words, Clark develops an ecological media theory of mind. It is a media theory of mind because non-human, non-mental media such as the technologies we use play a key role, according to Clark, in our cognition. It is an ecological theory because it argues that we can only understand mind in relation to various entities of our environment. It is in this sense that our minds are "extended minds." Our minds are not simply between our ears, *in* the brain, such that the brain is a centralized controller that manipulates representations, but rather minds are extended out into the physical media of the world. What does this mean?

First, it's important to note that Clark is not advocating an *idealist* thesis about the mind's relationship to physical entities in the world. The entities onto which our minds offload cognitive operations are not *constituted* by mind, nor are they *ideas* in disguise. They are real physical entities that make genuine contributions to cognition. Mathematical cognition provides a good example of what Clark is getting at. Most of us have great difficulty solving complex mathematical problems such as those found in geometry or calculus through purely representationalist and internalist means. Our short-term memory is such that we have trouble keeping all the steps of the proof or solution in mind. As a consequence, when we try to solve a proof solely in our heads, our chance of error increases significantly, and we find that our ability to solve the problem quickly diminishes significantly as proving a theorem or solving an equation often requires us to return to earlier steps. Thus, when we solve a problem in our head, we find ourselves perpetually rehearsing the steps in our head in ways that take significantly more time, while also eating up more calories (as cognition requires energy like anything else).

Clark argues that we respond to these limitations of memory and constraints of time by offloading elements of the problem onto *physical* media in the world about us, allowing that media to do the work for us. Take the following simple arithmetic problem:

$$
\begin{array}{r}
7^1{,}4^1 3\,2 \\
+\quad\ \ 674 \\
\hline
=\quad 8{,}106
\end{array}
$$

Rather than adding the complete units together in our mind, we instead allow the *paper* to do the work. We first focus on the relationship between 6 and 4, then 7 and 3, we carry the 1 of the sum 10 to 4 and add 4, 1, and 6, carry the one of 11 and then add 1 and 7 arriving at the sum 8,106. The advantage of solving the problem on paper is that we can focus on two numbers at a time, *ignoring* the rest of the numbers. The result is that we are able to solve the problem far more quickly than if we did it in our head and with a greater degree of accuracy. This is rendered possible by two things. First, through our inscriptions, the *paper* remembers for us. Once I have figured out the sum of 4 and 2, I can ignore 6 as the paper remembers it for me, and move on to finding the sum of 7 and 3. My cognitive load is thereby reduced. My brain is far less taxed as I have to remember less, freeing my mind up to do other things. Second, it is made possible by the *types* of symbols we use. Material symbols make a difference. Arithmetic would be far more difficult, if not nearly impossible, if we used Roman numerals or points to represent these numbers. The invention of Arabic numerals opened all sorts of mathematical possibilities as it allowed us to offload very complex thoughts (the number 7,432 represented through points, for example) on very simple symbols. This thesis is "anti-representational," not in the sense that it denies that mind uses and manipulates representations – clearly all sorts of manipulations are deployed in solving a problem of addition – but in the sense that it rejects the thesis that cognition solely consists in the manipulation of representations. The physical media themselves contribute to the activity of cognition.

Clark's thesis is that physical media such as paper and pencil and the symbols we use are not simply convenient prostheses that we could dispense with altogether, but that they are actual participants in our cognition. Cognition that takes place with pencil, paper and Arabic numerals is *different* from cognition that takes place purely inside the head. Put more dramatically, for Clark these are two different types of minds. What holds for solving mathematical equations holds for a variety of problems we face. Take the example of walking. A purely representational account of walking would generate nearly insurmountable problems as the mind would have to engage in so many operations in mapping the environment, our bodies, our movements, and how to get from point A to point B that little would be left for anything else. Fortunately, many of the problems of walking are solved by the sheer physics of our bodies, or how our bones, muscles, and nerves are put together and are able to respond to shifting environmental conditions without requiring much cognitive expenditure. The bones, muscles, nerves, and how they're organized do the work, diminishing the cognitive load of the brain. This is seen most dramatically when our bodies are removed from their native environment, such as when astronauts walk on the Moon. Our physiology is configured to be maximally responsive to the gravity of the Earth. In their Moon visits, astronauts encountered significant difficulty walking, often falling over or spinning out of control because of differences in the Moon's gravitational forces.

Clark develops his extended mind hypothesis in far reaching ways, covering not simply how cognitive processes are extended into physical media such as paper when solving mathematical equations, but also developing a novel theory of *belief*. In his now seminal essay co-authored with David Chalmers, "The Extended Mind," Clark argues that even beliefs can be extended in the world (Clark and Chalmers 2011: 226–30). In other words, he argues that beliefs and memories can exist *outside* our *brains* in physical media such as notebooks, computer data banks, and so on. To illustrate this thesis, Clark and Chalmers compare the hypothetically existing minds of Inga who has a normally functioning brain and Otto who suffers from Alzheimer's disease. Because Inga has a normally functioning brain, she is able to recall beliefs such as her plan to attend a particular art exhibition and the address at which that exhibition is located in her head alone. Otto, by contrast, assiduously keeps a notebook storing important information because he is aware of the forgetfulness wrought by his unfortunate condition. Clark and Chalmers argue that while the beliefs of Inga and Otto are stored in different places, the notebook and brain memory are nonetheless functionally identical. Even though Otto is unable to store his beliefs in his brain because he forgets them, those beliefs inscribed on the paper of his notebook are still *his* beliefs, and the notebook serves a role that is functionally identical to Inga's beliefs stored in her head.

In short, the extended mind hypothesis entails that we can have beliefs of which we are unaware and that exist outside our head. When we reflect on this thesis about the nature of belief, we'll note that extended or externalized beliefs of this sort are not restricted to extraordinary circumstances such as those of the Alzheimer's patient that keeps a notebook. With the rise of smart phones, for example, few of us bother to memorize phone numbers anymore but instead allow our phones to remember on our behalf. In a related vein, many of us keep diaries, daily planners, and notebooks in a manner similar to the fictional Otto to preserve our memories, important information, and our appointments. Similarly, many of us, of course, believe that the various elements that exist have the various properties that are listed on the atomic table of elements, yet few of us, unless we are chemists or physicists, have memorized all of the numerical properties listed on that table. Rather, when an occasion arises requiring us to recall the atomic properties of, say, iron, we consult the atomic table of elements on the Internet or in a chemistry textbook. In these instances, the Internet and chemistry textbook store the belief for us. We don't know *what* our belief is, nor do we store it in our mind, but we do know *that* we have this belief and know where to go to retrieve this belief should circumstances require. As a writer, I forget much of what I have written. Nonetheless, my published texts remember for me. Confronted with a text I have forgotten, I say to myself "oh yes, I believe that," even though I might not recall having written the text at all or its general line of argument. To be sure, in the intervening time I might have changed my beliefs and no longer advocate claims I made in the past, but it's difficult to see why this is any different than changing beliefs in the head.

Although Clark does not himself make this argument, it is not difficult to see how this thesis can even be extended to affects (in the sense of ways we feel or emotional responses). Žižek gives a nice example of externalized and extended affect in *The Sublime Object of Ideology*. There he discusses the phenomenon of canned laughter on television shows. Rejecting the hypothesis that canned laughter is a cue to remind us to laugh on the grounds that we seldom laugh when this laughter takes place, instead he argues that canned laughter *relieves us* of the obligation to laugh. As Žižek remarks, ". . . even if, tired from a long day's stupid work, all evening we did nothing but gaze drowsily into the television screen, we can say afterwards that objectively, through the medium of the other, we had a really good time" (Žižek 1989: 33). Here, strangely, even though we didn't directly feel the affect, the feelings of amusement and enjoyment were nonetheless ours. It just happens that the affect, in this case, is out there in the world, in the television show, rather than inside us.

Clark's extended mind hypothesis raises a number of interesting ethical and political questions. If beliefs can be extended and externalized in physical media such that we can have beliefs without knowing those beliefs, just how do we determine which beliefs are ours and which are not. Is it possible for us to be committed to beliefs of which we're entirely unaware? We are, of course, familiar with the idea of possessing beliefs of which we're unaware from psychoanalysis and cognitive science. However, an externalized and extended belief is something very different. Where unconscious beliefs presumably reside in our brains, externalized and extended beliefs are outside of us, out there in the world inscribed in paper, the brains of other people (people who remember things we've said), computer data banks, and so on. It is easy to see how we can simultaneously have a belief in the atomic table of elements without knowing *what* is contained in that table, just as it is easy to see how we can believe something we've inscribed in a notebook or saved on a computer or smart phone, but forgotten.

Yet, what about more exotic cases of extended belief? Suppose a particular person attends a church, but knows little of the theology of this church and even, without realizing it, advocates a different theology. It is likely that this is not an uncommon occurrence. It's probably unusual for people to extensively acquaint themselves with the theology and doctrines of their religion. How many Catholics, for example, actually bother to read the Catechism and the Church-sanctioned theology of their religion? Are there not many circumstances where a person attends a church while nonetheless advocating very different religious and metaphysical beliefs? Among my Christian fundamentalist students, for example, I have encountered many who believe in things like reincarnation, evolution, and climate change despite the fact that these positions are officially rejected by the doctrine of their particular denomination.

Two questions arise here. First, just what beliefs are *our* beliefs? We might wish to say that the person's beliefs are whatever they consciously advocate. Consequently, when we get a Baptist fundamentalist Christian that believes in the theory of evolution while nonetheless attending a Baptist church, we might conclude that this person really believes in evolution, not the creationist doctrine advocated by their denomination. Yet in participating in the church through their donations, attendance, and involvement in church events, is not this person implicitly affirming the doctrines of that denomination regardless of whether they endorse them in their heart? We wish to say that belief is what is in our heart of hearts, but following Žižek, belief seems to reside more in what we *do* than in how we theorize or conceptualize what we do in our hearts (ibid.: 31–3). Our beliefs are not inside here, in our minds, but rather out there in the actions we engage in, the institutions we support and participate in, the authorities we recognize, etc. I might wish to tell myself that I support the theory of evolution, that I don't share my church's positions, yet in contributing to the church, participating in its events, and so on, it is actually the creationist standpoint that I advance in the world, not evolutionary theory. Clark's extended mind hypothesis allows us to understand how this is so by underlining the manner in which many of our beliefs are externalized and out there in the world in other authorities, institutions, bits of paper and books, and so on.

This is no small matter, for generally we see ourselves as ethically responsible for our beliefs. Under this model, if I participate in an institution like a church that promotes egregious views such as homophobia and derogatory attitudes towards women, I am responsible for these beliefs even if I don't adhere to them in my heart. The case is similar with our participation in corporations through both our labor and purchases. The extended mind position regarding the status of belief would seem to entail that when I buy products from particular corporations or work at various corporations, I hold some responsibility for the social, labor, and environmental policies of this business. Even though I do not endorse these policies in my heart, I am nonetheless furthering these positions in the world through my work and purchases.

Clearly there will be degrees of culpability here. Ordinarily we relate our culpability for beliefs to the degree of freedom we have with respect to these beliefs. In cases of severe paranoid psychosis, for example, we have a hard time holding the person responsible for their delusional formations because they are unable to think otherwise. By contrast, we hold racists responsible for their racist beliefs because they have ample freedom to change those beliefs. Evaluating a person's responsibility for extended beliefs would thereby depend on how much freedom a person possesses with respect to these beliefs. Take the example of a person living under an oppressive, totalitarian government responsible for all sorts of human rights abuses. It is difficult to suggest that this person endorses that government because they pay their taxes, use the government-provided infrastructure, and so on. Such a person simply has no other choice. Similarly, it is hard to hold a person responsible for participating in a corporation when they live in a small remote town where there is only one place to buy goods and no other place to work.

The point here is that in evaluating ethical and political

culpability for beliefs, it is not enough to focus on what is between our ears, in our hearts, or inside our brains. An extended mind approach to belief suggests that at a more fundamental level we also need to look at the institutions and organizations in which we participate and how our participation furthers those particular beliefs, rather than the ones to which we commit ourselves inside our heads. A number of our beliefs are out there in the world in ways of which we are unaware, and it is these beliefs that we most often need to address.

In a related vein, the extended mind hypothesis significantly challenges the assumptions of humanistic political theories. In the context of the United States, these political theories begin from the premise of an ideal conception of human beings that are all more or less equal in their talents, capacities, and ability to reason. Based on this theory, it concludes that our political work is done when we protect the rights of these beings, ensuring that everyone is able to exercise their freedom so long as they do not harm others. However, if minds are not simply what are in the head, but are a relation between brain, body, and entities in the world, the unicity of the term "human" and therefore claims that all humans are equal are significantly called into question. Mind–body assemblages that have guns and steel possess different powers than assemblages that have swords and spears. Assemblages with access to the Internet have different powers with regard to employment and information than assemblages that only have access to libraries and newspaper wants ads. The engineer armed with a complex calculator is able to do things that the engineer with a slide rule is not.

The problem with humanistic political orientations is that they tend to treat as the same and equal what is in fact different and dissimilar. If it is true that mind isn't simply between our ears, and that the media we use contributes to the *type* of being that we are, then it follows that there are many more beings inhabiting our collectives than we ordinarily recognize as a function of the technologies or media to which various human bodies are coupled. Political humanism risks treating assemblages as equal that are, in fact, unequal, thereby ignoring social injustices and inequalities reinforced through media access that some assemblages enjoy and that others lack. A cyborg-informed political theory – to use Donna Haraway's term (Haraway 1991) – would, by contrast, begin with the premise that the minimal units of societies are not humans but assemblages individuated by powers. Starting from this premise, it would thereby be attentive to the various heterogeneous, machinic-assemblages that populate our social world and the inequalities that emerge between these assemblages as a result of access to different media and the powers that emerge from couplings with media. As a consequence, cyborg politics would be better equipped to recognize inequalities and devise strategies for overcoming them.

Entropy

All corporeal machines and many incorporeal machines contend with the problem of entropy. Here it is important to proceed with caution, as the term "entropy" signifies different things in different theoretical contexts. For many, the first thing that comes to mind when hearing the term "entropy" is thermodynamics and heat death. In this context, entropy refers to the manner in which closed systems lose available energy for work. For example, not all of the energy produced by a steam engine is available for work insofar as some of it dissipates into the environment. Where new energy is not produced through adding additional fuel, energy will eventually dissipate altogether and there will therefore be no additional energy available for work. If the universe itself is treated as a closed system, it is often suggested that it will suffer heat death, such that all energy eventually dissipates and no new causal events will be possible. If this is true, life will disappear, stars will blink out, atoms and particles will fall apart, and forces like gravity will cease because all of these things require energy. The universe will become a cold, motionless void.

Although related, this is not the concept of entropy discussed here. In information theory and biology, entropy refers to something different (see Peirce 1980: 78–106). In those contexts, entropy refers not to the tendency of closed systems to lose energy or their capacity for work, but to a measure of *probability* among elements within a system. A system is *highly entropic* if an element of that system has an *equal probability* of appearing *anywhere* in that system. As Luhmann puts it, ". . . a system is entropic if information about one element does not permit inferences about others" (Luhmann 1995: 49). If, in such a system, inferences cannot be made about the other elements, then this is because there's an equal probability of those elements appearing anywhere else in the system. A system is *lowly entropic* if there is a very *low probability* of an element appearing at a particular place within the system. In other words, a low entropy system is a system where information about one element enables inferences about others. Such a system is organized or structured. Finally, a system is *negentropic* if it engages in active *operations* to *maintain* a state of low entropy across time.

These heuristic definitions are very abstract, so I'll give some examples to illustrate them. Gases enclosed in a plastic bottle are an example of a high entropy system. This is because there is an equal probability of any particular atom of the gas appearing anywhere in the bottle. The case is similar with people milling about in Times Square in New York. This system is highly entropic because there is a high likelihood of a person appearing anywhere in the system. By contrast, a society is a low entropy system because it is stratified into different classes, identities, functions, roles, and so on. Claiming that a society is stratified or differentiated is equivalent to claiming that there is a *low probability* that people will *indiscriminately* appear *anywhere* in the social system. People of such and such a class will tend to congregate together, people with such and such a social function – say government officials – will be localized here rather than there, and so on. In other words, a low entropy system is highly organized and differentiated. It is structured. Similarly, biological bodies are low entropy systems. Cells in organic bodies are differentiated into different types and are localized in various regions of the body. This differentiation and distribution is improbable, unlike the distribution of particles in a gas cloud where molecules of a certain type are just as likely to appear anywhere in the system. Finally, a message sent from a sender to a receiver is often a low entropy system by virtue of the fact that the way in which the data, bits, or units are arranged or organized has a very *low degree of probability*. In a sentence, for example, the way in which the letters of the words follow one another, coupled with the way in which words follow one another, displays features not of equal probability, but *rarity* or low probability. The larger the sample of a message we have such as the difference between a single word, a sentence, a paragraph, and then an entire text, the more equal probability is reduced and the more we infer that we are in the presence of an *order* or organization. In other words, order, organization, is the opposite of "equa-probability." This low probability is what allows the cryptographer to begin distinguishing between message and noise, thereby discerning that we are in the presence of an organized being, a message, rather than chaos. Recognizing the presence of that order as a result of the low probability of elements being sequentially organized in this way does not tell us the *meaning* of the message, but does at least tell us that we're in the presence of a message rather than noise.

A *negentropic* system is a system that engages in operations that prevent evolution from a low entropic system to a high entropic system. Let's return to our gas in a plastic bottle. When this gas is introduced into the bottle, it *starts* in a state of low entropy. *Initially*, the gas is *localized* towards the top of the bottle as it is introduced into the system. Within the space of the bottle, this is an *improbable* localization of the gas. There is a low probability that molecules of the gas will be found anywhere in the bottle. As this system evolves, it shifts from a low entropy state where the gas atoms are localized in a particular region of the bottle, to a high entropy state where there's an equal probability of finding a gas atom at any location in the bottle. From T_1 to T_2 there are no operations that maintain the improbable organization of the gas molecules in their initial state.

This example allows us to discern the difference between a negentropic system and a mere low entropic system. A low entropic system is one that merely maintains a particular organization at a particular temporal moment. The destiny of such systems is often to evolve to a high entropic systems. By contrast, a negentropic system is a system that engages in *operations* that stave off – at least for a time – transition to a high entropic state. A negentropic system engages in operations to reduce and exclude noise, thereby maintaining the improbability of its organization. The cells of a body, for example, continuously die, yet that body continuously reproduces cells of various types, related in a particular way, so as to maintain the organization of that body. The same is true of political collectives, institutions, and organizations. In all of these cases we encounter entities that engage in operations that strive to preserve their organization and stave off noise or high degrees of entropy.

"Improbability" and "low entropy system" are synonyms of one another. Likewise, "machine" and "improbability" are synonymous. A machine is improbable in the sense that it is an organized or a low entropy system. In such systems inferences can be made from one element to another, which is to say that there isn't an equal probability of the elements appearing anywhere in the machine. Nonetheless, many corporeal and incorporeal machines face the perpetual threat of entropy or disintegration. As Luhmann writes:

> . . . *reproduction* is a continuous problem for systems with temporalized complexity. This theory is not concerned, like the classical theories of equilibrium, with returning to a stable state of rest after the absorption of disturbances, but with securing the constant renewal of system elements – or, more briefly, not with static but with dynamic stability. All elements pass away. They cannot endure as elements in time, and thus they must constantly be produced on the basis of whatever constellation of elements is actual at any given moment . . . [W]e will call the reproduction of eventlike elements *operations*. (Luhmann 1995: 49)

I will have more to say about time in Part 2, but for the moment it can be said that time is, in part, the duration required for a machine to produce the elements that compose it. As a consequence, there is not one homogenous milieu of time defined by a common metric of moments shared by all machines, but rather time is pluralistic and varied, differing from machine to machine. Being is composed of different rhythms of duration, some nested within one another, unfolding at different rates. Insofar as machines are composed of durations, we can also say that they are processes.

The elements that compose corporeal and a number of incorporeal machines, along with how they are related to one another, are in a constant state of disintegration. They come into being and pass away. Moreover, in interacting with other entities, machines threaten to pass into a greater state of entropy, effectively undergoing decomposition. Machines resist entropy in one of two ways, though it is likely that there is a variety of differences in degree between these two poles. On the one hand, most inorganic corporeal machines resist entropy through the agency of *forces*. The molecules that compose a rock are held together or resist dissolution through those forces studied by physics and chemistry. The upshot of this is that unlike organic and social corporeal machines, inorganic corporeal machines do not engage in further operations to maintain their organization across time or duration. For example, if a rock is chipped by another rock, it does not regrow the piece of itself that it lost. Similarly, rocks do not, for example, engage in operations to maintain a stable temperature in response to temperature fluctuations in their environment. Most inorganic corporeal machines, then, maintain their organization in time, but without active operations striving to maintain their form. Their form or low entropic state persists through the forces that act within them.

By contrast, organic, cognitive, and social machines engage in constant operations to both reproduce their parts and to maintain their organization. The cells of an organic body are perpetually dying. Organic bodies engage in operations to reproduce those cells they lose through this death. They do this by transforming the inputs that pass through them (nutrients) into new bone, liver, blood, muscle, and nerve cells. However, they don't simply reproduce these cells, but reproduce the relations between the cells in a way that maintains the organization of the organism across time. If a dog is cut, its wound heals and in largely the same form or organization that its body possessed prior to being wounded. The activities through which an organic body produces its cells (in development), reproduces its cells, and reproduces relations between those cells, are the operations through which it resists entropy. When machines operate in this way, they are negentropic.

The case is the same with social systems. Take a city. A city is not a brute thing that just sits there, but is a negentropic process that is simultaneously in a constant state of disintegration and perpetually maintaining its organization across its duration. A city is, in the first place, a low entropic system, which is to say that it is a particular organization. There is, of course, the inorganic dimension of the city consisting of roads, buildings, street signs, street signals, pipes, electric cables, and so on. This infrastructure is in a constant state of disintegration and therefore requires a variety of different operations in order to maintain its existence throughout time.

Similarly, at the level of people, cities are composed of different occupations, different ethnic groups, different religious groups, different government roles, different economic classes, and so on. In a city like New York, people of one economic class, or one ethnicity, or one occupation tend to localize themselves in one area of the city; for example Wall Street for stock brokers and bankers, or in Chicago, the poor largely living on the South Side. These are all improbabilities. Why is it that beings that are more or less biologically the same differentiate themselves in these improbable ways?

Why is it that they don't mill about in a sort of Brownian motion where it is impossible to make inferences from one person to their relationship to other persons and different regions of the city? All sorts of operations must be at work maintaining this differentiation across time. People and social relations must be *formed* in certain ways for this differentiation to take place. This entails the agency of a variety of incorporeal and corporeal machines acting on human bodies, minds, and affects to both sort people into different groups and form them into various social types. Just as a growing tree draws on certain nutrients about it, forming these nutrients into different types of cells, these incorporeal and corporeal machines draw on human beings as a sort of nutrient that it then forms into social organs. This is necessarily an ongoing *process* because new people are born that need to find their place in the city, while others retire or die. If the city is to persist across time, it must engage in perpetual operations or processes to continue its pattern of organization across time or duration. As Althusser remarks, ". . . in order to exist, every social formation must *reproduce* the conditions of its production at the same time as it produces, in order to be able to produce" (Althusser 2001: 86, my italics). Human bodies, minds, and affects along with relations between humans must be formed or reproduced in various ways in order for a city to resist falling into entropic dissolution so that it might continue to exist across time.

The incorporeal and corporeal machines that carry out these structuring operations are quite varied. At the level of incorporeal machines, there are educational techniques that form people into members of the city and different occupations. These incorporeal educational machines play a role in teaching developing bodies the norms of the city, giving them the basic knowledge base to function in the city, and gradually play a role in differentiating people into different occupations. In this way, certain social differentiations are built, and people are formed cognitively and physically in ways that allow them to maintain the infrastructure of the city so that it does not disintegrate. The various training regimes for different trades like construction work, road work, collecting waste, etc., are also human-forming incorporeal machines of this sort. Setting aside whatever theological content they might have, churches, in their turn, are incorporeal machines that instill people with certain norms and form particular social groupings. Among the different classes, ethnic groupings, and religious groupings, we find more diffuse incorporeal machines that form people according to various linguistic dialectics, norms or ways of conducting interpersonal relations proper to those communities, and to expectations about what a life for a member of that community should be (gender roles, reproductive relations, duties, responsibilities, and so on). Likewise, various media systems such as television, radio, and newspapers form minds and affects, indicating what issues people should be concerned with, how they should dress, what norms they should obey, etc. These media systems play a role in the formation of shared public opinion and norms, allowing something of a unity to be formed out of a diverse multiplicity. The list of incorporeal machines formative of human beings and social relations could be expanded indefinitely. These incorporeal machines are literally like recipes that relate to human beings as ingredients, forming them in a variety of ways.

The incorporeal machines do not simply carry out operations that form people and social relations between people in particular ways, thereby reproducing social differentiation; they also have a regulatory function. Persons are never perfectly or rigidly formed by the incorporeal machines that strive to form their bodies, minds, affects, and relations to one another. This is true even in the most rigid and striated social assemblages such as totalitarianisms. There are always little acts of resistance, disobedience, deviance, and novelty. The incorporeal machines are both machines that strive to form bodies in ways that would erase these deviations, and are machines that respond to instances of these deviations so as to ensure that the social assemblage continues to function according to its organization and differentiation. We see this regulatory dimension of incorporeal machines most dramatically in cases of laws and mental health institutions. In the former case, laws punish people who have deviated with sanctions, the aim being to return behavior and social relations back to those patterns delineated by the social machines. In the case of mental institutions, those people who prove unformable in the ways prescribed and sanctioned by the social machines are locked up and subjected to intense pharmaceutical treatment so that they do not disrupt the city.

However, these regulatory or feedback mechanisms function in a variety of ways outside of laws as well. The unwritten norms of a community or neighborhood, for example, function as regulatory mechanisms of this sort too. These norms do not simply create dispositions for people to think, act, feel, and respond in particular ways, but also feed back on to people who have deviated from these behaviors, attempting to nudge them back in the direction of sanctioned behavior. We encounter an example of this in Spike Lee's 1999 film *Summer of Sam*. Set in the context of David Berkowitz's serial killings during the summer of 1977, *Summer of Sam* explores how an Italian Bronx neighborhood responds to the fear induced by these murders. Of particular interest here is the character of Ritchie played by Adrien Brody. After an absence, Brody's character returns to the neighborhood as a "punk." His mode of dress has changed, he has now adopted an English accent, and he flaunts the norms that structure the neighborhood. Initially his friends poke fun at him and ask why he now talks and dresses in this way. They question his masculinity, wonder if he is worshipping Satan, and one of his old friends expresses dismay that he is dating his sister. As the number of murders grows, they begin to suspect that he is the killer and begin to pursue him to put an end to the killings.

All of these responses are feedback mechanisms that attempt to draw the person back to the norms structuring the community. The mockery and challenges to Ritchie's masculinity are normalizing operations aiming to push him into the norms of speech, dress, and behavior structuring the neighborhood. When these regulatory responses fail, Ritchie's actual life comes to be in danger. If Ritchie won't obey the norms of the neighborhood, then he has the choice of either exile or death. Through these mechanisms, the neighborhood maintains its system of identities, behaviors, modes of dress, ways of speaking, and so on. In other words, Ritchie's character is seen as an entropic threat to the organization of the neighborhood and these responses are a series of negentropic operations aiming to prevent a growth of entropy.

However, social assemblages like cities are not sustained by incorporeal machines alone, but also by a variety of corporeal machines. Buildings are needed for people to live, work, and entertain themselves. Tools and technologies are required to produce and maintain the city. I'll have more to say about this in Part 2, but paths of transit, modes of transportation, and media that carry communication (telephones, fiber optic cable, postal systems, and so on) are of particular importance to the structure of cities. The manner in which roads, bus lines, and train lines are laid out serves as much a segregative as a connective function. All of these connecting threads are as much about time as they are about space. The layout of roads, for example, will determine how easily and in a timely fashion one can get from one portion of the city to another portion of the city, and therefore influence what groups interact with one another. While incorporeal machines structuring norms of various ethnic, religious, and class communities – all of which can overlap – play a tremendous role in forming human bodies, minds, and forms of affectivity, paths such as the layout of roads, as well of modes of transportation and media that carry communications, play a similarly significant role in the differentiation of groups and the structuring of social relations. Because there is no direct path from one region of the city to another or because transit from one point to another is time-consuming due to distance or traffic, populations of people undergo something like geographical isolation. These isolated populations then form normative incorporeal machines that differentiate them from other groups, thereby generating subcultures. The important point here is that machines such as roads are non-signifying media that play a key role in how particular fields of signifying machines develop. It is not how the road signifies that produces these incorporeal signifying machines particular to various communities, but rather how the system of roads draws certain humans together in a quasi-isolated population. As a consequence, the layout of roads plays a negentropic role in maintaining the organization of different communities by generating dense populations of people in the region of one another that then engage in communications with each other leading to the formation of identities and norms. Similar points can be made about modes of transportation and media through which communications are transmitted (by foot, horse, automobile, fiber optic cables, satellites, and so on).

Above all, cities require flows of energy and matter in order to maintain their organization and resist entropy. Cities, of course, require stone, brick, wood, plastics, metals, and a variety of other materials out of which to build and maintain infrastructure. However, cities also require flows of energy to persist across time. They require wood, coal, oil, electricity, the power of water and wind to heat homes, run transportation, and sustain various technologies. Yet they also require caloric energy. People must eat. This entails that daily food must flow into the city, be prepared or rendered suitable for consumption, and that it must be distributed to people throughout the city. This requires the development of all sorts of corporeal and incorporeal machines for transporting food, distributing it, and preparing it. For example, local markets arise as a way of distributing food, while different shipping routes are developed for bringing food into the city.

The necessity of energy and materials for the ongoing existence of the city across its duration entails two things. First, wherever there is the consumption of energy there is also the production of waste as an output. Sewage, gases, and by-products of how energy is operated on to do work in maintaining the organization of the city are all outputs of the various processes through which the city, its people, and social relations are produced. The oil in which various foods are fried goes bad and must be disposed of in some way. Cars produce various gases and oil by-products as a consequence of burning fossil fuels. And, of course, humans produce all sorts of waste as a result of consuming calories. With the use of energy to perform operations of work in the genesis of bodies, cells, human labor, and the activity of various technologies, waste becomes a problem for the city. What is to be done with all of this sewage, these by-products of consumption, these gases, these abandoned possessions, these by-products of production, and so on, that daily appear in the city? In response to the problem of waste in its variety of forms, entire occupations, incorporeal machines prescribing techniques of waste disposal, technologies, paths for disposing of waste (sewage pipes and tunnels, for example), and ways of transporting waste arise. Waste itself can rebound on the city, introducing entropy into the city-machine, through waves of epidemic sickness like typhus and cholera that plague cities with poor waste disposal, or through phenomena like smog that cause all sorts of respiratory problems. Production, consumption, and the transformation of energy into work and material bodies is never without its remainder, a sort of Lacanian *objet a* or surplus that unsettles the city.

Second, we also see that cities are necessarily selectively open to an outside from which they draw their flows of energy and matter so as to maintain themselves. Very little of the energy sources and materials that a city draws upon to both produce and sustain itself arise from within itself. Rather, cities must draw on material and energy resources from elsewhere in order to continue their operations. Cities draw their energies from farms in the countryside, food production facilities outside the city, electric and nuclear plants that produce electricity, coal mines, Middle Eastern oil field, oil refineries, and so on, all from outside the city. The same is true of the materials cities rely on to produce themselves. Stone, wood, metals, plastics, and yet more exotic materials come from regions throughout the world outside the city. And finally, of course, cities require flows of people to do labor in the city, to maintain it, to govern it, and so on. As a consequence, in order to sustain themselves and continue their operations, cities must develop relations to other regions of the world, shipping routes, ways of transporting materials, ways of preserving foodstuffs from far away, etc. Cities only exist in and through the operations that perpetuate them. In this respect, and as is the case with all machines, a city is more a verb than a noun. Cities only persist so long as they are able to continue their operations. Where those operations cease and where the flows upon which cities perform their operations are cut off, cities quickly fall into entropic dissolution.

We saw this with stunning clarity in New Orleans in response to Hurricane Katrina in 2005. Cut off from flows of energy and communication as a result of the hurricane, the ratio of entropy in the city quickly increased. People came to relate to one another in ways they wouldn't have before. Familiar functions and operations disappeared. And for a time, the city was unable to reproduce itself as New Orleans across time or its duration. The city shifted from a population that was functionally differentiated, to a population that became more like a gaseous cloud in Brownian motion. Inferences could no longer be made from one element to other elements because the organization of the city, its differentiated, its negentropic structure, had fallen apart. This negentropic set of operations fell apart not because people lost belief in the incorporeal machines or norms, laws, and identities that formerly organized them, but because the flows of energy and matter that previously flowed through the city allowing it to continue its operations ceased to flow. Divorced from these flows, the intricate organization of New Orleans quickly evaporated. Where the corporeal and incorporeal machines upon which people had previously relied to organize their existence disappeared, people had to forge new relations and machines.

From the foregoing it is hopefully clear that entropy cannot be treated as a *normative* category. We cannot say that low entropy is a "good" while high entropy is a "plague" or "ill." Entropy, low entropy, and negentropy, are phenomena of being, not moral *preferences*. To be sure, a world – if it could even be called a world

– defined by absolute entropy would be intolerable for humans and other beings. The complete absence of order, organization, and the ability to make inferences from one element or event to another would be a miserable existence that would very likely lead to death and that would leave little time for anything else. It is because we and other organisms and institutions can anticipate certain regularities or low entropic states in our environment that we can free ourselves up for other tasks. We don't have to think much about this, because it is a fairly stable phenomena, and therefore can occupy ourselves with other things. On the other hand, negentropic mechanisms can be deeply oppressive. We saw this in the case of Ritchie's character in *Summer of Sam*, where he suffers both verbal abuse and later physical abuse up to the possibility of his own death because he had rejected the norms organizing identities, behaviors, and social relations in his community. In our view, when thinkers such as Foucault and Althusser speak of power and ideological state apparatuses, what they're really referring to are negentropic operations of this sort. They're referring to operational feedback mechanisms that regulate and normalize human bodies . . . *or else.* Low entropy, negentropic systems can be every bit as harrowing and oppressive as systems characterized by absolute entropy. In this regard, our political struggles are often a question of how to introduce *more* entropy into a system, how to loosen up striations or overly rigid machines so as to open the way to new and different forms of life and existence.

But finally, systems that are characterized by too little entropy, systems or machines that are too negentropic, also fare very poorly in navigating their environments. It will be recalled that machines only share selective relations to their environments and that these selective relations always involve risk. If the structural openness to an environment (other machines and flows from other machines) involves risk, then this is because the environment of a machine is always more complex than the machine. As a consequence, if the selections that machines make in forming their openness to the environment always involve risk, then this is because a machine's operational closure and selective openness to its environment always face the possibility of being blind to flows from other machines that could destroy it or of being unable to adapt to changes in its environment that would similarly bring about its demise. We see this, for example, in the case of the relationship between social machines and climate change, where a variety of social machines operate on the premise that climate will continue as it always has in the past. Unable to register changes in climate because they occur at such large scales and so diffusely, social systems like cities risk sawing off the branch upon which they sit and bringing about their own destruction.

A degree of entropy within a machine amounts to *plasticity*. A rigid machine is a machine whose entropy is so low that it's selective openness to its environment is more or less fixed – again there are different degrees of rigidity – and that can only operate on inputs in a fixed and mechanical way. As a consequence, such machines are unable to develop new forms of openness to their environment and create new operations for responding to the new and unexpected. Plastic machines are machines that contain a reservoir of entropy or are machines that are not rigidly organized. Because of this, they have degrees of freedom that allow them to develop new forms of openness to their environment, as well as new ways of operating on the inputs that flow through them. At present it appears that this sort of plasticity is unique to organic machines, cognitive machines, and social machines. Nonetheless, it increasingly looks like inorganic technologies such as artificial intelligences are developing this sort of plasticity as well.

In another register, entropy is central to both political theory and practice. At the most abstract level, all political questions and struggles are issues of entropy and negentropy. Social systems are negentropic machines that structure human identities, lives, cognition, affectivity, and ways of relating to one another. They operate between extremes of chaos – not to be confused with anarchism – and totalitarianism, functioning in ways that aim to minimize deviation from the structure of their operations. Emancipatory political struggle is first an attempt to introduce entropy into a social machine, striving to obliterate negentropic mechanisms that prevent other forms of life, association, relations, and affectivity. A successful political struggle is, in part, one that introduces entropy into a social system. Second, such political struggles introduce new forms of structural openness into a social system, as well as new operations. For example, the civil rights movements of the 1960s generated new forms of structural openness within the American social system through the recognition and inclusion of silent and invisible minorities within the social assemblage, while an anarchical social system introduces new types of operations through the formation of immanent governance by a community not mediated by the machine of the state.

Machine and entropy are two central concepts of onto-cartography. The first concept reminds us that things, objects, entities, or substances are processes composed of operations acting on inputs producing outputs in the form of qualities, actions, and products. Additionally, in the distinction between virtual proper being and local manifestation, we are reminded that machines always contain a virtual reservoir of potential qualities, actions, and products in excess of whatever qualities, activities, or products happen to manifest themselves at a given point in time and space. In this way we are called upon to attend to the interaction of machines with other machines providing inputs, so as to mark the manner in which relations to other machines bring about variations in the manifestations of a machine.

By contrast, the concept of entropy reminds us that machines require *work* if they are to continue their existence throughout time. With the exception of rigid incorporeal machines like mathematical equations, the vast majority of corporeal and incorporeal machines are perpetually beset by the threat of entropy. What has been said here of cities is largely true of all machines whether they are inorganic machines like comets, organic corporeal machines like rhinoceros beetles, or incorporeal machines like discourses. For example, incorporeal machines like conversations threaten to cease or to become so scattered that they no longer have any unity or organization. A conversation might cease if its degree of entropy is too low, as in those instances where two people continuously say "please" and "thank you." In the absence of any conversational moves introducing novelty among the participants, the conversation quickly dissipates like so much morning mist as no new information or play occurs calling for a response. By contrast, a conversation that descends into complete randomness in the utterances of the participants proves unable to form a unity *between* the participants, thereby preventing a conversational machine over and above the participants to emerge. What we here get are two or more people speaking in the same spatial and temporal vicinity of one another, but not speaking *to* and *with* each other. Each person's utterances could just as easily be made in the absence of the other people.

Just as Althusser contends that societies must *reproduce* their conditions of production in order to continue existing, all of these machines must engage in operations that allow them to reproduce their pattern of organization across time. Here "reproduction" is not to be conceived as the production of *copies* of itself as in the case of two capybara producing offspring or an amoeba dividing into two, but rather as the continuation of either a low entropic or negentropic organization across time. At each moment, these sorts of machines threatens to disintegrate into a plurality of machines, thereby losing their organization.

This reproduction of organization across time requires work both in the sense that the natural sciences conceive of work and in the sense of labor in the social sciences. Work, of course, requires energy. It is intriguing that the concepts of work and energy are almost entirely absent in the history of philosophy. We find brief glimmers of it here and there in concepts such as Schopenhauer's will and Nietzsche's will to power, yet these concepts remain all too vitalistic and romantic to really capture the idea of work. We encounter a more sophisticated concept of work in Marx with his emphasis on production; however, Marx's concept of work is largely restricted to the sphere of human economic production and attentiveness to work in Marxist thought was quickly eclipsed by the Frankfurt school that came to focus more on incorporeal machines found at the discursive and ideological level than production. We again find concepts of work in Foucault and Bourdieu's concepts of power; yet again power is restricted to the domain of society and social structuration, rather than being developed as a general concept pertaining to low entropic and negentropic systems including machines ranging from the inorganic to the technological.

The concept of entropy reminds us that machines, as low entropy entities, are improbable and that they require energy and work to continue to exist. The vast majority of machines are in a constant state of disintegration and are also threatened from without by dissolution. Far from being static lumps that just sit there, machines must instead engage in constant operations to continue their existence from moment to moment. Where those operations cease, the machine also ceases. One of the central tasks of onto-cartography is thus the investigation of those operations by which machines stave off entropy and forestall dissolution. Sometimes this investigation will be for the sake of improving a machine. For example, machines like revolutionary political movements might be particularly interested in the operations that allow them to persist and continue so as to forestall their destruction through the people that compose the movement becoming individual units that depart from the political project. Through an investigation of the negentropic operations of such a machine, more effective techniques of maintaining unity and purpose might be devised. Badiou's analysis of fidelity to events and truth-procedures in *Being and Event* seems devoted to such a project (Badiou 2005: part v). The case is similar with medical investigations of the body that seek to determine optimal diets and exercise regimes so as to produce health. An understanding of negentropic operations and how they act on inputs can allow us to devise more durable machines.

On the other hand, an understanding of the negentropic operations of a machine can allow us to devise strategies for demolishing those machines. This is of crucial importance in a variety of political struggles. Revolutionary machines do not simply strive to create new social machines, but also aim to demolish a variety of existing, oppressive social machines such as the state, white male privilege, patriarchy, capitalism, and so on. To accomplish these aims, revolutionary machines must develop knowledge of the negentropic machines that allow these reactionary machines to persist across time, structuring lives, cognition, associations between people, etc. The work of theorists such as Foucault, Butler, Marx, Latour, Haraway, Adorno, Althusser, Deleuze and Guattari, and so on, can be seen as so many investigations of negentropic operations designed to produce a cartography of power that would allow us to strategically intervene in these machines and demolish them.

Note

1. This discussion of emergence is inspired by the work of Dave Elder-Vass. For a more detailed discussion of emergence in these terms see Elder-Vass (2010: ch. 2).

Part 2

Worlds

5

The Structure of Worlds

Ecologies of Worlds

The central project of onto-cartography consists in the analysis or cartography of worlds. A cartography is a mapping. We must exercise care here, for while geography provides us with exemplary instances of cartography, not all cartographies are geographical. Anatomists, for example, are cartographers of the body, mapping relations between bones, muscles, nerves, and organs. As DeLanda argues, complexity theorists develop cartographies of attractors governing systems, along with potential bifurcation points in those systems (DeLanda 2005: ch. 1). As Deleuze suggests following Lautmann (Lautmann 2011), mathematicians are cartographers of "problem spaces" (Deleuze 1995: ch. 4). Linguists are cartographers of phonemes and other linguistic entities, while Marx – in his historical work – was a cartographer of social relations under a variety of systems of production. The list could be expanded indefinitely. Foucault presents us with cartographies of knowledge (Foucault 1994) and how power structures social relations (Foucault 1995). Cartography is a central project of geography, but not all or even most cartographies are geographical. Wherever there is a map – even where we don't call it a map – there is a cartography. To map is to produce a cartography. While onto-cartography overlaps with cartographies as developed in geography, and while, as we will see, it necessarily contends with issues of time and space as is the case with geography, the object of onto-cartography is something other than the mapping of geographical, spatio-temporal relations. What onto-cartography maps are relations between machines or networks of machines composing a world.

However, in order to articulate the project of onto-cartography it's necessary to first clarify the concept of "world." A world is not a planet such as the planet Earth. Planets are machines within a world, components of a world, but are not themselves worlds. Similarly, worlds are not networks or systems of signs referring to one another, as in the case of Heidegger (Heidegger 1962: 91–148). Heidegger describes how a particular machine, Dasein, is structurally open to a world, but does not give an account of a world. He confuses openness or access to a world with a world itself. To be sure, Dasein throws a net of meaning as conceived by Heidegger over those flows to which it is structurally open, but this system of meaning, of signs referring to one another, is not a world. So radical is our thrownness in a world, so radical is the facticity of a world into which we are thrown, that it cannot be in any way reduced to our access to it or how we signify or intend it. In this regard, Descartes was closer to the true being of world (Heidegger 1962: 114–22) than Heidegger. Far from being something characterized by "everydayness" or familiarity, world in its ontological being is something that no mode of access structures or dominates. World is that which *intrudes* on the networks of meaning we throw over it; it is what Lacan sometimes refers to as the Real. It is not the network of meaning produced as a synthesis of the Imaginary and the Symbolic. In this regard, worlds are non-subjectivizable and are the ungrounded ground of all systems of meaning beings such as ourselves or dolphins might throw over it. We might cease to exist and along with us all meaning, but worlds would remain. As Sartre taught in his discussions of being-in-itself (Sartre 1956: 617–24), worlds are indifferent to our existence. Incorporeal machines that produce meaning or sense are machines among other machines in a world, not the ground of world. As a consequence, world, in its ontological being, is not what Husserl refers to as a "*horizon* of lived experience" for the *cogito*. To be sure, as the neuro-philosopher Thomas Metzinger argues, all experience for beings such as ourselves is organized around *gestalt* structures between foreground and background such that, *for us*, foreground always refers to a background functioning as the horizon of the experience we are having now (Metzinger 2009: ch. 2). But a world *itself* is not to be conflated with how we consciously experience the world, nor with the structure of our intentionality. Once again, this conflates how a particular being, the *cogito*, is structurally open to a world with the world itself. As an aside, we are, for this reason, unable to follow Graham Harman in his argument for the withdrawal of entities insofar as Heidegger's analaysis of *aletheia*, presence and absence, or revealing and concealing, is undertaken from the standpoint of phenomenology or the lived experience of Dasein. There is no reason to suppose that a phenomenological analysis can tell us about the being of beings or machines, as phenomenological analysis only tells us how *we* encounter beings, not how beings in and of themselves *are*. We require a different sort of argument to establish that machines are operationally closed or withdrawn than the sort provided by fine-grained analyses of lived experience.

In a similar vein, worlds are not compossible systems of "sense" as argued by Deleuze (Deleuze 1990: chs 16–17). Sense or incorporeal machines are *components* in many worlds, but are not a *condition* for worlds. Again, equating worlds with compossible systems of sense, no matter how anti-humanist and anonymously it is conceived, confuses worlds with how they are encountered for particular machines – in this case, linguistico-social machines – and what worlds are in themselves. For the same reason, worlds cannot be equated with a "transcendental" that indexes multiplicities to a system of identity as in the case of Badiou (Badiou 2009: 101–2). While the "transcendental" might adequately describe how a social system or, as Badiou calls it in his earlier work, "encyclopedia," codes and structures inputs from an environment in reproducing itself, this transcendental can in no way be equated with a world. Rather, the transcendental is a sieve or series of operations through which a social machine encounters a world.

Again and again we see the same error of conflating worlds as they are in themselves with worlds as they are encountered through the structural openness and operations of particular machines: Dasein, lived body, *cogito*, language, social systems. But while we do not doubt that each machine, and especially organic and cognitive machines, encounters world in its own particular way, we nonetheless contend that no world can be equated with or reduced to these modes of access or correlation to a world. This conflates what a world *is* with how a particular machine has access to a world. Without denying the veracity and importance of all these different analyses, a world is not a particular machine's openness to a world, nor its way of operating upon and structuring inputs from other entities within a world.

No, a world is a loosely coupled assemblage of machines interacting with one another through the mediation of other machines in an ecology. Insofar as all machines participating in a world have their own mode of access to that world, their own structural openness and ways of operating on inputs from other machines in that world, there is no machine that could totalize or function as a condition for all of the other machines that exist in this world. In this regard, worlds are non-subjectifiable, and evade all totalities based on social constructivism. To be sure, subjects, lived bodies, Daseins, *cogitos*, and social systems all apprehend the other machines that compose a world in their own way, but none of them are the condition or ground of a world. Worlds evade all such possibilities of mastery, grounding, or centering. To be in a world is to be decentralized, to lack all mastery, and to be a participant in an assemblage, network, or composition that exceeds society, culture, and oneself. It is a failure to engage in alien phenomenology, post-humanist phenomenology, or second-order observation that leads us to miss the being of world. Descartes, in his so-called "ontic" understanding of world – and here we must add that world is not a "phenomenon" as Heidegger would have it – is closer to the truth of what worlds are than the phenomenologists. In this regard, we have no direct access to worlds. We can only infer their being and organization, without directly experiencing them. Indeed, analyses based on "everydayness," "lived experience," and semiotic structurations of ways in which we have *access* to worlds are doomed to miss world, conflating how we experience world with what worlds *are*. To proceed based on analyses of givenness is a surefire way to miss the being of world altogether. *A world is an ecology of loosely coupled machines linked by machines without any of these machines totalizing world.*

In this regard, worlds are not *containers*. Despite what Columbus said, all worlds are *flat*. There is not one thing, a world, and then another thing, machines *in* this world. As an ecology, a world is nothing more than the machines that compose the world. To be sure, there is void for, as Lucretius argues:

> . . . not all bodily matter is tight-packed
> By nature's law, for there is a void in things.
> . . .
> By *void* I mean vacant and empty space,
> Something you cannot touch. Were this not so,
> Things could not move. The property of matter,
> It's most outstanding trait, is to stand firm,

Its office to oppose; and everything
Would always be immovable, since matter
Never gives way. But with our eyes we see
Many things moving, in their wondrous ways,
Their marvelous means, through sea and land and sky.
Were there no void, they would not only lack
This restlessness of motion altogether,
But more than that – they never could have been
Quickened to life from that tight-packed quiescence.

(Lucretius 1969: 29–30)

Without void there could be no movement or change; yet void is literally nothing. It is an emptiness that resides both within all machines insofar as all machines are composites, and is that within which machines reside. A world, by contrast, is nothing more than couplings among machines effected by machines.

For this reason, worlds are not *geometrically* flat, but *ontologically* flat. They are ontologically flat in the sense that there is no supplementary dimension over and above the machines themselves that totalizes machines. Nor are there any sovereign beings like God, power, force, Platonic forms, the Good, *cogito*, transcendental subjectivity, language, signs, life, and so on, that function as hierarchs of being, determining all other beings. As Ian Bogost puts it, ". . . all things equally exist, yet they do not exist equally" (Bogost 2012: 11). Alternatively, ". . . there is no hierarchy of being" (ibid.: 22). To be sure, machines are unequal among *themselves* in all sorts of ways. Some machines exercise greater power over others and play a more significant role in structuring relations between machines, but there is no ontological "great chain of beings" as conceived by Lovejoy (Lovejoy 1936). In a hierarchical or vertical ontology, some beings such as God or Platonic forms are able to affect all others, without themselves being affected in turn. In a flat ontology, by contrast, there is no machine that is beyond being affected by other machines. While machines cannot be affected by all other entities insofar as they are only selectively open to their environment, as in the case of the neutrino that can't be affected by the majority of matter that makes up the furniture of our daily life, every machine is nonetheless open to being affected by some other entities. Consequently, if a God exists, he is not a sovereign like Leibniz's grand architect that designed and produced this world as the best of all possible worlds, but rather is a tinkerer like the rest of us that must contend with the exigencies of other machines. Such a God could both be affected by other machines and would have to contend with the manner in which machines have their own resistances, their own tendencies, their own powers that usurp his intentions. A flat ontology is thus an *anarchic* ontology. There is no ultimate ground within a world for machines. There are only immanent planes of machines affecting and being affected by one another without a supplementary dimension that structures all their interactions. An ecology is a network of machines without a single governing principle. Hence all ecologies are anarchic.

Up to this point, I have used indefinite articles and the plural when referring to worlds. Why is this? With Deleuze (Deleuze 1990: chs 15–17) and Badiou (Badiou 2009), onto-cartography begins with the premise that there is not *one* world, but rather a plurality of worlds. In other words, machines do not add up to a totality that forms a *universe*. There is only a pluriverse. There are two reasons for this. First, as we have seen, machines are external to their relations. No machine relates to all other machines, but rather each machine only relates selectively to other machines. Indeed, as we will see, it is even *possible* that there are machines that are completely unrelated to other machines. I refer to these as "dark objects." Because worlds are nothing more than the machines that compose them and because machines are not related to all other machines in an organic whole, it follows that it is possible that there is a plurality of worlds. A world would here be an assemblage of loosely coupled machines that is discontinuous with other assemblages of machines.

Second, if it is possible that there is a plurality of worlds, then this is because there is no action at a distance. In order for machines to relate or interact they must be capable of touching in some way. This can take the form of direct contact as in the case of a cat sharpening its claws on a couch, or it can occur indirectly through the mediation of another machine. The distinction between direct and indirect interaction is premised on locality. Two entities interact directly when they occupy the same locality. The cat is directly scratching the couch and this is possible because geographically the cat and the couch are in the same locality. By contrast, the Sun and Earth cannot directly touch one another because of the vast distances that separate them. Rather, the Sun affects the Earth only through *another term*, the photons of light that the Sun emits. It is the photons of light that directly affect the Earth, not the Sun itself. The Sun interacts with the Earth and other planets through, among other things, the machinic mediation of photons of light. Unlike the cat scratching the couch, it does not directly interact with the Earth, but rather relates to the Earth through a machinic mediator or medium. When two people speak to one another, their interaction is mediated through machines such as soundwaves traveling through the air, text messages, telephones, Internet chat rooms, letters, and so on. In short, the relation between one machine and another machine with one another from a distance is not a binary relation, but rather a triadic relation: p → q → r, where machine p is related to machine r through the medium of machine q.

Often the relation established by machine q between machines p and r is itself dependent on additional media. Thus, for example, soundwaves (q) cannot relate two people (p, r) without the additional medium of air. Speech and birdsong are not possible in a vacuum such as outer space. Similarly, the relationship between two people through a text message is not dependent on the text message alone, but also requires media such as the device through which the message is sent like a smart phone, the software that allows the text message to be composed and sent, satellites and cell phone towers that transport the message, as well as all the energy required to sustain the operations of these various machines. Nor is this restricted to technological relations. Machines function as media for other machines regardless of whether those machines are technological, cultural, or natural. It is well known that astronauts suffer bone and muscle degeneration from prolonged time spent in space. Presumably this would be no less true of pig bodies in outer space than of human bodies. Phenomena such as this show us that the Earth is a medium for organic bodies. It is not simply that organic bodies produce themselves through genetic algorithms acting on food passing through the body to produce proteins. Rather, relation to a medium such as the Earth plays a role in how those muscles and bones developed. Absent the Earth's gravity, absent this medium, bone and muscle develop poorly.

In this regard, indirect relations between machines have a structure similar to commodity fetishism as described by Marx. As Marx explains, commodity fetishism is a phenomenon in which a "... definite social relation between men themselves which assumes ... the fantastic form of a relation between things"

(Marx 1990: 165). Marx's point is that in our dealings with commodities we take ourselves to be relating to the thing alone, the commodity itself. We go to the grocer and buy a roasted chicken, believing that there is nothing *social* about this relation insofar as it is simply a relation between us and the chicken. Yet the commodity embodies an entire set of social relations that are the medium of the chicken, insofar as it was produced by people under certain conditions, within a particular legal system, within a particular network of distribution, and so on. As Deleuze and Guattari remark, ". . . we cannot tell from the mere taste of wheat who grew it; the product gives us no hint as to the system and the relations of production" (Deleuze and Guattari 1983: 24). The "mediasphere" of the chicken and wheat is veiled in the thing, withdrawn from view.

From an epistemological standpoint, the same is true of all mediated relations between machines. Our tendency is to miss the network of mediation, the world, which conditions the local manifestations of machines. Thus when we text back and forth to each other we attend only to the text message, treating the message as arising solely from the other person, ignoring the series of machinic mediations that enable this indirect relation between two people. Likewise, when we investigate the local manifestations of a tree, noting the qualities of its leaves, bark, how robustly it has grown, the shape it has grown into, etc., our tendency is to treat these local manifestations as arising solely from the genetics of the tree or some sort of vital principle that resides within the tree, ignoring the machinic encounters with wind, rain, air, soil nutrients, sunlight, other plants, animals, and so on, in generating this local manifestation. What we get in these instances is a sort of ontological fetishism that focuses on the individual tree, ignoring how that tree's local manifestation was a product of a world. Onto-cartography, in part, seeks to overcome this ontological fetishism through the investigation of how worlds preside over the local manifestations of machines.

The claim that there is no action at a distance is the claim that no two entities can affect one another without some sort of material medium to link them. This is true even of incorporeal entities such as mathematical equations, ideologies, texts, and so on. To affect other machines such as human beings, these incorporeal machines must become embodied in a corporeal body such as writing, soundwaves, smoke signals, or digital pulses of electricity to travel from person to person. No machine is able to affect another machine without a material mediator passing between them that is itself a machine of some sort. Even our ability to see another machine such as a cloud must be materially mediated. It is not the *cloud itself* that I see, but photons of light that have bounced off the cloud and traveled between me and the cloud.

This entails that material relations between entities are necessarily bound up with time and space. If there is no action at a distance, then this is because there are no *instantaneous* interactions between machines at a distance from one another. Machines that function as material media or mediators between machines must *travel* across space in order to affect another machine. This travel takes *time*. As a consequence, when we look up at the night stars or the person sitting across a table from us, we're seeing them not as they are now but as they were in a more or less remote past. The speed of light, of course, is simply the upper limit of the rate at which two machines at a distance can interact. Speeds of interaction will be variable depending on the medium that carries a flow of matter, energy, or information. Flows transported by wind, airplanes, ocean currents, letters, illuminated texts, horseback, automobiles, fiber optic cables, tin cans linked together by string, and so on all have variable speeds, ranges, and rates of movement.

This material dimension of machinic mediators is the second reason that onto-cartography begins with the premise that there is a plurality of worlds rather than a single unified universe containing all machines. On the one hand, machines are only selectively open to flows from other machines. Once again, the neutrino, while a material entity, is unable to interact with most matter that makes up the familiar furniture of our daily life. Where two entities are unable to interact we should conclude that they belong to two different worlds. On the other hand, insofar as flows take time to travel from one machine to another, there are a number of machines that never interact with one another and that, for all intents and purpose, are incapable of encountering one another. For example, it's entirely likely that at this very moment a massive star millions of light years away is going supernova. However, given that light from this supernova will take millions of years to reach us, it makes little sense to claim that we and the supernova belong to the same world. There's simply no possibility of material interaction between us and this supernova because we will be dead well before that light travels here.

The rate at which material mediators travel thus places significant constraints on both how machines can interact and the size of worlds. Plato recognized this issue with respect to the size of cities in Book IV of the *Republic* (Plato 1989: 423a–d). If a city is too small it lacks the labor power to sustain and defend itself. If a city is too large, then the people that inhabit the city can no longer form a unity among themselves, but instead become a mere multiplicity. In other words, a city that is too large is subject to a high degree of entropy. Part of Plato's point here has to do with material *media* of interaction between citizens of a city. A city that is too large is a city where the material media of communication relating people are unable to adequately link people together spatially or in a timely fashion, generating shared identity, purpose, and solidarities among the citizens. As a consequence, such a city ends up forming distinct groups that are differentiated from one another and that therefore no longer possess a shared sense of belonging to the city. They literally end up belonging to different worlds.

This situation arises not from the meaning of the messages transmitted among the people or what those messages convey, but from the *materiality of the media* that transport these messages. If the medium that links identity-forming communications between people consists of soundwaves alone, that city will only be able to reach a particular size. The reason for this is twofold. On the one hand, soundwaves can only travel a certain distance within the range of hearing before dissipating or becoming inaudible. Such cities are literally limited by earshot. Messages can, of course, be repeated from person to person. However, on the other hand, as a message is repeated it undergoes a high degree of entropic variation as in the childhood game of telephone where the message with which the game begins and the content of the message after ten or fifteen people have repeated it are quite different. In other words, messages transmitted through speech lack *durability*. Because of this, a city based on communication through speech will have difficulty engaging in citizen-forming operations when the city reaches a certain size because it is unable to maintain the durability of its messages across wide reaches of time and space. It will therefore have difficulty coordinating action among its citizens because of the time it takes for speech to travel and the variation it undergoes.

The upshot of this is that the ideal size of a city – if such a thing really exists – is not a fixed target, but rather varies depending on the sort of media upon which a society is based. Societies based on speech, writing, television, smart phones, internets and so on, will all have different structures and forms of organization as a result of the machinic media through which they transmit their messages to their elements. The difference between a society based on medieval illuminated texts and one based on the printing press, for example, is not simply a difference in degree, but a difference in kind. In the first instance, the great time it takes to produce copies of a handwritten text ensures that this text will travel very slowly throughout the culture and will be accessible to only the wealthy or those who have access to a library such as monks, priests, and prestigious scholars. As a consequence, these texts will have limited capacity to engage in operations of social genesis. By contrast, the rate at which texts can be produced through a printing press allows them to circulate much more widely because the labor to produce them is diminished, their cost falls, and multiple copies can be easily made and distributed. The invention of the printing press thus intensifies operations of social genesis, opening the possibility of spatially greater and more distant social relations.

The scale of social relations is therefore deeply bound up with the sorts of media on which a society relies. We saw this in the case of the Arab Spring of 2010 and the Occupy Wall Street movement in 2010. As has often been noted, social media such as Facebook and Twitter, along with communications technologies like smart phones, played a key role in these political movements. It's not that these media and technologies single-handedly kicked off these movements, but rather that they opened the way to new forms of association, organization, and strategization that did not exist in the previous world. Most importantly, these media allowed groups to circumvent corporate and government-run media machines, giving these groups greater control over messages and allowing for the possibility of identifications and coordinated action between groups of people that had never met. These political movements could now become more responsive to unfolding events in the "meat-world," reporting information that indicated where people needed to appear, as well as police responses that needed to be avoided. Messages could be anarchically composed allowing for shared identification and participation spanning the entire globe that, in turn, placed pressure on governments and corporations. Finally, as a result of these technologies and media of communication, political movements became far less dependent on party systems. In earlier worlds, parties were required as media for the distribution of communications and organization because it was difficult for geographically separated groups to communicate with one another. With the rise of these new technologies, it became far easier for groups to communicate without the mediation of parties, thereby allowing them to develop their own visions of what needed to be done, their own aims and values, and their own strategies. As McLuhan argued, the medium is the message.

As an aside, we should here note that the appearance of new material mediators introduces *entropy* into worlds. With the advent of mediators such as writing, the printing press, and smart phones, older worlds are no longer able to negentropically perform operations as they once did. New linkages between machines are forged, reducing the strength of old relations and operations. Far from being a negative thing, entropy here contributes to the formation of new worlds and social relations. It is what allows creativity to occur within a world.

These reflections on the role of material meditators between machines in worlds lead onto-cartography to reject Luhmann's thesis that societies are composed *solely* of communications (Luhmann 2002c). It is not that Luhmann is wrong to recognize the importance of communication for social assemblage, but that he is mistaken in his suggestion that material mediators don't play an equally significant role in the form that social relations take. Technological media, the layout of roads, rivers, and power lines, tornadoes and hurricanes, resources, and so on, all play as significant a role in the form that social assemblages take as communications. Communications are only one element among others in social assemblages.

We must beware of treating worlds as fixed or static structures. Similarly, we must take care not to treat worlds as enumerable sets. Worlds are closer to a gaseous cloud in Brownian motion or fireflies flickering to each other, than to a fixed geometrical lattice like the iron supports of a radio tower. Worlds are, as Timothy Morton suggests, a mesh (Morton 2010: 28 – 38), but this mesh is dynamic and ever changing as a result of interactions between machines that compose the world. Worlds are fuzzy and without clearly fixed or defined boundaries and elements. This is not to say that worlds are characterized by *absolute* entropy, only that they lack fixity. Whenever we substantialize "world," treating it as a thing rather than a fuzzy process, we miss the being of world. While all worlds possess their regularities and tendencies or vectors, no world can be pinned down once and for all. With each interaction between machines composing a world, the configuration of machines change. Some machines depart from a world through leaving it or being destroyed, while new machines appear like satellite technology that reconfigures relations among a variety of other machines. In other instances, events descend upon worlds, sending ripples throughout all the machines as in the case of revolutions, Hurricane Katrina, and the stock market crash of 1929. Within worlds, some machines endure longer than others, like the planet Earth or certain social institutions like a university, while others disappear almost as quickly as they appear.

These observations allow us to distinguish between worlds and machines. A world is not a giant machine. We are only before a machine in those instances where a certain number of the elements that compose a machine – which are themselves machines – are structurally coupled in such a way that their separation entails the destruction of that machine. While worlds are indeed compositions of machines, they differ from machines in that the machines that compose them are separable. Trees can be uprooted from one world to another. Persons can travel to distant planets. Rocks can be blown off the surface of Mars by meteor impacts, landing on the planet Earth. In each of these instances, the machines that have travelled from world to world will undergo different local manifestations as a result of falling into a new media ecology, while the world and be moved from which they departed will continue to exist. Worlds too, of course, can be destroyed, but they differ from machines insofar as the relations between the elements that compose them are *external* or *separable* relations. This is why phenomena like revolutions and climate catastrophe are possible. A political revolution is the complete transformation of social relations organizing a world. Such revolutions would not be possible unless relations between machines in a world could be severed and reconfigured. Likewise, if something like climate catastrophe is possible, then this is because machines necessary for the functioning of other machines in an ecology can be destroyed, as in the case of bees disappearing, or because new toxic machines like carbon emissions can be introduced into an ecosystem, creating an ecology inhospitable to those machines that populate that world. In both cases, this is only possible where relations are external to machines.

In its most basic formulation, onto-cartography is the mapping of ecologies of machines in a world. However, because machines are dynamic assemblages, these maps are not maps of fixed entities and relations as in the case of the anatomy of an organic body, but rather are maps of the *vectors* along which a world is unfolding. Within this topology of a world, some machines will be more stable and enduring than others, while there will also be trajectories of development unfolding within the world. Likewise, some machines will be more dominant or influential than others. It is these dynamic structures presiding over local manifestations that onto-cartography seeks to map. However, insofar as worlds are fuzzy ecologies characterized by bewildering complexity, we must always remember that, as Bateson observed, ". . . the map is not the territory" (Bateson 2000: 455). The territory is the world itself. The cartography is itself an incorporeal machine in the world that it maps. Like all machines, maps only possess selective relationships to their environment or the ecology of machines they map. They literally select certain vectors within the ecology to map, while ignoring others. This difference between map and territory must always be borne in mind, lest we forget that we might be ignoring important actants within the ecology of machines we're mapping. Moreover, insofar as a map is itself a machine within the world that it maps, we must remember that this map also has the capacity to affect other machines; indeed, as we see in the case of cartographers such as Foucault, Butler, and Marx, one of the central aims is to affect or change the worlds we map. In this regard, we must be attentive to the ways in which our maps act on the world and circulate throughout the world, and whether or not our maps are even composed in ways conducive to producing the sort of change we aim for.

Content and Expression

The ecologies of many worlds contain elements of both content and expression that are of particular interest in the investigation of social and political assemblage. First presented in *Kafka: Towards a Minor Literature* (Deleuze and Guattari 1986: 3–8), the concepts of content and expression constitute a radical reworking of Louis Hjelmslev's concept of the sign (Hjelmslev 1969: 41–60), liberating content and expression from exclusive enclosure in the domain of the semiotic so as to apply to a wide domain of non-semiotic machines. Deleuze and Guattari are careful to note that "[c]ontent

Table 5.1 Structure of expression and content

	Form	Substance	Matter
Plane of expression	Form of expression	Substance of expression	Matter of expression
Plane of content	Form of content	Substance of content	Matter of content

is not a signified nor expression a signifier . . ." (Deleuze and Guattari 1987: 91), but rather "[t]he two formalizations are not of the same nature; they are independent, heterogeneous" (ibid.: 86). The two planes of content and expression are distinct and autonomous domains – not unlike Spinoza's attributes without the parallelism – and both have their own organization, being, and processes. While they can intermingle and interact in all sorts of ways, one plane cannot be reduced to another, nor does either plane dominate or overcode the other.

Deleuze and Guattari remark that "Hjelmslev was able to weave a net out of the notions of *matter, content,* and *expression, form,* and *substance* . . . [T]his net had the advantage of breaking with the form–content duality, since there was a form of content no less than a form of expression" (ibid.: 43). We can represent these relations schematically as in Table 5.1.

The plane of content refers to corporeal machines, ". . . actions and passions, an intermingling of bodies reacting to one another . . ." (ibid.: 88), while the plane of expression refers to incorporeal machines, ". . . acts and statements, . . . incorporeal transformations attributed to bodies" (ibid.). Elsewhere, Deleuze gives a nice example to illustrate the difference between content and expression. As he writes in *Foucault*:

> The content has both a form and a substance: for example, the form is prison and the substance is those who are locked up, the prisoners . . . The expression also has a form and a substance: for example the form is penal law and the substance is "delinquency" in so far as it is the object of statements. (Deleuze 1988: 47)

In this example we see that we are dealing with two quite distinct domains. At the level of content, the prison and the inmates it imprisons are corporeal machines with their own distinct organization, powers, interactions, and so on. It is an ecology of relations between material entities. The form is the manner in which the prison is structured or organized, while the substance of the prison is the prisoners that are imprisoned there. By contrast, the regulations that govern the prison, its laws, the verdicts that befall prisoners when they violate regulations, the roles that they're given (launder, cafeteria duty, etc.), and so on, belong to the domain of incorporeal machines. These regulations are the form of expression for the prison insofar as those regulations constitute an incorporeal domain of signs, while the substance of expression is, in this case, the abstract "semiotic object" of "delinquency." Delinquency is not a particular person or group of persons, but rather a category that social systems at a particular point in history deploy to group certain corporeal bodies or humans.

Each of these domains has its own form or organization, as well as its own objects. Proof of this autonomy and difference can be found in the fact that each of these planes can change, while the other remains the same. The prison can be demolished and a new one with a very different architecture and made of very different materials can be erected in its place (content), while the regulations governing the prison remain the same (expression). Likewise, the regulations governing a prison can be changed, new ones can be put in their place, while the architecture and materials of the prison remain the same. In this regard, we cannot say that expression *represents* content – that content is the signified of expression – nor can we say that content is an effect of expression as Lacan seems to suggest when he claims that "the universe is the flower of rhetoric" (Lacan 1998: 56). The idea that the universe is the flower of rhetoric seems to suggest that the universe – material beings – are somehow generated out of language as effects of how the signifier carves up the undifferentiated plenum of the "real." In Deleuze and Guattari's schema, however, the domain of language and signs (expression) and of material bodies (content) are heterogeneous, divergent, independent, and have their own principles of organization.

On the one hand, the plane of content is composed entirely of bodies or corporeal machines – in the widest sense possible, up to and including the *materiality* of signifiers when they're uttered – that affect and are affected by one another. Insofar as most worlds contain no intelligent, organic life, the plane of content is far more ubiquitous throughout the pluriverse. In other words, most worlds are composed of content *alone*. On Neptune, for example, there is nothing but content, corporeal machines, or bodies affecting and being affected by one another. There is no expression or semiotic machines that incorporeally transform these corporeal bodies on the planet. Deleuze and Guattari give us a nice example of how corporeal machines within the plane of content interact when they write that

> ... an organism befalls the body of the smith, by virtue of a machine or machinic assemblage that stratifies it. "The shock of the hammer and the anvil broke his arms and legs at the elbows and knees, which until that moment he had not possessed. In this way, he received the articulations specific to the new human form that was to spread across the earth, a form dedicated to work ... His arm became folded with a view to work." (Deleuze and Guattari 1987: 41)

Deleuze and Guattari's point is that the smith's body takes on a new form and set of dispositions as a result of his interaction with other corporeal bodies or machines such as the hammer, the anvil, the metals he works with, the heat of the forge, and so on. His muscles form in a particular way different from that of, say, a bodybuilder, as a result of laboring at the anvil with his hammer all day. The repetition of these movements with the hammer and anvil creates certain muscular *dispositions*, the capacity for certain operations, or leads to the genesis of certain powers. As a result of these constant movements, his bones perhaps suffer damage, leading to hairline fractures that constantly heal and then occur once again (will he suffer arthritis in the future?). Similarly, it's likely the manner in which he stands at the anvil day after day generates postural dispositions or a tendency to stand in a particular way. This can be seen in the case of people who live their lives at sea on barges and tugboats such as my grandfather. Their movement and manner of holding themselves is absolutely distinct. They walk a bit like a crab, their legs squarely apart, their shoulders slightly hunched, arms at the side. They have folded the movement of waves into their bodies, generating a form of walking and standing that allows them to traverse the surface of boats without falling over or stumbling. So inscribed is this movement of waves in their musculature that they are eventually unable to walk or hold themselves in any other way even on dry land. The sailor's body literally becomes a wave made flesh. The point here is that these bodily *forms*, these forms of content, have nothing to do with the signifier, language, or signs. While sailors and smiths certainly underwent a training that involved expressive components, and while they are subject to regulations and standards that involve expressive components, these changes in their bodily dispositions, powers, and qualities are not the result of semiotic machines, but of physical, affective, encounters between corporeal machines. They are the result of corporeal machines affecting and being affected by one another, modifying the operations and powers of each other as a result of their encounters.

On the plane of expression, by contrast, we get something very different: semiotic machines and incorporeal transformations. A semiotic machine is a machine that effects transformations on inputs through signs and sign systems. While we do not here follow Deleuze and Guattari in all they argue about language, signs, and expression, they define an incorporeal transformation as a linguistic or semiotic event that intervenes within bodies, transforming their status and powers within a semiotic system. Unlike the relationship between a smith, the anvil, and the hammer, an incorporeal transformation changes nothing *material* in the corporeal machine upon which it falls. The corporeal machine remains exactly what it was before qua corporeal machine. Moreover, we would look in vain to find a *quality* in the corporeal machine that corresponds to a semiotic, incorporeal transformation. There is no material quality, for example, that corresponds to being a newly elected president. Were we to encounter such a person on the street and had we no knowledge of that country's government, we would find no qualitative property that marks this person as a president. What has changed in an incorporeal transformation is not a being's material powers and qualities, but its social being. Lacan gives us a nice example of this when discussing the agency of the signifier in the world and unconscious (Lacan 2006: 416–17) – see Figure 5.1.

Lacan's point here is that there is no *material* or *corporeal* difference between these two doors. It is not the powers of the *doors* that create this dramatic difference between the lady's room and the men's room; the difference between these two doors did not arise from how these two doors *corporeally* affect the bodies of men and women. Rather, it's only a signifier, an agency from the plane of expression, that differentiates these two doors. Once the *signifiers*, the *signs*, "*hommes*" and "*dames*" befall the doors, they take on very different *social* functions. The doors remain the same doors they always were before, and if all signifying machines were

HOMMES   DAMES

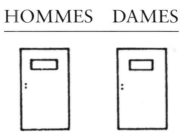

Figure 5.1 Lacan's two doors

to disappear as the result of an apocalypse like a completely successful plague, the doors would remain. What wouldn't remain is the manner in which their incorporeal transformation through a signifying act sorts bodies, assigning these bodies to pass through that door, those bodies to pass through that door. It's the signifier that introduces the difference here, a particular incorporeal machine, not the doors themselves. *Incorporeal transformations transform not the thing itself, but rather how other machines relate to the machine or thing.* In short, incorporeal machines pertain to the way in which one type of machine – cognitive, social, semiotic, and linguistic machines – relate to another machine. They change not the powers of the corporeal machine itself, but rather how one corporeal machine relates to another corporeal machine. As a result of the semiotic machine, I can now only pass through the door named "*hommes*," and I will suffer sanctions if I pass through the other.

Without using this terminology, Baudrillard makes similar points about expressive machines and incorporeal transformations in works like *System of Objects* (2006) and *For a Critique of the Political Economy of the Sign* (1981). As he remarks in the context of an analysis of consumption, "[a]n accurate theory of objects will not be established upon a theory of needs and their satisfaction, but upon a theory of *social prestations* and *signification*." He continues, "[t]he fundamental conceptual hypothesis for a sociological analysis of 'consumption' is *not* use value, the relation to needs, but *symbolic exchange* value, the value of social prestation, of rivalry and, at the limit, of class discriminants" (Baudrillard 1981: 30–1). Baudrillard is both right and wrong. He is wrong to suggest that the theory of needs, use-values, or symbolic exchange-values is a theory of *objects* or machines. Corporeal machines are what they are regardless of how we use them, need them, or symbolize them. Baudrillard here conflates a discussion of the *being* of objects with how we signify, use, or consume them. What Baudrillard in fact analyzes is the manner in which one type of machine relates to another type of machine. In the case of an analysis of objects in terms of needs and use, we're talking about how corporeal machines such as humans relate to other corporeal machines such as food, screwdrivers, automobiles, water, and so on. In the case of an analysis of objects in terms of symbolic exchange-values, we're talking about how incorporeal expressive machines, semiotic machines, imbue other machines with significance pertaining to status and class. For example, a Mercedes is not simply a mode of transportation that one uses to get from point A to point B, but is also a marker of prestige and affluence. Nothing in the automobile itself changes when it undergoes this incorporeal transformation, but what does change is how we relate to the object and the person that drives it.

Marx makes precisely this point with respect to the phenomenon of value in *Capital*. As he remarks, "[s]o far no chemist has ever discovered exchange-value either in a pearl or diamond" (Marx 1990: 177). It is sometimes suggested that Marx rejects the independence of objects or machines through his analysis of commodity fetishism. Here one might refer to Marx's thesis that commodity fetishism occurs when a ". . . definite social relation between men themselves . . . assumes . . . the fantastic form of a relation between things" (ibid.: 165). We think that we are merely buying a car, a thing, ignoring the fabric of social relations between humans out of which this car was produced and through which it takes on its value. From here it is but a short step for the hasty reader to conclude that things are, in fact, an illusion and that what is truly real are social relations. However, Marx does not reject the independent existence of things, objects, bodies, or machines. As he remarks later, "[t]hings are themselves external to man, and therefore alienable" (ibid.: 182). Just as the worker is alienated from the products of his labor in the process of production, things are alienated from *themselves* in becoming commodities and taking on value. It is not that things, machines, or objects are unreal and social relations are truly real. Corporeal machines are entirely real and have their own independent existence. Rather, it's that in becoming commodities and taking on value, things or machines have been alienated in the operations of another machine: an incorporeal, expressive, social machine of production. They have become inputs for this incorporeal machine, transformed by the operations of that machine so as to take on a status that is nowhere to be found among the properties or powers of the thing.

Once we look, we find these incorporeal machines and their transformations pertaining to the plane of expression all over the place. When two people get married, we are before an incorporeal transformation. Nothing changes here materially in their bodies, in their corporeal being, yet how they relate to one another, how others relate to them, their legal status, all change significantly. The case is similar with enunciations like "I love you." Materially the two lovers remain the same, yet everything changes in how they relate to one another and what they can expect from one another. When a person is granted a degree, citizenship, or given a promotion they undergo incorporeal transformations. In racism, distinctions between races are incorporeal transformations. Declarations of war and crisis are incorporeal transformations. Sentences decided in court and verdicts of guilt and innocence are incorporeal transformations. As Saussure noted, even bus schedules are the result of semiotic machines. There is nothing about the material being of the bus that makes it the same 8.00 a.m. bus. From day to day, two buses that are entirely different corporeal machines, two entirely different bodies, can be the 8.00 a.m. bus. Rather, it is an incorporeal system of expression that determines whether a bus is the 8.00 a.m. bus or not. Proof of this lies in the fact that even when it is a materially different bus or when the bus is six minutes late, the bus still remains the 8.00 a.m. bus. Even sortings of kinds, types, statuses, and so on are incorporeal transformations.

For all incorporeal transformations there is a historically informed "grammar" and system of categorization. "Grammar" refers to the structure or form of operations presiding over the incorporeal transformations. The grammar of the fifteenth-century legal system, for example, is different from the grammar of the twenty-first-century legal system. Not only are there different procedures for determining guilt and innocence, but there are different sortings of crimes. Similarly, medical diagnostic systems, systems of social statuses, positions and occupations, governments, and so on, change. The grammar of an expressive system refers to the manner in which all of these sortings and operations are related to one another, while the substance of an expressive machine refers to the different abstract objects it recognizes. In

Deleuze's example cited earlier, for example, "delinquency" was cited as the substance of the expressive system of the penal system. "Delinquency" refers not to any particular person or set of bodies, but rather to an abstract category that can perform incorporeal transformations on a variety of different corporeal bodies. The substance of expression refers to the *abstract* types that an expressive machine carves out in the world, while the form of expression refers to the manner in which these substances are structured, the grammar of their relations to other expressive substances, and the organization of the system of expression in that ecology.

The key point is that planes of expression and content exist on a single immanent plane in the worlds where they appear. While the two planes interact and influence one another, they do not determine or overcode one another. The plane of content for a particular world does not determine the plane of expression, nor does the plane of expression determine the plane of content. In this regard, we cannot say that the plane of content is infrastructure, while the plane of expression is superstructure (Deleuze and Guattari 1987: 89). Sometimes the plane of expression will outpace the plane of content, engendering semiotic revolutions, revolutions in thought and social relations, as in the case of the bourgeois revolution during the Enlightenment. Here revolutions had taken place in the domain of thought, how social relations *should* be organized, the nature of personhood (a substance of expression), while the plane of content had not yet changed. City structures, labor structures, modes of production, techniques of production, technologies, and so on, had not yet created an assemblage of corporeal machines adequate to the incorporeal transformations that had taken place at the level of expression. People continued to live the same stratified and rural social ecology that they had for centuries. The revolution was restricted to people like Rousseau and Voltaire. But *nonetheless*, these incorporeal transformations at the level of expression provided an impetus for corporeal transformations at the level of content. The dreams of expression generated experiments in the formation of new corporeal machinic relations.

The same is true of the plane of content. Material transformations and technological transformations can outpace expressive transformations as in the case of new distributive technologies that don't register at the level of politics or social organization. Here the arrangements among corporeal bodies can be completely transformed as in the case of the factory that brought men and women together, that brought people of different ethnicities and from different regions of the countryside together, without the systems of expression yet registering this. We likely saw this in the case of World War II with women. When the men went away to war, the women took over the factories, took over jobs that men would have traditionally had, took care of household finances, disciplined and raised the children, made decisions about what to buy, and so on. The entire dimension of contents or relations between corporeal bodies changed. Yet the plane of expression did not change for another couple of decades. Why? The men came home, consigned the women back to the home and took their jobs. We can imagine that the children of these marriages witnessed mothers disgruntled by the freedom that they had lost, while they witnessed fathers ravaged by the effects of war with "post-traumatic stress disorder," alcoholism, and a series of expressive norms pertaining to male and female social roles they had carried with them from a period *prior* to the war. It was as if, when they returned, they were people transported from a different time in social history, carrying a set of norms out of pace with the new social relations that had developed in their absence. They were living in a different time that was still strangely present. Witnessing this discontent, this conjugal strife, the children perhaps began to envision the possibility of other gender relations at the level of expression. Why shouldn't women be able to work? Why should they need a husband to have a bank account? Why shouldn't relations in a marriage be equal? Why should marriage be necessary at all? Between the transformations effected through the factory during World War II and the invention of the pill, this later generation brought about a revolution at the level of the plane of expression in accordance with transformations that had already taken place or had been registered as possible at the level of the plane of content. The two planes develop independently of one another, while nonetheless influencing each other.

It is difficult to determine just how far planes of expression extend. We have seen that worlds containing both a plane of expression and a plane of content are the exception rather than the rule. Nonetheless, it is not clear that the existence of planes of expression is restricted to worlds composed of humans. It is likely that planes of expression are to be found throughout the animal kingdom in the way that cephalopods signal to one another through their changing colors, the way in which bees dance for one another to signal where nectar is to be found, whalesong, birdsong, communities of non-human primates, communications between members of wolf packs, and so on. While these are certainly different types of expressive machines with different powers and capacities, it does not appear that expression is restricted to the world of humans.

As computer technologies become more intelligent it appears that they are also developing expressive machines as well. When I buy a book online from Amazon it recommends other books I might be interested in with uncanny and disturbing accuracy. It is not human social-machines that have performed this sorting of taste and interest, but rather a computer program that monitors the purchasing habits of readers with one another to determine the likelihood of other readers being interested in similar books. Here we have computers expressively communicating with computers. Humans are a part of the equation insofar as they provide the input into these expressive computer machines, but it is the computers that carry out these operations. We can imagine this being taken one step further with computers gathering data on the demand for particular books based on purchases, relaying this information as an input to another computer, then giving commands to print additional copies of particular books while diminishing the printing of others. Like Lawrence Lasker's 1983 film *WarGames*, humans here will have been completely taken out of decision-making processes regarding production. Something like this seems to be going on with search engines like Google. When we conduct an online search we have the impression that *we* are choosing which links to follow when they appear on our browser. And indeed, in part, we are. What we have not chosen, however, are the *choices* themselves. Rather, the links that appear and their order of priority results from a computer algorithm based on the frequency of visits to various sites online. By ranking and presenting links in this way, search engines like Google produce a certain conformity of information, ensuring that, like ants following trails of pheromones left by other ants, other people will follow the same links. Here we have a technological expressive machine structuring human relations to information.

The possibility of expressive technological machines sounds rather grim and Orwellian, and indeed there is much opportunity for abuse and social control here. However, it is also important to note that "big data" also possesses utopian and emancipatory potentials. The standard argument against socialist planned economies is that they are non-responsive to the needs of production, distribution, and consumption, failing pitifully to produce the goods needed for consumption. Consumption needs are just too complex and aleatory to be planned in advance. Thus, the argument runs, capitalism is to be preferred because through its capacity for self-organization it is able to coordinate production with demand. However, in its ability to track extremely complex and fluctuating patterns of demand, big data opens the possibility of responses to problems of distribution and production. In this way, big data opens the possibility of cutting capitalist middlemen and speculators out of the picture.[1] Here we should recall that technologies, like any machines, are *pluripotent* in that they can be appropriated in a variety of ways. An oppressive appropriation of a machine is not an *intrinsic* feature of the machine appropriated, but rather a function of the machine that appropriates the machine. Insofar as all machines are separable from their relations, all machines can be put to other ends.

The planes of content and expression have both a synchronic and diachronic dimension. The synchronic dimension of content and expression refers to how these planes are organized at any given point in time and space, how machines on the plane of expression and on the plane of content are related to one another, and how the two planes intermingle and affect one another. The diachronic dimension, by contrast, refers to how machines operate on one another, producing and assembling other machines. As Deleuze and Guattari observe:

> Double articulation is so extremely variable that we cannot begin with a general model, only a relatively simple case. The first articulation chooses or deducts, from unstable particle flows, metastable molecular or quasi-molecular units (*substances*) upon which it imposes a statistical order of connections and successions (*forms*). The second articulation establishes functional, compact, stable structures (*forms*), and constructs the molar compounds in which these structures are simultaneously actualized (*substances*). In a geological stratum, for example, the first articulation is the process of "sedimentation," which deposits a succession of sandstone and schist. The second articulation is the "folding" that sets up a stable functional structure and effects the passage from sediment to sedimentary rock. (Deleuze and Guattari 1987: 40–1)

The first articulation refers to a machine that *selects* inputs for operations. Here we encounter the *substance* of either a content or expressive machine. The second articulation refers to the *structuring* of these operations or the production of a *form*. Those elements that are selected for these operations are referred to as *matters*. In *A Thousand Plateaus*, Deleuze and Guattari suggest that matters selected to become formed substances are themselves *formless*, remarking that ". . . *matter* . . . [is] . . . the unformed, unorganized, nonstratified, or destratified body without organs and all its flows: subatomic and submolecular particles, pure intensities, prevital and prephysical singularities" (ibid.: 43). However, insofar as there are no unformatted machines, this distinction is, in our view, purely relative. Machines are formable such that they are capable of becoming other machines, without being formless. A matter is a formed substance in and of itself that takes on a new form as a result of passing through another machine.

These points can be illustrated through Deleuze and Guattari's example of the *formation* of sedimentary rock. On the one hand, we have a machine that *selects* matters to become formed substances at the level of content. For example, the machine that selects might be a river whose water flows at a regular rate. Because the river flows at a particular rate, it picks up sand and pebbles of a particular size, depositing them downstream, perhaps where the river bends and slows. As such, the river is a machine that has selected certain matters to become substances (first articulation). Over time, the sand and pebbles accumulate, exerting more and more pressure. At this level, we get a passage from a mere accumulation of sand and pebbles to the formation of a new machine: sedimentary rocks (second articulation). Sedimentary rock is a new machine, but it is a formation produced out of other machines acting upon one another.

As Deleuze and Guattari note, the diachronic processes of the two articulations are extremely varied. They share common features with one another, but involve very different organizations and processes. For example, an educational-machine such as an elementary school will have both its first and second articulation, producing new machines in the form of students that have certain cognitive, affective, normative, class, and nationalistic features, but this machine will be far more complex than a river, involving a variety of interlocking machines at the level of both expression and content. At the level of expression, for example, there will be a legal or normative machine that selects which children (matters) can enter the school to begin the process of articulation. This expressive machine will only select students of a particular age, and might exclude children with certain disabilities, for example. In the case of a private school, the expressive machine might select children based on special talents, religious belief, economic status, and so on. This will be the first articulation selecting students to become substances within the educational machine. As the children enter the educational machine and begin the process of formation (second articulation), there will, of course, be all sorts of expressive machines deployed upon them. These expressive machines will include the curriculum, teaching techniques, and the regulations governing behavior. However, there will also be all sorts of machines at the level of content or corporeality that act on the students as well: how desks are arranged, physical activity, school lunch diets, and so on. These machines of content and expression will vary from educational machine to educational machine. As the students pass through these machines they are gradually structured or formed both physically and cognitively. Foucault masterfully analyzed complex machines of this sort in works such as *Discipline & Punish*.

We must never forget that from a diachronic perspective, machines have a *history*. This is as true of nature as it is of culture. In Nora Ephron's 1996 film *Michael*, the archangel Michael counts the invention of standing in line among his major contributions to culture. While standing in line appears obvious to us, it was nonetheless an expressive machine that had to be invented. The same, however, is true of natural machines. Darwin pointed the way to an investigation of the machinic operations and processes through which species are produced. Geologists investigate the machinic processes through which types of rocks, mountains, and continents are produced. Contemporary astrophysics shows us how different atomic elements are produced in the furnaces of stars. Recognizing that machines are the result of a genesis in no way entails what Graham Harman has called an "undermining" of objects (Harman 2011: 8–10). For Harman, an object is undermined wherever we deny its independent and autonomous reality, instead reducing it to a more basic reality. Thus, for example, we would be undermining the existence of iron atoms if we claimed that the iron atom is not truly real, but that what is really real is the subatomic particles or perhaps strings of which it is an *effect. Both* iron atoms *and* subatomic particles are truly real insofar as iron atoms have powers that do not exist at the level of the subatomic particles. Pointing out that iron atoms are the result of a genesis that takes place in the hades of massive stars does not undermine the independent reality of iron atoms *once* they are produced.

From the discussion of entropy in Part 1, we will recall that low entropy and negentropic entities are *improbable*. Not only does this mean that most machines must engage in constant operations to endure through time, but it also entails that machines have a *genesis* or come into being in natural and cultural history. Emphasis on the improbability of machines reminds us not to take machines as eternal and unchanging givens, but to attend to the history of how they came into being. Rather than taking the manner in which society is stratified into classes at a particular point in history, for example, recognition of the improbability of machines councils us to investigate the machines and processes through which this particular negentropic distribution was both historically produced and the machinic operations through which it continues to maintain itself in the present. If recognizing the diachronic dimension of natural and cultural machines is particularly important, then this is because it shows us that things can be *otherwise*. For example, recognition that a social machine is the result of a history, and that things have been different in the past, allows us to both critique currently existing social machines and imagine the possibility of other social machines.

Within the social and political dimension, onto-cartography seeks to investigate expression and content in their synchronic and diachronic dimension. It is of crucial importance to remember that social worlds pertaining to humans are composed of elements of both content and expression. Between the Frankfurt school, the structuralists, and the post-structuralists, Continental social and political thought has focused overwhelmingly on the plane of expression to the detriment of the plane of content. There have been, of course, notable exceptions to this statistical dominance in the work of Bruno Latour and the actor-network theorists, Isabelle Stengers, Donna Haraway, and Michel Serres, the new materialist feminists as exemplified in the work of thinkers such as Jane Bennett, Stacy Alaimo, and Karen Barad, and more recently the speculative realists. However, a focus on the plane of expression has nonetheless been hegemonic in cultural studies. This comes, of course, as no surprise given that these investigations are conducted within the humanities where there is naturally a focus on the plane of expression. Similarly, much theoretical work in Continental social and political thought is deeply informed by the trauma of the Nazi regime's use of propaganda to control people during World War II, as well as the rise of new forms of expressive media such as radio, television, and more recently the Internet that have had an unprecedented effect on social relations. It is not surprising that, given our historical moment, social and political theorists would be particularly focused on how semiotic machines are organized, what they contribute to the organization of social relations, how they function, and how they form us cognitively and affectively. Nonetheless, onto-cartography recommends that if we wish to understand social and political assemblages and develop effective strategies for changing them, it is necessary to investigate the interrelations of both content and expression and how they condition social relations.

Note

1. I owe this insight to a talk by Nick Srnicek (see Srnicek 2012).

6

Topologies of Space and Time

Space

Insofar as onto-cartography maps relations and interactions between machines functioning as media for one another in worlds, questions of the nature of time and space necessarily arise. These are massive, intricate, and incredibly complex topics that could easily take up multiple book length studies of their own, so there's no way they can be done full justice here. As a consequence, I will here restrict myself to the discussion of those features of space and time most relevant to the practice of onto-cartography. In what follows I have bracketed analyses of spatiality and temporality as developed within the phenomenological tradition. Not only have these analyses been done exceptionally well elsewhere, they are working at a different level of reality than that investigated by onto-cartography. For an excellent phenomenological analysis of the lived experience of space I refer readers to Edward Casey's *Getting Back into Place* (Casey 2009). Casey also provides a valuable account of how space and place have been conceived throughout history in *The Fate of Place* (Casey 1999). For an excellent survey of the various ways in which temporality has been conceived in the Continental tradition from the standpoint of humans, I refer readers to David Hoy's *The Time of Our Lives* (Hoy 2009).

It is not that phenomenological analyses of spatiality and temporality are mistaken. Indeed, they have significantly contributed to our understanding of how *humans* experience time and space. Rather, it is that these analyses focus on how one type of machine, humans, temporally and spatially operate on inputs that flow through them. Here I take these analyses as entirely valid accounts of the operations of these types of machines. However, insofar as onto-cartography begins from a post-humanist perspective premised on alien phenomenology, it cannot restrict discussions of space and time to how one type of machine operates temporally and spatially. Rather, onto-cartography requires a theoretical framework broad enough to analyze spatio-temporality for a variety of different types of machine. It also requires a framework capable of thematizing spatio-temporal relations among and between machines in a world, rather than a framework that focuses solely on how particular machines – generally living, human, and social machines – experience the world temporally and spatially. In other words, it requires a mode of analysis that is resolutely what Heidegger disparagingly referred to as "ontic."

Before proceeding, an additional caveat is necessary. While I treat space and time separately in the two sections that follow, the two are not separate in reality, but only in thought. In reality – as the following analysis makes clear – there is only *spatio-temporality*. There is no space that does not have its temporal dimension and implications, nor is there any time that does not have its spatial dimension and implications. Space and time are necessarily and *ontologically* bound up with one another like two sides of a coin or, better yet, a Möbius strip. It is this inseparability of space and time that accounts for the perpetual spatialization of time that Bergson so decried (see Bergson 2010). The spatialization of time, just like the temporalization of space, is not a glitch but an *ontological* feature. It is not that *we* spatialize time because we are geared towards action as Bergson suggests, but rather time and space are already inextricably bound up with one another as unitary phenomena. In short, our tendency to use spatial metaphors to describe time is not a mistake, but a feature of spatio-temporality itself. As a consequence, the best we can do is describe spatial and temporal *tendencies* of these unitary phenomena, keeping and mind that the two are always interrelated.

Questions of time and space are, in reality, questions of stability, instability, entropy, movement, and becoming. A space is not a container, but rather is a milieu of stability. As Lucretius taught, all beings are in motion. Not only are they falling through the void, but they are also in motion even when they sit still. As he writes:

It's no wonder
That while the atoms are in constant motion,

Their total seems to be at total rest,
Save here and there some individual stir.
Their nature lies beyond our range of sense,
Far, far beyond. Since you can't get to see
The things themselves, they're bound to hide their moves,
Especially since things we *can* see, often
Conceal their movements, too, when at a distance.
Take grazing sheep on a hill, you know they move,
The wooly creatures, to crop the lovely grass
Wherever it may call each one, with dew
Still sparkling it with jewels, and the lambs,
Fed full, play little games, flash in the sunlight,
Yet all this, far away, is just a blur,
A whiteness resting on a hill of green.

(Lucretius 1969: 60–1)

Like the movements of sheep on a far away hill that seem to be standing still because of their distance from us, the elements that compose the table upon which I write are in motion, yet this motion is hidden because it occurs at such a small scale. As Serres will write elsewhere, ". . . vortex[es] . . . [are] none other than the primitive form of the construction of things, of nature in general . . ." (Serres 2000: 6). A vortex is a flow of matter about an axis. It has pattern, it has organization, but it is in a constant state of motion. Later Serres will describe this in terms of a child's top:

Throw this toy and describe . . . what happens. It is in movement, this is certain, yet it is stable. It even rests on its point or its pole, the more so as its movement is rapid. All children know this. But its rest is still more paradoxical. The top may move about, by translation, without losing its stability. (Ibid.: 28)

This is how it is with all machines or objects. Their stability is not something other than their motion, but rather arises from their motion. They are, one and all, vortexes.

Yet if it is true that all machines are in motion both as falling through the void and within themselves as dynamic stabilities, why does all of being not degenerate into absolute entropy? It is not motion and change that are mysterious, requiring recourse to a divine being such as Aristotle's unmoved mover to explain how motion *enters* the universe; rather it is stability and endurance that

requires explanation. Motion and change are ontologically primitive. It is stability and endurance, the existence of objects, things,
or machines, that is surprising. It is stability and endurance that
are *improbable*. Why does everything not evaporate like morning
mist? Space will be part of the answer to this question, for far
from being a milieu of absolutely open movement, space is a space
of *constraint*. As Serres will observe, "[f]lows circulate on paths"
(ibid.: 51). Flows, matter, and machines move along paths. But
what is it that creates these paths? Why do machines not proliferate *randomly* in all directions? Why do statistical probabilities,
patterns, organizations, persistences, emerge within matter?

> All movement is . . . related to stability: it takes place more or less
> easily. In the first physical model, this signifies the encounter of an
> element with another atom, with other atoms: these hinder the first
> in its journey to rest. Collision is nothing but a hindrance, a brake, a
> difficulty, to the precipitous rush towards its base. These constraints
> are necessary so that movement *only be* maximal. All in all, in a region
> of space, objects as entanglements and complexes, are throughout no
> more than temporary obstacles, thick shields, either more or less solid,
> more or less resistant to the general tendency of each of its elements
> to dissolve towards equilibrium. They impede each other with shocks,
> frictions or viscosities. (Ibid.: 47)

Space is not an empty field, but is rather a field populated by
machines of all sorts. As these machines encounter one another,
they encounter resistances, torsions, densities, and so on. A
machine will generally follow the path of least resistance, before
coming to a state of rest because its movement is impeded by
another machine. Spaces are composed of paths and flows. Paths
are not something other than machines that flow along them, but
rather are themselves densities and fluid vectors produced by other
machines. Not only do these paths define trajectories or vectors
along which machines move, but they generate turbulence that
contributes to the formation of vortexes or machines. If, then,
there are stabilities and endurances in worlds of perpetual motion,
then this is because the paths structuring these worlds have a relative stability that allows certain turbulent vortexes to persist and
to persist in a particular way.

Based on the foregoing, we can begin to develop an onto-
cartographical concept of space. Crucial to this account of space

is the distinction between Newtonian and topological space. Roughly, Newtonian space is conceived as a homogeneous container within which all entities are contained. Under this conception, there is space and then all of the entities contained in space. Here, while spatial relations change between entities, space itself always has one and the same structure and there are invariant metrics governing this space. For example, under this conception of space, the city of Austin, Texas is necessarily closer to me than Cairo, Egypt because there is a constant metric that grids all space. In Newtonian space, entities can move freely in any direction. In other words, space isn't characterized by varying degrees of density and fluidity.

In a topological conception of space, matters are very different. Where a Newtonian conception of space conceives space as a *pre-existent* container in which machines are housed, a topological conception of space treats space as *arising from* machines. In a topological conception, *space is conceived of as a network of paths between machines or nodes* produced by machines. The first point to note here is that under a topological conception of space, there will not be a single, all-embracing space containing all machines. Insofar as space is composed of paths there will be different spaces depending on the structure of paths between machines. Second, notions of proximity and distance become different under a topological conception of space. Take the diagrams of topological or network space shown in Figure 6.1.

Here we have three different spatial fields hypothetically structuring different worlds. In each of these worlds, relations of proximity and distance are quite different than what we find in Newtonian space. In a centralized topology, the central node or machine is equally proximate to all other nodes, while all the other nodes are equally proximate or distant from one another. Where node 6 and 3 would be further apart than nodes 2 and 3 in Newtonian space, in this topological space, all three nodes are equally proximate in that they must pass through the same number of nodes to reach one another. By contrast, in a decentralized topology, we get a different type of distance. While nodes 9 and 30 would be metrically close to one another and node 4 would be quite distant from node 9 in Newtonian space, in topological space they are quite distant from one another, while node 9 is closer to node 4 than node 30. The reason for this is that node 9 must only pass through one node to reach node 4, while it must pass through four nodes to reach node

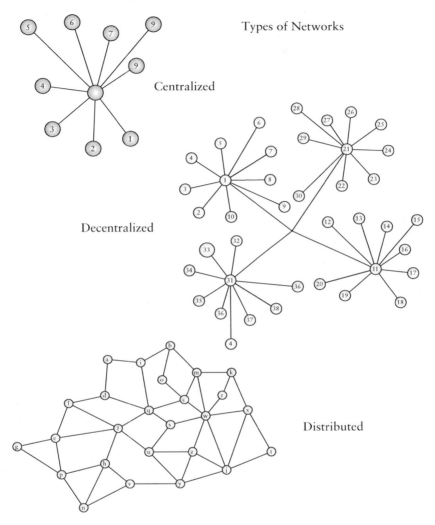

Types of Networks

Centralized

Decentralized

Distributed

Figure 6.1 Types of networks

30. In other words, there is no *direct* path between 9 and 30, rendering them topologically distant from one another.

Here we see one way of understanding Graham Harman's thesis that ". . . space is not just the site of relation, but rather of relation *and* non-relation" (Harman 2011: 100). Topological space separates as much as it relates. This is not simply because machines are, to use Harman's language, withdrawn from one another or operationally closed such that they never directly relate, but also

because relations between machines are mediated by paths or
other machines. A discontinuity between worlds or spaces consists
in the absence of a possible relation or interaction between two
machines.

We must be careful not to take the term "path" too literally, conceiving them as passages on the surface of space. While
machines such as roads, mountain passes, hallways, and ocean
currents are all paths, there are paths and nodes that do not exist
on the surface of other machines (such as the planet) at all. Here
music and radio is a valuable example. Like any other machine, a
song must travel along topologically structured paths in order to
interact with other machines such as persons. In our contemporary world, this path is commonly through the medium of radio.
However, while being transmitted by radio or electromagnetic
waves is a necessary condition for a song belonging to a particular
topological space, it is not a sufficient condition. Right now all
sorts of radio waves are passing through me, yet I do not share
a direct relation to them because they are unable to affect me. In
order for a song transmitted by radio to affect other machines in
a spatial assemblage, it must pass through certain nodes. First it
must be sent through the node of the radio tower. Then it must be
received through the node of a radio. In order to be received by the
node of the radio, the radio must, of course, be tuned to the proper
channel. Finally it must be received by another machine such as a
person. If that person is deaf or if the volume is too low, then the
song will be unable to interact with the recipient. Here, then, we
see that topological space requires both a medium through which
machines are related such as radio waves or the surface of the
earth or ocean, as well as the possibility of structural openness of
machines to the machines that travel along these paths.

While we believe that she associates space too closely with narrative, stories, or the plane of expression, when properly situated
within a post-humanist, machinic framework, Doreen Massey
nicely sums up space as conceived by onto-cartography. As
Massey writes in her magnificent *For Space*:

> *First*, . . . we recognize space as the product of interrelations; as con-
> stituted through interactions, from the immensity of the global to the
> intimately tiny. . . *Second*, . . . we understand space as the sphere of
> the possibility of the existence of multiplicity in the sense of contem-
> poraneous plurality; as the sphere therefore of coexisting heterogene-

ity. Without space, no multiplicity; without multiplicity, no space. . .
Third, . . . we recognize space as always under construction. Precisely
because space on this reading is a product of relations-between, relations which are necessarily embedded material practices which have
to be carried out, it is always in the process of being made. It is never
finished; never closed. (Massey 2005: 9)

While there is a sort of "ur-space" that Lucretius referred to
under the name of the void, this ur-space is not a homogeneous
container, but rather is the *potentiality* of relation between unrelated machines. Space proper consists of discontinuous topological fields produced through interactions between machines. It is
thus crucial to note that spatial fields are not static and fixed like
Newtonian space, but are in a constant state of change, production, and becoming as a result of the interactions that take place
within them. What was dense and impassible for one machine a
moment ago can become a path later through the operations of
machines acting upon it. Nodes or machines that were previously
unrelated can come to be related through the medium of other
machines within the spatial field as in the case of Internet blogs
bringing people together that would have never otherwise encountered each other. New machines can appear within a topological
field, reconfiguring existing relations within a spatial network. We
saw this earlier with respect to the invention of the printing press.
Through this technology, expressive machines such as books were
able to travel far more widely and to reach a broader population
because it became possible to easily produce copies and books
became much more inexpensive. Moreover, machines are able to
affect other machines indirectly in topological fields. A deaf man
might not be able to directly hear a song, but he can be indirectly
affected by the song through how the song affects others that have
heard it. In other words, a direct relation between two entities is
not a condition for belonging to the same spatial field. All that is
required is that machines within that topological field be able to
indirectly affect one another.

Above all, topological or spatial fields are milieus of becoming
and movement. On the one hand, paths determine the possibilities
of movement for a machine. *Statistically*, a machine's movement
will be a function of the paths open to it. Metrically, in Newtonian
space, two destinations might be very close to one another, yet
the paths structuring the topological field might be such that

movement from one place to another within a network is very difficult or impossible. To take a very literal example, one might not frequent a particular restaurant because, while metrically close, the paths structured by roads between home and this restaurant render it "out of the way."

A more significant example would be class distribution in Atlantic City, New Jersey. Gambling was legalized in Atlantic City on the premise that casinos would bring in revenue that would both create jobs for people already living there and stimulate the impoverished economy of the city. In other words, the idea was that casinos would hire people from the city and patrons of these casinos would spend their money at other businesses in the city creating the demand for more jobs.

Ultimately these arguments where based on a Newtonian conception of space where metric proximity was seen as sufficient for establishing relations between machines. In reality something quite different happened. The casinos came in, but did little hiring among the "locals" and money failed to "trickle down" to the other businesses in the region. The reason for this was that the casinos were constructed in such a way that those visiting – generally from *elsewhere* – could remain within the casino without ever leaving it. When you visit Atlantic City, you drive directly to the casino of your choice, park in the casino, and spend all your time within the casino. If you wish to go to another casino, there are bridges – paths! – between the casinos that link one to another. Moreover, the casinos provide for all of your needs with their shops. As a consequence, the patrons of the casinos seldom descend into the larger city to buy goods. The economy instead remains contained within the casino system.

Here we quite literally have city like that described in China Miéville's novel *The City & The City* (Miéville 2010). There Miéville depicts a strange world in which two distinct cities occupy one and the same geographical space while still being two cities. As a result of this, all sorts of expressive or semiotic machines are necessary to maintain the two cities as separate and distinct. Miéville's two cities in the same geographical space are not merely the stuff of science fiction, but are a reality all over the world. Whether we are speaking of situations like Atlantic City, class differences within cities, or cities that practice some form of apartheid, we find these sorts of distributions where two groups are metrically close to one another in Newtonian space, while nonetheless they are as far away as the moon due to how the paths are structured in this topological space. As a result of cultural, economic, and semiotic agencies, the people that live outside the casinos might as well be on another planet despite their close metric proximity to the casinos because the paths by which they can reach the casinos are indirect and long.

From the foregoing, it is clear that the paths organizing movement in a topological space have natural, technological, and expressive components. It is not simply corporeal machines that structure the paths along which other machines move, but also incorporeal machines. Returning to the example of Lacan's two doors, the signifiers "men's" and "women's" structure the paths along which human bodies move. Now men and women are segregated into two different spaces. Passports are semiotic machines that open people up to all sorts of movements from one country to another, while the presence or absence of papers determine whether or not immigrants can work and receive services in a foreign country. The DSM-IV is a semiotic machine that generates paths of treatment through its naming and categorization of different types of disorders, but it can also close off paths as in those instances where a person is deemed a danger to him or herself and institutionalized. National borders are themselves expressive or semiotic machines that structure people who might live very near one another while not having the proper paperwork that would allow them to relate to each other. All of these expressive machines and many others besides structure space and movement in their own particular ways. Nor are expressive structurations of space restricted to humans. The manner in which animals mark territory, for example, is also a formation of paths for other animals.

Yet topological fields or spaces are not merely milieus of movement, they are also milieus of becoming. As we saw in Part 1, the local manifestations and becomings a machine undergoes are often a function of the flows it receives as inputs from other machines. A local manifestation is the result of how a machine operates on an input producing a quality, activity, or material product. For example, a mug will now be this shade of blue, now that shade of blue, depending on the wavelengths of light it interacts with. Here an entity does not become insofar as the virtual structure of powers that underlie its local manifestations remain the same. By contrast, a machine undergoes becoming when the inputs that pass through it – whether arising from outside the machine or inside the machine – transform the structure of powers that govern a machine's operations. A machine becomes when it acquires or loses powers, rendering it capable of new operations. The becomings a machine undergoes will often be a function of the topological field in which it unfolds. In other words, it will be a function of the inputs and paths to which it is proximally open. Thus, for example, a person raised at this place or node within a topological field will be different than the very same person had they been raised at another node in the spatial field. The reason for this will be that, depending on where the person is located in the topological field, they will encounter different inputs or flows at the level of both expression and content from other machines. They will encounter different nutrients, different corporeal relations at the level of content, different semiotic machines at the level of education, mass media, normative practices, and so on. These encounters will play a key role in the powers or capacities that a person develops.

Kim Stanley Robinson depicts this point beautifully at the level of the plane of content in his novel *Red Mars* (Robinson 1993). Discussing the offspring of the humans from Earth that colonize Mars, he observes how slender and tall these genuine Martians are. Why are these Martians tall and slender in comparison to their Earthling parents? Mars is about half the mass of the planet Earth. As a result, it has a very different gravitational structure. Human bodies that are born and develop in such a field would likely grow taller because of the manner in which their developing bodies interact with this gravitational differential. This would affect not only the height that persons could reach, but would also affect how their muscles and bones develop. Indeed, later in the series, those genuine Martians that return to Earth risk death because the virtual proper being of their bodies has not become or developed in such a way as to deal with the thicker atmosphere and greater gravity that we know. These powers or capacities weren't *intrinsic* to the bodies that developed on Mars, but were the result of the spatial milieu in which these bodies developed. It is not that the Martians had different genes than their parents, but that they developed differently when exposed to a different ecology of machinic inputs. Had they developed in a different spatial milieu, they would have had different powers.

These observations regarding the relationship between topological fields and the powers of machines reminds us that powers are not fixed *essences* inhabiting machines. As the developmental systems theorists teach, it is not enough to investigate machines in isolation to understand their being and potentials; it is necessary to investigate the entire system or relation between machine and environment to understand why machines have the powers they have and why they have developed as they have (see Oyama et al. 2001). As Harman often puts it, machines harbor hidden and volcanic powers waiting to be unleashed. They can undergo surprising local manifestations when placed in new topological fields, but can also become in entirely different ways, developing or not developing powers that they would not otherwise have had. This is the problem with variants of biological racism and sexism: they confuse sociological phenomena with biological phenomena, treating the characteristics of various peoples as intrinsic essences of their biology. Not only do they have a mistaken conception of biology, treating genetics as a fixed map or blueprint that ineluctably unfolds like a master plan rather than as a set of potentials that can be activated in different ways under different environmental conditions, but they have a mistaken understanding of how machines relate to topological fields in which they're enmeshed. As Mary Wollstonecraft noted long ago, it is not that the women of her age were *naturally* prone to emotion, inability to reason well, obsession with romance, and so on, but rather that in being denied education beyond basic reading and mathematical skills necessary to run a household, and in being consigned to the mind-numbing drudgery of housework and raising children, they were denied paths of becoming that would allow them to develop their intellectual powers (Wollstonecraft 2009). Women were caught in a field of expressive and corporeal paths that structured both their movement and their becoming, a topological field that still exists in a variety of ways today. Change that topological field and you also change the becomings to which things are open.

As Massey argues, topological fields are in a constant state of construction. In Part 1, we saw that most machines face the problem of entropy. They must engage in perpetual operations in order to maintain their existence. This is no less true of worlds and topological fields composing an ecology of machines than it is of machines themselves. Roads must be maintained, satellites require upkeep, nations must perpetually police their boundaries, people must continue to communicate, every generation must be "interpellated" and take their place within existing class, ethnic, and occupational structures, and so on. Topological fields are both in a constant state of disintegration and construction. Just as machines themselves are improbabilities from the standpoint of their continued and organized existence, spatial fields are improbable in their organization.

This is not cause for despair, but hope. The fact that topological fields must perpetually struggle with entropy also entails that they can be *changed*. No topological field – no ecology of machines – is so rigid, so enduring, that it cannot become otherwise. Even the most iron clad totalitarian regime can be made to collapse. Indeed, it is paradoxical that regimes such as this are strangely *more fragile* than more loosely organized ecologies.

On the one hand, a totalitarian or authoritarian ecology can be defined as a spatio-temporal field that attempts to reduce entropy to zero. It is the dream of an ecology that would never be beset by noise nor deviation from its order. The maintenance of any form of organization requires *energy*. Improbability or organization doesn't come for free, but requires the constant work of operations, and work requires some flow of energy in order to maintain itself. An authoritarian or totalitarian organization is one that must perpetually maintain the strict regulation of paths between different people and institutions, as well as the constant upkeep of expressive categories organizing the identity of peoples and non-human machines of the world. This requires the formation of expressive and corporeal machines that intensely regulate and monitor motion, and that also carefully form the cognition and affects of the populace. From an energetic standpoint, such regulation is costly, leaving little opportunity to engage in other operations. Additionally, highly striated systems of this sort have a tendency to engender resentment among the people subjected to them, which in turn boil over into micro- and macro- acts of resistance and subversion. The old adage about extremely strict upbringings tending to produce rebellious children holds both for families and larger-scale social systems. On the other hand, rigid social systems that attempt to reduce entropy to zero often prove inflexible in responding to events in a changing environment. Because the expressive web thrown over the world as a system of categorization and meaning rigidly pre-delineates – at an epistemological level – what is and what is not, what can happen and what cannot, such systems have a very difficult time responding to novelty and the unexpected. It is these two factors that constitute the fragility of rigid social ecologies.

When encountering any organized topological field, it is necessary to account for how such an improbable organization exists and how it is able to maintain itself. Why do people not just mill about, mixing occupations, economic status, ethnicity, religion, gender, and sexual orientation like particles in a gaseous cloud, rather than organizing into stratified social relations? Why do people of one economic class tend to settle in this part of a city and members of another in that part of the city? Why are there more Evangelical Christians in the South, rather than an equal distribution throughout the entire country? Why do trees of a particular type tend to grow in one area, rather than forests being a completely random mixture of different trees? How does one species become dominant in a particular ecosystem? What are the *processes* by which these improbabilities are produced and maintained?

Sometimes these distributions will arise from the nature of the machines in the topological field themselves. We don't find palm trees in Alaska because they lack the sort of virtual proper being that would allow them to grow there. However, much of the form that space takes arises from interactions between machines. These interactions can be thought in terms of the concepts of structural coupling and feedback. As we saw earlier, structural coupling is a relation in which one or two entities are dependent for stimuli or flows from one another in order to engage in their own operations and becomings. These operations can be bidirectional or unidirectional. A structural coupling is bidirectional when *both* entities involved in the relation require flows from one another to exist as they do. An example of such a bidirectional structural coupling would be the relation between the micro-fauna of the stomach and the human body. The human body requires these parasites in order to digest as it does, while the parasites require the human body to provide them with the food they consume. As a consequence of this coupling, the development and evolution of these beings are bound up with one another.

A coupling is unidirectional, by contrast, when a machine draws flows from another machine without the machine from which it draws flows drawing flows from it. A good example of such a coupling is the relation between the redwoods of California and the Pacific Ocean. Because there is very little regular rainfall in

Northern California, sequoias have had to devise other strategies for acquiring water to grow. To solve this problem redwoods have drawn on the mists that roll off the Pacific Ocean daily and that drift quite far inland. In other words, redwoods have become structurally coupled to these mists as a source of water, while the Pacific Ocean is not coupled to redwoods. If some blight destroyed redwoods, those mists would occur as they did before.

This unidirectional coupling has had a significant effect on both the becoming of redwoods throughout their biological history, as well as their spatial distribution or geography. At the level of evolutionary becoming, sequoias learned how to absorb water primarily through their leaves rather than their roots. No doubt this is part of the reason that redwoods grow so tall. Those trees that grew taller would have an advantage over their fellows because they would be better able to draw water from incoming mist. Over time, natural selection favored those redwoods most capable of absorbing water through their leaves, as well as those that grew the tallest. If those that did not grow as tall weren't favored, then this wasn't simply because they had a difficult time absorbing water from the morning mists, but because their ability to absorb sunlight was diminished by the taller trees.

However, this becoming or the development of these powers had consequences for the spatial distribution of redwoods. On the one hand, because sequoias draw their water primarily from mist rolling off the Pacific Ocean, they can only grow so far inland. The boundary of their geography becomes the point where these mists stop. On the other hand, because redwoods chose to develop their leaves as water absorbing machines rather than their roots, they cannot be transplanted to other geographies where this kind of mist does not regularly occur. We might think that they could be transplanted to a region that has heavy rainfall, but sequoia have developed the structural openness of their leaves in such a way as to specifically be open to water in the form of mist, not rain. This topological field and the structural couplings that take place within it accounts for both the becoming and geographical distribution of sequoia. It also entails that the future of redwoods is bound up with that of the Pacific Ocean. If, for example, climate change transformed the environmental conditions that produce this mist, the sequoia would likely become extinct. When we keep in mind that a whole host of other machines or plants and animals are structurally coupled to the redwoods for their existence, we see that such a change would generate a cascade effect throughout this entire topological field.

The phenomena of feedback is yet another reason geographical distributions take the form they take. Feedback comes in positive and negative varieties. Negative feedback consists of regulatory actions that maintain a certain type of organization in a stable state. Thermostats, for example, engage in activities of negative feedback of this sort. When the thermostat is set at a particular temperature, the heater will kick in until a certain temperature is registered by a thermometer. At this point it will shut down, thereby maintaining a more or less consistent temperature in a room. Our bodies work in similar ways, shivering when cold to produce heat, sweating when warm to cool us down. In other words, negative feedback is an interaction in which a system maintains a particular equilibrium. By contrast, positive feedback is a form of interaction in which an organization spins out of control. Rather than reaching a point of equilibrium where a system maintains itself in a particular organization, a positive feedback relation is one in which disequilibrium continues to intensify. This, for example, is one of the worries about global warming. As average global temperature continues to increase, more glaciers and tundra melt. As more glaciers and tundra melt, the planet absorbs more heat because the Earth develops a greater albedo, absorbing more of the Sun's energy rather than reflecting it back into space, and more frozen methane gases are released making it more difficult for the Sun's energy to be reflected back into outer space. Rather than the planet maintaining an average temperature, its temperature instead continues to rise and rise. Such is an example of positive feedback.

When thinking about positive and negative feedback we must take care not to understand these terms *normatively*. As philosophers such as Serres have shown (see Serres 2007), disequilibrium and noise can be a *new* source of order. In other words, positive feedback can be generative of new possibilities of organization. Likewise, systems characterized by negative feedback or equilibrium systems can be oppressive. "Harmony" is not necessarily a "good." As a consequence, positive and negative feedback should be strictly taken as descriptive and analytical categories, not as normative categories defining what is desirable (negative feedback) and undesirable (positive feedback). It is disappointing that ontological categories are so often translated into moral categories.

Negative feedback plays a powerful role in maintaining the patterns of various vortexes and geographical distributions. Thus, for example, one particular species in an ecosystem might evolve a set of powers that gives it a particular advantage in capturing prey. Because more food becomes available to it, it also ends up reproducing in greater numbers. As a result of its increase in numbers it now over-hunts its prey, causing famine among its kind, that, in turn, takes pressure off the prey allowing them to return in greater numbers. An equilibrium is then reached in the geographical distribution of predator and prey through feedback mechanisms. Feedback mechanisms also play an important role in the geographical distribution of wealth and poverty. It is sometimes said that wealth attracts wealth, while poverty attracts poverty. The reason for this is that as wealth increases links or paths are forged that attract more wealth to this node, while poverty is characterized by an absence of paths that ensure that the offspring of the impoverished will be similarly lacking in opportunity. As a consequence, wealth and poverty become geographically distributed as in the case of the population distributions between the north and south side of Chicago. When a person attempts to transition from a state of poverty to wealth, all sorts of feedback mechanisms emerge. They encounter a great deal of density making such a transition incredibly difficult. Wealth and poverty are not just privation and excess, they aren't just the presence and absence of property, they are also geographies. The person striving to move to a different economic status faces feedback loops from family and friends pulling them back to their home territory, the absence of clear paths of opportunity, as well as an absence of knowledge pertaining to cultural codes in wealthy populations.[1] They thus encounter two forms of negative feedback: attractive and repulsive feedback mechanisms. On the one hand, obligations to family and friends from the spatial node from which they originate, coupled with the exigencies of daily life when living in a state of poverty, attract them back into this node of the socio-economic network like the sticky threads of a spider web. On the other hand, cultural codes, incorporeal machines, governing the other node to which they wish to move push back against them, repulse them, closing doors of opportunity. As a result, the wealthy tend to remain wealthy and the poor tend to remain poor. Gabrielle Muccino's 2006 film *The Pursuit of Happyness* is the exception rather than the rule.

From the foregoing it becomes clear that onto-cartographical space should be thought more as a *process* than a container that is always-already there. Topological fields both arise from machines and condition the becomings and movements of machines, rather than existing as a fixed container for machines. The mapping of spatializing, machinic processes – so central to the discipline of geography – is crucial to the project of onto-cartography. Such a mapping is necessary to understanding the ontological constitution of machines, their becomings, and their movements. Above all, however, understanding how vector fields are organized is crucial to intervening politically in these fields in ways that might allow alternative forms of social life to become possible. It is high time for critical and emancipatory theory to become geographical.

Time

Just as onto-cartography rejects the notion that there is one homogeneous space containing all entities, arguing instead that there is a plurality of heterogeneous spaces that are also internally heterogeneous, onto-cartography rejects the notion that there is one time containing all entities. In the same way that spaces arise from machines rather than containing them, times arise from machines as well. There is a plurality of times. In the *Critique of Pure Reason*, Kant famously remarked that

> [t]ime is nothing other than the form of inner sense, i.e., of the intuition of our self and our inner state. For time cannot be a determination of outer appearances; it belongs neither to a shape or a position, etc., but on the contrary determines the relation of representations in our inner state. (Kant 1998, A33/B59–B50)

In part, onto-cartography here follows Kant's thesis with three important qualifications. First, where Kant treats time as the form of *our* inner sense (i.e., rational beings), onto-cartography *pluralizes* temporalities. *Every* machine has its internal form of temporality and these temporal rhythms differ among themselves. Recognition of this has important implications for our understanding of how different types of machines interact with one another. Consequently, second, onto-cartography cannot share Kant's thesis that "[d]ifferent times are only parts of one and the same time" (ibid.: A31/B47). There is not one time that contains all temporal rhythms, but rather a plurality of heterogeneous times that never unify to form a totality or whole. Machines operate and unfold with different temporal rhythms. Finally, third, time is not simply the inner world of various machines, but is also their duration in their outer world. Machines become at different rates and exist for different durations. There are machines that disappear almost as quickly as they appear such as certain subatomic particles, while there are other machines that exist for millions of years such as a galaxy or a planet. Insofar as machines are processes, they are temporal through and through.

What, then, does it mean to claim that there are multiple times and that times arise from machines? The thesis of onto-cartography is that time is the rate at which a machine can engage in operations. Here it is important to distinguish between phenomenological conceptions of time, organized around discussions of how humans retend and anticipate various impressions, as well as around discussions of futurity and historicity, with the onto-cartographical conception of time. Once again, the issue isn't that these analyses are *mistaken*, but rather that they are focused on the way in which *particular* machines – Dasein, the *cogito*, the subject, etc. – operate temporally. On the one hand, there are machines such as crystals or stars that do not operate through historicity and futurity as thematized by Heidegger, Husserl, or Derrida at all. These entities certainly *have* a history and a future, but they do not intend the world – indeed they do not intend at all in the phenomenological sense of the term – in terms of historicity and futurity. It would be strange to speak of rocks as having "existential projects" or *projecting* a future and drawing from a past. Nonetheless, these entities have their own specific sort of temporality. They exist in and through time with a rhythm or duration unique to them such as the rate at which an element decays. On the other hand, there is a variety of living entities, institutions, social phenomena, and so on, that have different structures and rhythms of temporality. Onto-cartography takes phenomenological accounts of temporality as valid as descriptions of how humans experience time, but requires a framework robust enough to capture these other forms of temporality. Consequently, at the most basic level, time can be thought as the rate at which entities are capable of engaging in operations, but this must be qualified with the recognition that the nature of the operations engaged in by various entities differs from entity to entity. There are many different forms temporal operations take, of which the human is but one example.

We have seen that machines are structurally open to the world in a selective fashion. No machine is open to *all* flows that radiate throughout a world. Cats can hear things that humans cannot register at all. Dogs can smell things that are invisible to cats. Mantis shrimp can see wavelengths of light completely hidden to other types of organisms. One chemical element can be affected by others in ways that another cannot. Machines are only ever selectively open to their environment. Time is one of the ways in which machines are selectively open to their environment or other machines. Not only are machines only open to particular *types* of flows from other machines, but they are only open to flows at particular *rates* or speeds. Thus, for example, humans perceive at a rate of 60 Hz. Hertz measure the frequency or cycles per second of a particular phenomenon. Houseflies perceive at a rate of 200 Hz, while honeybees perceive at about 300 Hz (Mineault 2011). The rate at which an organism can perceive is also the rate at which it can carry out cognitive, affective, and locomotive operations on an input. Above these thresholds and well below them, the organism will be unable to consciously register motion. However, here we must proceed with caution as matters are complicated. As Mineault notes, older fluorescent lights oscillated at a rate of 120 Hz, well above the rate at which humans can *consciously* perceive motion, yet studies have shown that they nonetheless cause headaches and cognitive deficits. This suggests that systems or machines themselves can be composed of a variety of different temporalities.

The rate at which a machine can register inputs is also its capacity for encountering events in its environment as information. As Bateson defines it, ". . . information is definable as a difference which makes a difference" (Bateson 2000a: 315). Information is not an *intrinsic* feature of the flow a machine receives as an input, but rather only takes place when the flow selects a *new* state of the machine for operations. For example, when someone repeats the same thing twice, it no longer functions as information because it selects no new system states. However, whether or not something can function as information at all will be partially dependent on the rate at which a machine can register inputs as inputs. If it is so difficult to swat a fly, then this is because flies can register motions issuing from us at a much faster rate, while we cannot do likewise with the motions of the fly. What seems still to us is pervaded by motion to the fly. The fly is thus able to register certain things as information that we don't discern at all.

What we have here is an intersection of two very different temporalities, two different rates at which machines can engage in operations. This will have important consequences for how entities interact with one another. Issues such as this, for example, lie at the heart of attitudes towards climate change by both people and governments. Climate change happens so slowly and gradually that it is not registered by people and governments. As we walk by a glacier on a daily basis, it seems to be largely unchanged. Likewise, from year to year, season to season, the weather seems to be more or less the same. Even though things are constantly changing, their change takes place at a rate that is difficult to register by these machines. As a consequence, it becomes difficult to believe that these things are indeed taking place. We require special technologies and the accumulation of data in order to transform these slow-moving events into information.

These problems are particularly acute in the case of governments such as that of the United States. Not only does the US government as a machine have difficulty registering something like climate change because of the slow rate at which this change takes place, but the rate at which operations take place in the various governmental branches themselves pose problems that make it difficult to respond to long-term problems like climate change. In the United States, representatives serve two-year terms, senators six-year terms, and presidents four-year terms. This has significant temporal consequences for the sorts of issues that the government can address. The relative shortness of these terms entails that politicians must begin campaigning for their next term almost as soon as they enter office. This makes long-term planning very difficult, because politicians end up focusing on the immediate issues and controversies of the day.

This problem is exacerbated when the political system is coupled to the contemporary mass media system. As sociologist Niklas Luhmann argues, in-depth reporting is organized around the code of information/non-information. Information is that which is selected to be reported. In order for the news system to continue, it must perpetually find information to report (Luhmann 2000: 25–41). However, here we must remember that information is not *fact*, but a difference that makes a difference. As Luhmann puts it, "[i]nformation itself can only appear as (however small) a surprise" (ibid.: 27). For the news system, information is that which *deviates* from the *norm*, the expected, the ordinary course of things. The news system must perpetually find that which is the exception rather than the norm to continue its operations. As a consequence, rather than tarrying with an issue and working through it, the news machine instead favors constant change. It will therefore favor controversy, disagreement, the new, and so on, rather than the gradual building of knowledge that we find in the sciences. When such a machine is coupled to the political system we get into a scenario where politicians must perpetually respond to the controversy of the day rather than engage in long-term issues and planning. Only in this way will they be able to ensure their next term. The result is that it becomes very difficult to respond to very slow-moving processes from other machines.

On the one hand, then, a machine can be unable to engage in operations on flows issued from other machines because those flows either move too slowly or quickly to be registered. On the other hand, machines can be captured in the temporal rhythms of other machines such that the activities of one machine become structured by another. This is often the case in our interactions with institutions. The rate at which a government institution can engage in operations and register information differs from that at which a human being can do so, and is often far slower. Thus, for example, a person might have lost a beloved family member in another country, but lack a passport. The person's ability to respond to this event will be structured by the temporality of the State Department's processing of paperwork.

In *The Structures of Everyday Life*, the great historian Fernand Braudel discusses an interesting example of couplings between human and non-human temporalities when discussing wheat and rice (Braudel 1981: 108–57). Wheat and rice each have their own temporal rhythms that contribute to structuring life and social relations in their own particular ways. For both grains there is a time of development. With wheat you get about one harvest a year and the grain is particularly susceptible to disease and climate fluctuations. This entails that for societies highly dependent on wheat and similar grains such as Europe through the eighteenth century, societal rhythms will become organized around periods of intense planting and harvest, with a great deal of empty time in between.

The temporality of these grains will, on the one hand, necessitate the invention of food preservation technologies so as to weather those periods where the grain is still growing or when the ground is fallow, while on the other hand, it will free up a great deal of time for other activities. Moreover, because of the properties of these grains, large labor forces will not be required to cultivate and harvest them, allowing for agriculture to be organized around family farms. Much of European society will thus come to be organized around the rhythms of these grains.

In the case of rice, matters will be very different. Rice is both a very hardy grain and yields two to three harvests a year. Thus, where civilizations based on grains similar to wheat tend to be beset by famines and the social turbulence this causes, there is an abundance of food for those civilizations that rely heavily on rice. However, this abundance comes at a price. Rice is extremely time-consuming to plant and harvest. As a consequence, societies based on rice will tend to favor collective farming as a means of planting and harvesting enough rice. This, in its turn, will encourage stratification within society between those who farm and a priestly or noble class that keeps track of rice reserves and distributes them. Among the farmers, time for other activities will be limited.

Matters become far more complicated in the case of machines capable of memory. Memory comes in a variety of forms, ranging from types such as genetic memory where a particular part of the genetic code refers to a trait acquired in the distant past, to freer and more conscious forms of memory such as those found in advanced species like lions and humans, social institutions, and increasingly with various forms of computer technology. With memory, time ceases to be linear and becomes parallel and crumpled. As Serres has noted, such time must be thought topologically. He writes that

> [i]f you take a handkerchief and spread it out in order to iron it, you can see in it certain fixed distances and proximities. If you sketch a circle in one area, you can make out nearby points and measure far-off distances. Then take the same handkerchief and crumple it, by putting it in your pocket. Two distant points suddenly are close, even superimposed. If, further, you tear it in certain places, two points that were close can become very distant. This science of nearness and rifts is called topology, while the science of stable and well-defined distances is called metrical geometry. (Serres and Latour 1995: 60)

In the case of machines without memory, an event is only temporally related to the event that directly preceded it:

$$E_1 \rightarrow E_2 \rightarrow E_3 \rightarrow E_4 \rightarrow E_n$$

In this form of metric time, E_4 is only directly temporally related to E_3. E_2 is gone.

With machines capable of memory the situation is markedly different as the past *persists* in the present. Now E_2 can directly influence E_4, leaping over, as it were, E_3. Freud expresses this topological form of time beautifully at the beginning of *Civilization and Its Discontents*:

> ... [L]et us, by a flight of imagination, suppose that Rome is not a human habitation but a psychical entity with a similarly long and copious past – an entity, that is to say, in which nothing that has once come into existence will have passed away and all the earlier phases of development continue to exist alongside the latest one. This would mean that in Rome the palaces of the Caesars and the Septizonium of Septimius Severus would still be rising to their old height on the Palatine and that the castle of S. Angelo would still be carrying on its battlements the beautiful statues which graced it until the siege by the Goths, and so on. But more than this. In the place occupied by the Palazzo Caffarelli would once more stand – without the Palazzo having to be removed – the Temple of Jupiter Capitolinus; and this not only in its latest shape, as the Romans of the Empire saw it, but also in its earliest one, when it still showed Etruscan forms and was ornamented with terracotta antefixes. Where the Coliseum now stands we could at the same time admire Nero's vanished Golden House. On the Piazza of the Pantheon we should find not only the Pantheon of to-day, as it was bequeathed to us by Hadrian, but, on the same site, the original edifice erected by Agrippa; indeed, the same piece of ground would be supporting the church of Santa Maria sopra Minerva and the ancient temple over which it was built. (Freud 2001a: 70)

Here Freud nicely illustrates Serres conception of time as a sort of crumpled handkerchief. Where, in a linear, metric form of time, events in the past are gone and no longer influence the present, topological forms of time are capable of bringing events from the remote past into contact with the present. An event E_3 that directly precedes E_4 can be topologically remote from E_4, while E_1 can be extremely close and present.

The condition under which this is possible is the existence of some sort of medium of inscription. As Freud will note elsewhere, for memory and time to function in this way, they must be preserved as memory-traces in a medium (see Freud 2001c). Only in this way can the past leap over the intervening sequence of events and directly influence the present. This medium can be genes, the brain, paper, computer databases, recordings, and so on. In each case we have the preservation of a trace that can be reactivated in the present.

This form of temporality is ubiquitous among living entities, social institutions, and certain technologies. Dormant genes – often referred to as "junk DNA" – can be reawakened under certain circumstances. A dog that was repeatedly beaten in its youth might encounter every subsequent person as a potential danger. Nations operate according to the constraints of their constitutions, written hundreds of years ago. Likewise, the religious live according to holy books thousands of years old. Computer systems such as that found on Amazon.com recommend books based on what others have bought in the past. As Badiou notes, lovers can organize their lives in fidelity to an encounter with one another, an event, that took place years ago (Badiou 2008). In each case, we get a folding of the past into the present such that the past continues to act in the present.

Mnemonic machines allow us to define the difference between trivial and non-trivial machines. As articulated by Heinz von Foester, a trivial machine is a machine in which a given input invariably produces a particular output. For example, you flip a switch and the lights turn on. By contrast:

> Non-trivial machines, however, are quite different creatures. Their input-output relationship is not invariant, but is determined by the machine's previous output. In other words, its previous steps determine its present reactions. While these machines are again deterministic systems, for all practical reasons they are unpredictable: an output once observed for a given input will most likely be not the same for the same input given later. (Foester 1971: 8)

In the case of non-trivial machines, the output transforms the internal operations of the machine such that in encountering the *same* input on a different occasion, the machine will respond differently or produce different outputs. Part of the reason for this lies in the form of temporality characteristic of mnemonic machines. Insofar as inputs leave a memory-trace in mnemonic machines, those traces modify the way in which the machine functions, rendering it capable of novel responses in new instances.

Insofar as mnemonic machines are non-trivial machines, we must therefore take care to note that repetition of the past in the present is not a *brute*, *mechanical*, or *rote* repetition of the same. As Deleuze notes, "[r]epetition changes nothing in the object repeated, but does change something in the [machine] which contemplates it . . . Whenever A appears, I *expect* the appearance of B" (Deleuze 1995: 70, my italics). Because I expect the appearance of B following A, I can now modify my response to A, my operations, when encountering A. Later Deleuze goes on to remark that:

> Repetition is never a historical fact, but rather the historical condition under which something new is effectively produced. It is not the historian's reflection which demonstrates a resemblance between Luther and Paul, between the Revolution of 1789 and the Roman Republic, etc. Rather, it is in the first place for themselves that the revolutionaries are determined to lead their lives as "resuscitated Romans", before becoming capable of the act which they have begun by repeating in the mode of a proper past, therefore under conditions such that they necessarily identify with a figure from the historical past. (Ibid.: 90)

How can repetition produce novelty? Recall that in the case of trivial machines, input and output are strongly correlated such that given a particular input we necessarily get a particular output. As a consequence, trivial machines are necessarily determined strictly by the historical present. In the case of non-trivial machines, by contrast, the relation to the past provides *distance* with respect to the present. The machine is no longer determined strictly by events in the present, but rather draws on a reservoir of past events that allow it to rise above that present. The machine can now look at the present not from the standpoint of the present, but rather from the standpoint of Roman Republicans. Yet why is this not just a repetition of the Roman Republic in the present? Although the revolutionaries draw on this event from the past, that event is synthesized with the experience of the present. Moreover, in repeating the Roman Republic in the present, the revolutionaries had to act in a different world, a different configuration of machines, that required the invention of new corporeal and incorporeal machines unknown to the Roman Republicans.

The existence of topological time raises significant difficulties for historicism, whether at the level of psychic systems, social systems, or cultural artifacts. Historicism begins from the premise that cultural artifacts, events, actions, and institutions are to be explained in terms of the historical setting in which they occur. For example, the work of Shakespeare is to be explained in terms of the *contemporary* events, norms, and circumstances in which they were written. Clearly, because these events occur in a world, in an assemblage of machinic interactions, there has to be some truth to this thesis. However, simply because two or more machines are contemporary to one another we cannot assume that they determine one another. Because non-trivial mnemonic machines can pull upon a remote past, they can be determined by events outside the contemporary in ways that allow them to leap over the present. A revolutionary can be in "closer" communication with Roman Republicans than her present. From an onto-cartographical perspective, it is thus necessary to investigate the crumpled handkerchief of time and how a machine interacts with a past.

As a consequence, we cannot assume that just because two events are contemporary they are of the same time. Time is not smooth and distributed in the same way throughout a world, but is rather lumpy, discontinuous, and heterogeneous. Many of us, for example, will be familiar with the tenured professor that stopped reading a few decades ago and who continues to think of philosophy in terms of existentialism as it was understood in the 1950s. While this professor is present and contemporary, he is of a different time than those about him. A similar example would be the different temporal fields of the Amish and people who live in a city nearby. Likewise books written in recent history can be less contemporary than books written in the remote past. This might be the case with a work like Sartre's *Being and Nothingness* when compared with Lucretius' *De Rerum Natura*. While I do not share this sentiment, it seems that Sartre's work has fallen out of favor. Despite its fairly recent publication in 1943, for many readers there's a sense in which it is experienced as antiquated and unable to respond to the questions of the present. By contrast, works like Serres' *Birth of Physics*, Greenblatt's *Swerve*, Jane Bennett's *Vibrant Matter*, as well as a host of references to Lucretius by

Althusser, Badiou, Deleuze, and a variety of other thinkers, suggest that *De Rerum Natura* is undergoing a sort of renaissance. As a thinker that had fallen into obscurity between the heyday of post-structuralism between the 1960s and 1990s, who was unable to resonate with the present of that time due to its focus on language, his work has suddenly popped back into presence as highly relevant.

This example should lead to caution in conceiving the way in which non-trivial mnemonic machines relate to the past as a *fixed* feature of the past. There is something holographic about the way in which non-trivial mnemonic machines relate to the past. If you tilt a holograph one way one image appears. If you tilt it another, another image appears. Events and texts can fall into obscurity at one point in time, only to become centrally important at another. A particular book or passage of the Bible, for example, can go largely ignored and forgotten. However, under the right circumstances it can become the crucial text defining how to read the rest of the work and how one is to live a pious life. As Deleuze noted, it is not repetition in the *object* that is important – nothing changes in the repeated object by virtue of being repeated – but rather how the machine that contemplates the repetition regards the object. Every being of the past can pass from a state of complete obscurity to crucial importance. When a machine of the past rises into prominence in this way, it is this historical machine that defines the coordinates of the contemporary, not the contemporary that defines the machine. The resurrection of this historical machine leads the machine that draws on it to act on the contemporary in new and unexpected ways.

Like space, time is populated by a variety of different types of temporal paths. This variability of temporality holds for trivial and non-trivial machines, as well as corporeal and incorporeal machines, though there will be a variety of different temporal operations along these paths. Einstein demonstrated this most dramatically in the case of trivial and corporeal machines. The closer a machine is to a massive object, the slower time will pass. Likewise, the further a machine is from a massive object, the faster a time will pass. Alternatively, the faster a machine moves, the faster time will pass. Here we get a clear example of time arising from machines rather than being a container for machines. For corporeal machines, time contracts and dilates as a function of mass and speed (Pogge 2009). This gives rise to a strange situation in which two machines are contemporary with one another while nonetheless being at different times. Astronomer Richard Pogge illustrates this point nicely with respect to global positioning systems (GPS). Time passes more quickly for the satellites upon which GPS is dependent than airplanes and cars because they are further from the mass of the Earth. This leads to differences in determining the location of a machine on the surface of the planet and how it is calculated by the satellite. Indeed, these differences in temporal frame of reference add up to an error rate of about 10km a day. In order for the satellite and the vehicle on the ground to accurately interface with one another, the satellite must take account of this difference in temporal frames of reference and compensate for it. Here we have a strange situation in which the satellite and the vehicle on the ground are "present" to one another, while the satellite is actually in the car's future and the car is in the satellite's past. In order to bridge this difference in rhythms of time, a temporal path must be constructed through the compensations of the clock.

We saw an example of temporal paths earlier in the case of human beings relating to machines like governments and other institutions. Humans have their time, institutions have their time. Generally the time of a bureaucracy or an institution is slower than that of a person. In order to interact with an institution, humans must thus follow the temporal path of the institution and organize their lives around that of the institution. For example, one must first pass through the operations of an insurance company before it can be determined whether or not one will be able to undergo a particular operation. Similarly, we saw that the rate at which messages can travel makes a difference as to how assemblages can be structured. Military campaigns, for example, will be organized differently depending on whether messages are carried by horseback, or whether they're carried by radio or satellite. In the first instance, responses to the enemy will be slower because of the speed of the horse and the time it takes for the orders to proliferate throughout the spatially disconnected soldiers. In the latter case, entirely new forms of strike and coordination become possible because of the speed at which information about the enemy and orders can be transmitted.

Finally, in the case of contemporary entities that animate different historical planes of the past, temporal paths must be forged in order to allow these machines to interact with one another.

Returning to the example of the Sartrean professor that has not kept up with subsequent debates in philosophy and, say, the contemporary speculative realists, all sorts of paths will have to be constructed in order for these two figures present to one another to meaningfully communicate with each other. Indeed, the two will be able to talk back and forth with each other, yet due to their different frames of reference or the way in which they structure operations on inputs, it is likely they will have a very different understanding of what is being discussed. As the prison captain said in Stuart Rosenberg's 1967 film *Cool Hand Luke*, "what we have here is a failure to communicate." It *appears* that the two people are communicating, but in fact they both understand each other completely in terms of *their own* historical frame of reference. Often we are completely oblivious to these forms of miscommunication because phenomenologically the person we're talking to is physically present. Their relationship to the past, in other words, is not given to our operations of perception. It is only through inference that we begin to discern that the other person is working with a different frame of reference. Once this is recognized we can begin to develop temporal paths – a sort of translation key – that allows these different relations to the past to be surmounted, thereby forming a new present.

These reflections also draw attention to the fact that machines are limited in the number of operations they can carry out. The choice to operate on one set of inputs entails that one cannot, at that time, operate on another set of inputs. The number of operations a machine can engage in is limited as a function of the complexity of the machine. Generally, the more complex a machine, the more operations it can simultaneously undertake. However, there is no machine that can engage in all operations at once. Institutions, societies, people, and governments can only attend to so many things at once. As a consequence, the choice of operations, the choice of inputs, always involves *risk* and *sacrifice*. For those machines capable of choosing operations and inputs – more advanced machines – choosing to operate on this input rather than that input entails risk insofar as it opens the machine to being caught unawares by those flows not attended to. We see a dramatic example of this in the case of the nineteenth-century potato famine. The failure to cultivate a variety of different types of potatoes and crops rendered the poor farmers entirely dependent on this one particular type of potato. Likewise, temporal selectivity involves sacrifice as attending to one thing entails not attending to other things. One thing rises into relief, while others fall into obscurity.

Fatigue is therefore a real dimension of non-trivial machines such as human beings. Fatigue signifies two things. On the one hand, fatigue refers to the number of operations a person can carry out in a minute, hour, day, week, month, and year. When the number of operations a person is called upon to perform exceeds a certain limit, everything frays apart. One reaches a point of operational saturation where one is unable to attend to any particular operation well. A person's capacity to operate is, in these circumstances, *exhausted* and the person is more or less overwhelmed by the world. In such circumstances, the person has been called upon to do too much within a particular span of time. In this regard, the person has lost his capacity to order and integrate his life. Every moment is taken up with attending to some input, to operating on some input, and inputs and operations crowd one another, all equally calling for attention, without the person being able to give their complete attention to anything. The world becomes a maelstrom demanding activity.

On the other hand, fatigue signifies physical and cognitive exhaustion. *Operations never come for free, but always require some sort of energy to take place. Order never comes for free, but always requires work and energy to be produced.* This is one of the reasons the concept of entropy is so important for onto-cartography. We recall that a high entropy system is a system with a random distribution of elements such as we find with gases in Brownian motion. With such systems, given the position of one element we can make no inferences about the positions of other elements because there is an equal probability that they will occur *anywhere* in the system. By contrast, low entropy systems are highly ordered systems in which, given the position of one element, we can make inferences about the position of other elements in the system. There is a *low probability* that other elements will be located *anywhere* in the system. Such systems are highly organized.

Organization never comes for free, but always requires work and energy to be maintained. Over the course of their existence, most machines are in a perpetual state of disintegration. Roads and buildings decay, relations between people fall apart, technologies wear out, the cells of bodies are perpetually dying, noise coming from within and without threatens to overwhelm every institution. Machines are perpetually falling apart. This entails that they must draw on energy and engage in perpetual work to maintain their organization. Roads, power lines, and buildings require upkeep. New generations of young must be educated or formed according to the norms and customs of a people. Communications must continue. Bodies must perpetually produce new cells to replace those that have died. All of this requires work and energy. Wherever we encounter a persistent low entropy system, wherever we encounter a machine, we ought thus ask what energy it draws upon to maintain that organization and what work it engages in to continue existing as it does.

In the case of machines such as humans and other animals, fatigue as exhaustion is a real feature of their being. There is a limit to the amount of work our bodies can do in maintaining themselves, as well as the amount of work we can do in operating on information and in maintaining those features of the world about us that concern us. Beyond that point, our minds grow fuzzy, unable to operate on any additional information, and our bodies grow weak. We fall to the ground. At a certain point we can go no further and we require rest and additional energy.

It is for these reasons that questions of time and fatigue are privileged sites of political thought. In his critique of the "scholastic disposition," the sociologist Bourdieu remarks that

> [t]here is nothing that 'pure' thought finds it harder to think than *skholè*, the first and most determinant of all the social conditions of possibility of "pure" thought, and also the scholastic disposition which inclines its possessors to suspend the demands of the situation, the constraints of economic and social necessity, and the urgencies it imposes or the ends it proposes. (Bourdieu 2000: 12)

Skholè refers to the Greek concept of leisure, rest, or free time. Bourdieu's thesis is that the position of the university professor, the social scientist, the critical theorist, and so on *forgets* the leisure upon which their practice is made possible and that this leads to systematic distortions in how they explain social phenomena. As he remarks further on

> [b]ecause he forgets what defines its specificity, the social scientist credits agents with his own vision, and in particular an interest in pure

knowledge and pure understanding which is normally alien to them. This is the "philologism" which, according to Bakhtin, tends to treat all languages like dead languages fit only for deciphering; it is the intellectualism of the structuralist semiologists who treat language as an object of interpretation or contemplation rather than an instrument of action and power. It is also the epistemocentrism of the hermeneutic theory of reading (or, *a fortiori*, of the theory of the interpretation of works of art conceived as "reading"): through an unjustified universalization of the presuppositions inscribed in the status of *lector* and in academic *skholè* – the condition of possibility of that very particular form of reading which, performed at leisure and almost always repeated, is methodologically oriented towards extraction of an intentional and coherent meaning – they tend to conceive every understanding, even practical understanding, as an *interpretation*, a self-aware act of deciphering (the paradigm of which is translation). (Ibid.: 53)

The *skholè* of the academic world or scholastic disposition cultivates a sense of the world as a text to be deciphered, as something governed by *codes* or *rules* structuring action, forgetting the real-time constraints that organize action. When seeking to explain why people tolerate oppressive circumstances and behave in ways contrary to their interests, for example, we posit an intelligible code, a belief, an underlying ideology, that would account for their action and the persistence of their behavior. Žižek, for example, goes so far as to suggest that we even find such intelligible codes beneath the different toilet designs of the English, French, and Germans (Žižek 1997: 5). We treat human action and social arrangements as arising from these intelligible codes alone, and treat people who follow these codes as being duped by false beliefs. Emancipatory critical response to such things thus comes to be conceived as a debunking of these beliefs.

The point here is not that people don't have many curious beliefs and suffer from a number of perverted ideologies. We have seen that incorporeal machines are among those machines that populate worlds. The point is that we tend to overestimate the degree to which these beliefs and ideologies organize social life. What is missed is the degree to which non-human machines contribute to this organization. As Latour writes elsewhere:

Between a car driver that slows down near a school because she has seen the "30 MPH" yellow sign and a car driver that slows down because he wants to protect the suspension of his car threatened by the bump of a "speed trap", is the difference big or small? Big, since obedience to the first has gone through morality, symbols, sign posts, yellow paint, while the other has passed through the same list to which has been added a carefully designed concrete slab. But it is small since they both have obeyed something: the first driver to a rarely manifested altruism – if she had not slowed down, her heart would have been broken by the moral law; the second driver to a largely distributed selfishness – if he had not slowed down his suspension would have been broken by the concrete slab. (Latour 2005: 77–8)

The theorist working within the scholastic disposition tends to only acknowledge the first source of organizational efficacy – the sign, the code, what can be interpreted and deciphered – as the ground upon which social relations come to be organized as they are. The agent behaves in a particular way because they acknowledge a code underlying a sign and act accordingly. The role that something like a speed bump might play becomes entirely invisible. Changing social relations becomes, as a result, merely a matter of changing relations to signs or codes.

Consideration of things like fatigue shows why we should be cautious with respect to forms of analysis premised on the scholastic disposition. The person beset by fatigue "tolerates" the oppressive social conditions they do, not because they *believe* in a code underlying social relations, not because they are duped by an ideology, but because they are dependent on this form of life for the energy that sustains them in their operations and because they have little time for anything else. A person wakes up, feeds his children, gets them ready for school, takes them to school, then goes to a job consisting of numbing intellectual or physical labor for eight to twelve hours. They come home and then face chores, making dinner, getting the kids to bed, and so on. With the brief minutes left over, they then lose themselves in drink, mindless television, empty books, and so on. Little *energy* is left over for anything else, much less understanding the intricacies of turgidly written critical theory addressed to experts, understanding why worlds are organized as they're organized, or overturning oppressive social systems. If people tolerate such unsatisfying conditions, it is not so much because they *believe* this is the natural order of things as a result of some ideology that dupes them – though often this is the case as well – but because they are dependent on this assemblage to provide them with the energy required to sustain themselves, their families, their shelter, their transportation, to pay back their debts, and so on. We are caught in temporal and energetic webs that structure our lives and what is possible. Despite its good intentions, emancipatory theories, with their focus on discursivity, often doubly alienate the people they seek to emancipate. We are first alienated in fatigue, in fields of temporality that saturate our being leaving us little to no time for anything else. We are then alienated by a moral condemnation that claims we are duped by ideology or that we are vapid consumerists, and that ignores the way in which the exigencies of the world in which we live structure how we live, what we can do, and what we are capable of enjoying.

If time is a central site of the political, then this is because time is the possibility of carrying out operations. A life that is saturated by the exigency of demands, pervaded by the necessity of carrying out operations, is also a life that finds it tremendously difficult to explore the possibility and construction of other operations and social relations. It is a life trapped in a web of existing relations of power. It is often said that idle hands are the devil's tools. From the standpoint of dominant power, this is entirely true, for with the emergence of open time, with freedom from labor and the exigencies of life in a world, people have the means to begin questioning existing social relations, existing spatial networks, and the time to begin building those networks. In other words, open time threatens power. If this is true, it then follows that creating time, opening time, is a project central to any emancipatory politics.

With respect to time, onto-cartography maps the rates at which different machines are capable of carrying out operations, hierarchies of machines temporally coupled to one another, the manner in which the operations and inputs chosen involve risk and sacrifice, and sites of fatigue that occur within various machines as a consequence of the number of operations they're required to carry out. In other words, onto-cartography, in part, seeks temporal maps structuring relations between machines in a world. These temporal maps are traced and drawn not simply for the sake of intellectual understanding, but are drawn as strategic maps for the sake of exposing risk as well as for the sake of devising strategies for creating time, opening time, that would allow people to begin constructing alternative forms of life within a world.

Overdetermination

The manner in which machines exist in spatio-temporal ecologies complicates the sort of causality presiding over their movements, local manifestations, and becomings. It is crucial to understand that the local manifestations of machines, along with their movements and becomings along spatio-temporal paths, are overdetermined. We must take care not to confuse overdetermination with Deleuze and Guattari's concept of "overcoding." A set of phenomena is overcoded when it is territorialized upon a *single* agency such as a sovereign (Deleuze and Guattari 1983: 199), such that all things flow to and from that agency. The purest case of overcoding in this sense would be all things being both for the sake of God, originating from God, and being sacrificed for God. Overcoding occurs when all things are seen as *issuing* from a single agency like Leibniz's God, capital, a privileged transcendental signifier, and so on (Deleuze and Guattari 1987: 8–9). Here overcoding refers to phenomena of unification around a center, the One, and ultimate grounds.

Introduced by Freud in *The Interpretation of Dreams*, overdetermination refers to the precise opposite (Freud 2001b: 307–8). A phenomenon is overdetermined not when it is determined by *one* cause or meaning, but rather when it is determined by a *variety* of causes or meanings. Overdetermination follows the logic of conjunction or the "and." The properties of a particular grape are the result of the grape's genetics *and* the soil conditions *and* the cultural practices or incorporeal machines defining how it is cultivated *and* the weather conditions that year, and, and, and. There is not one cause that determines the local manifestation of the grape, but rather a variety of causes intermingled with one another producing a novel output. Freud contends this is how it is in the case of dreams. Part of the reason that dreams are so enigmatic is that the manifest dream – what we recall the next morning and experience while dreaming – expresses a multiplicity of different meanings at the level of dream-content – the wishes that a dream satisfies – that are often contradictory or at odds with one another. By fusing together a variety of different dream-thoughts through operations of condensation and displacement, the dream both allows repressed wishes to be satisfied in a manner acceptable to the ego and superego, and allows a variety of divergent desires to be satisfied at one and the same time. Indeed, these desires can even be contradictory.

Freud gives a nice example of overdetermination of meaning in a dream when discussing one of his female patients who dreamt her sister's only remaining son had died and she was at his funeral (ibid.: 132–5). What possible wish could have been behind this dream? In the course of free association on the dream, the woman recalls a man that she had hoped to marry. Things had come to naught and she had since taken to catching glimpses of him at public events from afar such as lectures he would give. The last time she had seen the man was at the funeral of her sister's other son. At this point the meaning of the dream begins to become clear. It was not that she wished for the death of her sister's last remaining son, but rather that she wished to see this man again. If her sister's remaining son was to die, she would catch a glimpse of this man again at his funeral.

What really needs to be accounted for, however, is not the woman's desire to see the man again, but why her unconscious would create such a terrible setting for this wish to be satisfied. Why did her unconscious not conjure a more direct encounter in the manifest dream? Certainly, for example, we have all had dreams of eating food when we're hungry, where the wish seems to be directly and explicitly satisfied without concealment or distortion. Why did this woman's unconscious take such an indirect and devious route towards satisfying her desire to see this man again? Freud is unclear on this point, but we can hazard a few hypotheses. One possibility is that the woman's pride might have been wounded from being rebuffed by the man when she courted him before. The funeral of her sister's remaining son might have *simultaneously* been a way of satisfying her wish to see this man again *and* of punishing herself for continuing to desire him. A darker possibility would be that a situation such as the funeral of a beloved nephew would bring sympathy from the man, granting her wish not only to see him again but also to have his affection. Or yet again, perhaps the man had, in the past, shown more interest in her sister than her and the dream was a way of both seeing the man again and satisfying her desire to take revenge on her sister.

What we see in this dream is the overdetermination of meaning. There is not one simple meaning or desire that determines the dream, but a variety of conflicting desires that the dream simultaneously satisfies through condensation and displacement. On the one hand, the dream condenses many different desires into a single setting so as to simultaneously satisfy these wishes at the same time, while also veiling these desires. On the other hand, the dream displaces the wish to see the man onto the setting of the funeral, effectively repressing the conscious thought of the man. The man does not directly appear in the dream, but only comes to mind in her subsequent associations when analyzing the dream. Here we encounter the mechanism of displacement that allows the desire to see the man again to be displaced onto the last circumstance in which she saw him without directly representing him so that the thought of him might pass the guard of her unconscious dream-censor under cover. The funeral is also a condensation of her wish to see the man again and either her wish to be punished for that desire or also to earn his affection due to the circumstances. A variety of wishes are at work in the dream, thus rendering it overdetermined.

This is how it is with all machines. There is never a local manifestation, a movement, or a becoming that isn't overdetermined. The qualities of corn are not just the result of its genetic code, but rather result from its genetic code, the soil conditions, the weather, incorporeal machines presiding over how the farmer plants and cultivates the corn, insects, birds, mice, and wavelengths of light. What the corn becomes is a result of its *trans*-corporeal encounters, which is to say a *variety* of different causes. The case is no different with traffic. Traffic patterns result from incorporeal machines such as laws and traffic signs, the corporeal layout of roads, the dispositions of different drivers, the features of the cars on the road, events that take place on the road such as tires exploding, animals running across highways, or inattentive drivers suddenly swerving in the direction of another car. There is not one machine that overcodes all the others, determining how they move, become, or locally manifest themselves, but rather that movement, becoming, and local manifestations are a collaborative affair.

Matters are further complicated by the fact that when flows from other machines conspire together within a particular machine, what they produce is often a novel result that is unexpected. As Roy Bhaskar has argued, machines, or what he calls "generative mechanisms," can behave differently in open and closed systems (Bhaskar 2008: 53). I cannot give a detailed discussion of his argument here (see Bryant 2011: ch. 1); however, Bhaskar's thesis is that science engages in experiment so as to create *closed* systems in which we might trigger the events of which machines (which he calls "generative mechanisms" and "things") are capable. As Bhaskar argues:

> The intelligibility of experimental activity presupposes . . . the intransitive and structured character of the objects of scientific knowledge, at least in so far as these are causal laws. And this presupposes in turn the possibility of a non-human world, i.e. causal laws *without* invariances and experiences, and in particular a non-empirical world, i.e. causal laws and events without experiences; and the possibility of *open systems*, i.e. causal laws *out of phase* with patterns of events and experiences, and more generally of epistemically insignificant experiences, i.e. experiences out of phase with events and/or causal laws. (Bhaskar 2008: 35)

By "intransitive objects" Bhasker means objects that exist independently of the mind and culture, such as the sun or helium atoms. Bhaskar argues that these objects are "generative mechanisms" that are ". . . nothing other than a way of acting of a thing" (ibid.: 51). In other words, Bhaskar conceives generative mechanisms in terms of *powers* or capacities in a manner similar to that defended by onto-cartography's conception of machines (ibid.: 49).

The key point for Bhaskar is that generative mechanisms or machines can be *out of phase* with the events they are capable of producing. As he puts it, ". . . powers are potentialities which may or may not be exercised . . ." (ibid.: 50). There are two possible reasons for this: either the machine is *dormant* because it has not encountered the appropriate input to trigger its operations or powers, or there are other causal factors involved that either suppress the machine's power, disguise it, or, through a conjunction of causes, produce a different event than the mechanism would produce in isolation. This latter situation describes the behavior of machines or generative mechanisms in *open* systems where a variety of different generative mechanisms act in conjunction with one another. The task of the experimental scientist is to create a *closed* system where a particular generative mechanism is isolated from interaction with other generative mechanisms or machines so that the scientist might trigger the mechanism to discover what operations or powers belong uniquely to it. As we saw in Part 1, for example, oxygen and hydrogen – both generative mechanisms – behave very differently depending on whether they do or don't interact with one another. Alone they are gaseous and highly combustible, whereas when they bond they form a liquid that puts out many types of fires. In this latter instance, in an open system, the generative powers of hydrogen and oxygen are veiled. It is only when we isolate oxygen from hydrogen that we discover the powers of which it is uniquely capable.

Bhaskar contends that it is open systems rather than closed systems that are the rule in the natural and social world. It is rare to find generative mechanisms or machines in isolation from other machines, and generally it takes great effort to create closed systems in which we might discover the generative mechanisms unique to particular machines. The upshot of this is that the local manifestations of machines are, as a rule of thumb, products of overdetermination, of a variety of causal agencies beyond the machine in question itself, rather than of the machine taken in isolation. A machine's local manifestations are generally the result of its relation to other machines in a world, not of the machine alone. Recognizing this is of especial importance in understanding the behavior of organic and social machines. Because it is machines or individual things rather than their interactions with other machines in a world that we perceive – relations or interactions, as Hume argued, being invisible (Hume 1999: 108–18) – we have an unfortunate tendency to treat local manifestations as originating *solely* from the powers of the particular machine that manifests in this way, rather than treating these local manifestations as the effect of a conjunction of a variety of different machines acting in tandem or conjunction in a world. For example, we treat the way in which features or properties of an organism's phenotype manifests itself – such as hair color – as resulting solely from the organism's genes. In this instance, we treat the organism as being the result of a sort of master plan or blueprint defined by the genes. The problem here lies not in claiming that genes are *a* causal factor, but in arguing that the genes already contain *all* the information that will determine the local manifestation or form that the phenotype will take over the course of its development. However, as theorists such as Susan Oyama have compellingly argued – not simply abstractly, but based on empirical evidence as well – the qualities an organism comes to locally manifest are not simply a product of a genetic encoding – indeed, genes are activated differently depending on the environment within which they unfold processes of protein production – but rather as a conjunction of factors ranging from genes, the nutrients an organism encounters as it develops, whether or not particular proteins encounter one another over the course of their development, the presence or absence of light, temperatures, pressures, and so on (see Oyama 2000). The local manifestation of the organism is quite literally overdetermined.

What is true of organisms is true of the local manifestations of most machines. While the machines that locally manifest themselves indeed contribute to those local manifestations, the nature of those local manifestations does not arise solely from the individual machine, but from a conjuncture of machines acting in relation to one another in a world. As a consequence, agency within worlds or assemblages of machines ought to be conceived as *distributed*. As Jane Bennett writes, assemblages

> ... have uneven topographies, because some of the points at which the various affects and bodies cross paths are more heavily trafficked than others, and so power is not distributed equally across the surface. Assemblages are not governed by any central head: no one materiality or type of material has sufficient competence to determine consistently the trajectory or impact of the group. The effects generated by an assemblage are, rather, emergent properties, emergent in that their ability to make something happen (a newly inflected materialism, a blackout, a hurricane, a war on terror) is distinct from the sum of the vital force of each materiality considered alone. (Bennett 2010: 24)

The way in which a machine manifests itself in terms of its qualities, its properties, and its actions is seldom the result of its agency alone, but rather tends to be the result of many machines interacting with one another. Onto-cartography is the attempt to map this distributed agency of machines, but in cognizance that the map it produces is not identical to the territory.

In a machinic media ontology, overdetermination presents us with a Charybdis and Scylla that must be carefully navigated in the ethics of thought. Recognizing that most local manifestations are overdetermined by their interactions with other machines, we might conclude that machines are *nothing but* their interactions with other machines. In other words, we might conclude that they have no *autonomy* whatsoever. In this way we would reduce machines to their interactions or relations to other machines. We would then be led to conclude that no change is ever possible because a machine is nothing but its relation to other machines.

Recognizing that this is ontologically, empirically, ethically, and politically improbable – and even deplorable – we might take the opposite approach and hold that all machines are absolutely independent of one another, that they do not relate at all, and that what they are originates solely from each machine itself. Such an approach then leads to a rejection of how machines influence one another. This position, again, is untenable.

What we must recognize is, as Deleuze noted, that interactions are external to their terms. Machines enter into interactions, relations, with one another, but also harbor the power to break with those interactions. This is the central reason that the distinction between virtual proper being and local manifestation is marshaled. In interacting with other machines, machines do indeed undergo local manifestations that do not originate from them alone, but that arise from their relationality in a world. Nonetheless, machines always possess a virtual proper being that carries with it the capacity to enter into new relations while *remaining that* machine, and harbor inner powers that allow them to select the flows they engage with. This is especially true in the case of non-trivial machines that produce outputs that aren't simply responses to inputs, but that develop within themselves technologies that allow them to determine which flows – from both the present and past – they will respond to. Such machines carry within themselves – though to varying degrees depending on the complexity of the machine – the capacity to act on their world and select what they will take from the world, rather than simply being acted upon by the world.

A first ethical prescription for onto-cartography might thus be formulated as follows: *Never reduce a machine to its interactions or relations to other machines, but always recognize that each machine carries an excess capable of breaking with its circumstances.* Every machine possesses its degree of freedom, though this degree of freedom will vary depending on whether or not the machine is a trivial or non-trivial machine, a rigid or plastic machine. A clam, certainly, has more degrees of autonomy or freedom to both select its environment and act on it than a rock, while a dolphin has a greater degree of freedom than a clam. What we must recognize, however, is that every machine can break with existing contexts either through its own will or contingent natural events, and enter into new relations. In these new relations, the machine might very well display hitherto unexpected powers. We must thus take great care not to reduce machines to their relations.

Lucretius expresses this point with great beauty in *De Rerum Natura*. As he writes:

> Whatever exists you will always find connected
> To these two things, or as by-products of them;
> *Connected* meaning that the quality
> Can never be subtracted from its object
> No more than weight from stone, or heat from fire,
> Wetness from water. On the other hand,
> Slavery, riches, freedom, poverty,
> War, peace, and so on, transitory things
> Whose comings and goings do not alter substance –
> These, and quite properly, we call *by-products*.
>
> (Lucretius 1999: 33)

Lucretius's point is that there are properties that belong to the things themselves and properties that arise from the thing's relation to other things. The weight of a thing is a property of the thing itself (Lucretius was wrong about this), while whether or not someone is a slave is a by-product of how that person is related to other persons and social systems. Because "by-products" are not *intrinsic* powers of a thing, but are local manifestations produced as by-products of a machine's relation to other machines, it is possible to change and break with these relations while remaining *that* entity. Here Lucretius articulates the core of all revolutionary thought: relations between entities are *contingent* and can be *severed*, they are not *internal* and *inseparable*. This has always been the debate: are relations external such that they are contingent and a machine can break with them, generating new local manifestations and relations between machines, or are they *internal* and *essential* such that the being is what it is only as a function of the network of relations to which it belongs? All subsequent revolutionary thought has consisted in arguing the former, while all reactionary thought – prior and after Lucretius – has argued for the internality of relations, for the relational or "natural" being of machines.

A second ethical prescription would be the exact opposite: *While we must recognize the furtive powers or autonomy of machines, we must take care not to ignore the role that relations play in the local manifestations of a machine.* Individualism is often the ideology of reactionaries. Detaching a machine from the world or set of relations or interactions within which the machine operates, the reactionary then attributes the local manifestations of the machine to the essence of the machine. "The machine could not have acted otherwise, because it was in the essence of the machine to act in that way." In this way, the reactionary enjoins us to attend to the moral culpability of the machine alone, ignoring any context in which the machine acts. But we must also recognize that machines act in a world, in a set of relations to other machines, and that their local manifestations are generally overdetermined by these relations to other machines. Agency and local manifestations produced solely by generative mechanisms rather than conjunctions of machines are *rare*. Individual agency is not something that is *given*, but something won, often at great cost and in highly improbable circumstances. It is irrational and reactionary to treat the exception as the rule.

Third and finally, above all, we can conclude that ethically overdetermination enjoins us to *be cautious*. Our discoveries about how generative mechanisms behave in *closed* systems can lead us to believe that they will always behave in this way in *open* systems. Yet overdetermination teaches us that because generative mechanisms can generate new effects when they enter into interactions with other generative mechanisms such as what happens when hydrogen and water bond, we should exercise caution as to how a generative mechanism will behave when introduced into a new open system. As Spinoza said, "we never know what a body can do," and this is above all the case when machines are introduced to other machines. As a consequence, simply because a machine has produced local manifestations of one kind in a particular *closed* system, we shouldn't assume that the outputs will be the same when introduced into an assemblage of machines. Agency is distributed and the distributive nature of agency should lead us to exercise both a softer hand with the actions of particular agents and a caution when introducing agents into a new system.

Note

1. For a discussion of the importance of cultural codes with respect to class positions see Bourdieu (2002).

7

Gravity

The Gravity of Things

A delicate problem arose with the publication of Newton's *Philosophiae Naturalis Principia Mathematica* in 1687. On the one hand, Newton's concept of gravity gave us the first rigorously predictive theory of motion. For the first time in history, we were able to carefully predict the motion of planets, when comets would return, and where our cannonballs would land. With an equation composed of three simple letters, Newton was able to discover a set of constants underlying all motion ranging from the motion of the planets and stars to a leaf falling from a tree. The problem was that gravity's ability to exercise this influence on entities at a distance was entirely mysterious. How could the Moon, for example, influence ocean tides on Earth when there is no direct interaction between them? In *Principia Mathematica*, Newton had discovered much about how gravity *functions*, yet the *mechanism* of gravity remained unknown. Indeed, within the Newtonian framework we weren't to ask questions about *how* gravity functions at all. It was enough that Newtonian theory could make accurate predictions about the movement of planets, comets, moons, and so on. It was enough that it allowed us to get our cannon balls where we wanted them. How gravity was able to affect objects in this way was set aside as a question in the euphoria of the new predictability occasioned by these simple equations, these few letters and symbols, which now allowed us to predict the movement of objects.

The problem was simple. Naturalistic and materialist thought has always argued that in order for a causal interaction to occur between two entities, there must be a *direct* interaction. One entity must *touch* the other to affect in it. In a masterpiece that was nearly destroyed by the Roman elite and Christian church (see

Greenblatt 2012), the great Roman poet-philosopher Lucretius gives voice to this principle: "Our starting-point shall be this principle: *Nothing at all is ever born from nothing* . . ." (Lucretius 1969: 24). Such is the maxim of every genuine materialism. Lucretius's thesis was that in order for one entity to affect another there has to be a real material interaction between the two. With this axiom he challenged all superstition and broached the possibility of a rigorous science of causes. If Lucretius's first axiom was so anathema to all superstition, then this is because it undermined the idea of magic or action at a distance. For example, within a Lucretian framework, a spell or curse cast against another person in the absence of that person could have no effect because there is no material interaction between the enunciation of the spell and the person. You cannot step on a crack and break your mother's back. In short, any materialism worth its salt holds that in order for two entities to interact, they must either materially touch as in the case of a baseball hitting a window, or some sort of material information must pass between them as in the case of an electric current passing between the telephone of a person located in New York to another person's telephone located in Paris. Materialism means that there are no shortcuts where relations are concerned. In order for two things to be related, it is necessary for them to materially interact in some way or another.

It is on the basis of a thesis such as Lucretius's first axiom that Newton's theory of gravity was so disturbing. For like absurd beliefs such as the idea that you can step on a crack and break your mother's back, Newton's gravity appeared *occult*. How is Newton's thesis that the Moon and Sun are responsible for the tides any different than the idea that somehow a prayer at a distance can heal a person? How is it possible for one entity to affect another without the two touching in some way or other? Newtonians appealed to the concept of force to account for gravity, but it was difficult to see how force could be anything but an occult or magical agency insofar as no one could see how one thing could exercise force on another from a distance. How can one entity act on another without touching that entity?

It was in the context of questions such as these that Einstein's general theory of relativity constituted such a revolution. While Einstein, like Newton, did not yet provide a mechanism for gravity – we are only now beginning to unlock the mechanism of gravity through the discovery of the Higgs-Boson – he did go a long way towards demystifying the phenomenon of gravity by freeing it from the concept of force. Indeed, what Einstein showed is that gravity is not a force at all, but is rather a *curvature* of space-time produced by the mass of objects. Within the Einsteinian framework, gravity is not a force that *attracts* and *repels* other objects, but rather is an *effect* of how the mass of objects curves space-time. The Moon orbits around the Earth not because it is simultaneously attracted to and repelled by the Earth, but rather because the mass of the Earth curves space-time, creating a *path* that the Moon follows in its movement along a straight line, a line that is straight along the surface of a curve. To visualize this, imagine a bed sheet upon which a cantaloupe has been placed. The cantaloupe curves the surface of the sheet in such a way that if an orange is placed in the field of that curvature it will follow that path as it rolls along the sheet. Gravity is not a force, but is rather a field or a topology that other objects follow in their movement.

As Bruno Latour has noted, we encounter a similar problem in the social sciences and social and political thought. Latour distinguishes between what he calls the "sociology of the social" and the "sociology of associations." The sociology of the social appeals to the "social" as a sort of stuff or agency that explains states of affairs. As he writes

> [w]hen sociologists of the social pronounce the words "society," "power," "structure," and "context," they often jump straight ahead to connect vast arrays of life and history, to mobilize gigantic forces, to detect dramatic patterns emerging out of confusing interacts, to see everywhere in the cases at hand yet more examples of well-known types, to reveal behind the scenes some dark powers pulling the strings. (Latour 2005: 22)

According to Latour, the sociology of the social confuses ". . . what they should explain with the explanation. They begin with society or other social aggregates, whereas one should end with them" (ibid.: 8). Terms such as "power," "society," "structure," "context," "social force," and so on are treated as explanations, when they are the very thing to be explained. We thus get a situation similar to that of Newtonian physics. We appeal to social force or power as if these things explained the patterns we find in the world about us, when force and power are the things we need to explain. What we need to explain is what holds worlds together and why they hold together as they do, for as we saw, every machine and every world is haunted by the threat of entropy.

When faced with the question of what holds worlds together, onto-cartography's answer is gravity. However, while the concept of gravity developed here includes that examined by the physicists, it is much broader. In onto-cartography, the term "gravity" replaces concepts such as "force" and "power" common in the humanities and social sciences. The reason for this is twofold. On the one hand, the concept of "force" is too occult to be of much analytic use in the analysis of worlds. Just as the Newtonians encountered the problem of how two entities could influence one another when they don't materially interact, the concept of force as it is deployed in the social sciences leaves us with very little in the way of a material account of how society, signs, language, economics, and so on, can affect machines in the way they do. The situation is similar here to what Hegel describes as "formal ground" in the *Science of Logic* (Hegel 1969: 456–8). Hegel refers to these sorts of explanations as "tautological" because the ground given for the phenomenon is the same as the phenomenon itself, though in a veiled sense. By way of example he remarks that

> [t]he sciences, especially the physical sciences, are full of tautologies of this kind which constitute as it were a prerogative of science. For example, the ground of the movement of the planets round the sun is said to be the *attractive* force of the earth and sun on one another. As regards content, this expresses nothing other than what is contained in the phenomenon, namely the relation of these bodies to one another, only in the form of a determination reflected into itself, the form of force. If one asks what kind of a force the attractive force is, the answer is that it is the force that makes the earth move round the sun; that is, it has precisely the same content as the phenomenon which it is supposed to be the ground. (Ibid.: 458)

While we do not share Hegel's view that tautological explanation or formal ground is the special prerogative of the physical sciences, we do recognize the problem that he alludes to. When asked why, for example, social relations take the particular form they take such as a particular percentage of people in a state of poverty or unemployment localized in a particular geographical location, we're referred to social forces as the ground of this local manifestation. Yet all we've been given here is a tautologous explanation of the phenomenon or local manifestation that merely repeats, in different words, what was to be explained. We're not told *how* social forces do this. In short, we are given an *occult* explanation of the local manifestation we wished to ground (ibid.: 459). It is our hope that the concept of gravity as discussed in what follows goes some of the way towards ameliorating this problem.

On the other hand, the concept of power suffers similar problems. Not only does power tend to be deployed in an occult fashion to explain social phenomena, but it also suffers from the drawback of being overly anthropocentric in its connotations. The concept of power draws our attention to how narratives, signs, discourses, language, and human institutions are formative of social relations. It is not that this is wrong, but that – as theorists and historians such as Fernand Braudel, Marx, Bruno Latour, Deleuze and Guattari, Jane Bennett, Manuel DeLanda, Stacy Alaimo, and a host of others have shown – these explanations are too restrictive, largely ignoring the plane of content as discussed in Chapter 5. Social assemblages also take the form they have as a result of the distribution of rivers, ocean currents, disease epidemiologies, local resources, the configuration of mountain ranges, weather patterns, the distribution of natural resources, altitudes, and so on. The concept of power leads us to focus too exclusively on the plane of expression to the detriment of the plane of content. What we need to think, however, are the entanglements and interactions of machines from the plane of content and expression with one another. The rhetorical advantage of the concept of gravity over terms like power and force is that it gives an all-purpose term capable of straddling both humans and non-humans, the social and the natural, so that we avoid fixating on the cultural. Gravity is as operative in the world of a deep ocean volcanic vent as it is in the social dynamics of an institution like a government agency.

We must be careful not to take the term gravity too literally. What I wish to capture with the onto-cartographical concept of gravity is the way in which one machine influences the movement and becoming of other machines, as well as the interactions possible between machines. Thus, with Einstein, the onto-cartographic concept of gravity conceives gravity as the manner in which one machine bends the space-time movement and becoming of another entity. The similarities end there, however. For Einstein gravity pertains solely to the movement of bodies along a spatio-temporal trajectory produced by the manner in which that body bends space and time. Within an onto-cartographical context, by contrast, gravity refers to machinic mediations as diverse as how a particular signifier might organize a person's life, how features of a particular diet might play a key role in the development of their body, how particular discourses and institutions structure social relations, and so on. In short, there is, in the onto-cartographical sense, a gravity proper to phenomena as diverse as chemical, biological, meteorological, and semiotic processes. For example, the Sun exerts profound gravity on the planet Earth not simply because of the way in which it bends the fabric of space, determining the orbit of the planet, but also because all organic and social life is dependent on energy ultimately derived from the Sun. Questions of energy drawn from the Sun refer not so much to physics as chemistry and biology. Similarly, discursive entities exercise tremendous gravity over human lives. Steven Spielberg depicts this sort of discursive gravity to great dramatic effect in his 2004 film *The Terminal.* There the character of Viktor Navorsky is unable to leave the JFK International Airport because his home country of Krakhozia has fallen into a revolution, resulting in a breakdown of diplomatic relations with the United States. Here Navorsky has been caught in a gravitational field defined not by the mass of large bodies like the Moon, but rather by signifiers, revolutionary pronouncements and actions, diplomatic relations, the existence or non-existence of nations, and the policies of Homeland Security in the United States. This gravity is of a semiotic nature, and plays a key role in both the range of his movement, how his relations to other machines come to be organized, and his becomings.

The first point to note is that the social is not something *over and above* the beings that *compose* the social. Just as in the case of worlds where a world is nothing other than the beings that compose the world, the social is not a container. As Latour remarks:

> In most situations, we use "social" to mean that which has already been assembled and acts as a whole, without being too picky on the precise nature of what has been gathered, bundled, and packaged together. When we say that "something is social" or "has a social dimension", we mobilize one set of features that, so to speak, march in step together, even though it might be composed of radically different types of entities. This unproblematic use of the word is fine as long as we don't confuse the sentence "Is social what goes together?",

with one that says, "social designates a particular kind of stuff". With the former we simply mean that we are dealing with a routine state of affairs whose *binding* together is the crucial aspect, while the second designates a sort of substance whose main feature lies in its *differences* with other types of material. We imply that some assemblages are built out of social stuff *instead* of physical, biological, or economical blocks, much like the houses of the Three Little Pigs were made of straw, wood, and stone. (Latour 2005: 43)

There is no distinct sort of stuff that composes the social. Rather, the social is *nothing more* than the way in which different types of machines are bound together in an assemblage. The social *is* power lines, roads, mountain ranges, rivers, people, animals, factories, microbes, computers, spirits, money, satellites, soccer balls, gods, signs, laws, liturgies, sporting events, television shows, fluorescent lights, buildings, groups, institutions, flees, and rats. We are thus in a position to understand what Latour has in mind by the "sociology of associations." In a sociology of associations one investigates how machines are bound together, how they are associated to form certain low entropy and negentropic patterns. In a sociology of associations, the "social" as social context, social force, power, and so on, doesn't explain power lines, rather power lines, televisions, lights, coal-burning power plants, governments, people, etc., explain social context and power.

The second point we must understand is that because of this the social is not a *distinct domain* that we could investigate in isolation from other domains. The social is not some special sort of stuff, some special domain, that could be separated out for isolated investigation from chemistry, biology, electrical engineering, and so on. Wherever we have associations, we have the social. Thus we must reject that tradition that places the social on one side and the natural on the other. As Latour describes it

[a]ccording to tradition, the social actor endowed with consciousness, speech, will, and intention, on the one hand, has to be distinguished from the thing that obeys causal determinations, on the other. Although they are often conditioned, even determined, human actors can nevertheless be said to be defined by their freedom, whereas things obey only chains of causality. A thing cannot be said to be an actor, in any case not a social actor, since it does not *act*, in the proper sense of the verb; it only behaves. (Latour 2004: 73)

On the one hand, we are told that there is the domain of the social that is characterized by freedom, normativity, beliefs, intentions, will, ideologies, meaning, languages, laws, and so on. On the other hand, we are told that there is the domain of nature composed entirely of non-human things defined by mechanical causality. Investigations of the social are, within this tradition, to restrict themselves solely to the former. To investigate the social is here to investigate meaning, intention, norms, ideologies, and language.

But if it is true that the social is nothing over and above the beings or machines that compose it, domains can no longer be separated in this manner. While it is indeed true that a number of social worlds will contains beliefs, norms, representations, language, and ideologies as binding components in their assemblages, they will also contain automobiles, rice, twinkies, weather events, and a variety of other non-human actors. If we ignore the latter we will never understand why assemblages are organized as they are. We will never understand the gravity that binds machines together in a world. The social is not a specific sort of stuff, but is another word for the "ecological." A social assemblage is an ecology.

At this point, however, we must take great care not to confuse the thesis that flees, rats, malaria and bubonic plague bacteria, power lines, and Hurricane Katrina *belong* to the social, with the claim that they are *socially constructed.* In their influential book *The Social Construction of Reality*, Peter Berger and Thomas Luckmann attempt to demonstrate that the machines that populate the world are in fact *constructed* by society (see Berger and Luckmann 1967). In this way they subordinate all other machines to representations, norms, intentions, beliefs, and language. It is these agencies that are to explain everything else. In including non-human machines as members of social assemblages, onto-cartography claims something quite different. It does not claim that Hurricane Katrina is *socially* constructed, but that Hurricane Katrina is a *real* actor and participant in the production of social relations *as* a hurricane. The powers of Hurricane Katrina arise not from how we *represent* it, they are not derived from "society," but belong to the hurricane itself.

Matters here, however, are quite complicated. As Latour remarks, assemblages are ". . . *simultaneously* real, like nature, narrated, like discourse, and collective, like society" (Latour 1993: 6). The Tunguska meteor of 1908 was a real machine that had its own powers, that moved in its own way, and that affected Siberia and the rest of the world as a result of hitting the Earth. It also contributed to the organization of human activities in particular ways. For example, for weeks afterwards the sky throughout Europe was so bright that you could read a newspaper outside in the middle of the night. The Tunguska meteor would have produced these effects regardless of whether or not humans existed. Yet there was also a discourse surrounding the event ranging from theories as to why no solid meteor or impact crater was ever found in Tunguska, to speculations about the event being caused by the testing of nuclear weapons or even visitations from UFOs. As we saw in the last chapter, happenings in the world are over-determined or are the product of a variety of different intersecting machines. What's important is that we recognize that non-human machines are themselves real actors, with real powers that can't be reduced to how they are represented or talked about.

Two consequences follow from this. First, our social theory must become *post-human*. This in two ways. On the one hand, social theory becomes post-human insofar as the social is no longer understood as being composed solely of things issuing from humans such as signs, discourses, norms, and representations, but also as including non-human actors such as microbes, fiber optic cables, and mountain ranges. Understanding a social assemblage entails taking into account the role played by these entities as well. On the other hand, insofar as the social consists of *nothing but* relations or interactions between machines, rather than a special "stuff" like signs, norms, beliefs, and representations that issue from *humans*, it follows that there are *non-human* social assemblages. Tribes of bonobo apes, coral reefs, and Amazonian rain forests are all social assemblages because they are all formations in which machines are bound together in a world in a particular way. They differ, of course, from social assemblages in which humans dwell, but are no less social for all that. "Social" is just a synonym for "ecology."

Second, it turns out that the sociology of associations – another name for onto-cartography – is, in fact, an investigation of machines functioning as *media* for other machines. Our tendency is to think of media as machinic domains related to the five senses such as film, television, radio, the Internet, and print. While these media are without doubt examples of media, this definition is far too restrictive. First, it illicitly restricts media to the five senses, whereas media pertain every bit as much to the movements and becomings of an entity. An automobile or horse, for example, are no less media than newspapers. The soil is no less a medium for a cucumber plant than film is a medium for a story. Second, this conception illicitly restricts media to human beings, ignoring the manner in which machines function as media for other machines even where no humans are involved. Sharks are media for remora. Wind is a medium for pollens. The Moon is a medium for all sorts of insects. The Earth is a medium for the Moon. Indeed, even humans are media for other machines such as housecats, livestock, technologies, or plaintiffs. Wherever machines relate to one another we have media relations.

The concept of media refers not to something that relates to the five senses – though that too – but rather to any relation between machines in which one machine *mediates* the structural openness, movement, or becoming of another machine. As McLuhan argues, every mediation *both* affords *and* constrains the structural openness, movement, and becoming of another machine (McLuhan and McLuhan 1998: 98–9). In other words, when one machine affords possibilities for another machine, it also closes off other possible mediations for that machine. In drawing food from the scraps of a shark's feeding, the remora closes off other possibilities of acquiring food. Over great evolutionary time the remora might come to be so mediated by the shark that it is completely unable to live apart from the shark. Thus, as Latour remarks, media

> ... are defined above all as obstacles, scandals, as what suspends mastery, as what gets in the way of domination, as what interrupts the closure and the composition of the collective. To put it crudely, human and non-human actors appear first of all as trouble-makers. The notion of *recalcitrance* offers the most appropriate approach to defining their action. (Latour 2004: 81)

A medium is both what presents an obstacle to another machine, but is also something that affords a machine particular possibilities of action – such as the seeing-eye dog for the blind man – that would not be there in the absence of that machine.

In the onto-cartographical sense, gravity thus refers to the way in which the structural openness, movement, and becomings of one machine are mediated by another machine. Here onto-cartography follows Einstein's intuition concerning gravity and the structuration of time-space. For Einstein, gravity is not an independent *force* that attracts and repulses machines to and from one another, but rather is a curvature of space and time produced by the mass or velocity of a machine. As a result of this curvature of space-time, other machines are led to follow the path of this space-time. This is how it is with all assemblages of machines. Machines are bound together in a variety of different ways and form associations as they do because other machines structure the space-time paths along which they move. In other words, machines create *fields* that organize the structural openness, becoming, and movement of other machines. The difference here is that where Einstein's account of gravity pertains only to mass, the onto-cartographical concept of gravity refers to physical motion, as well as fields produced by signs, chemistry, the topography of surfaces, technologies, and so on. Once again, the term "gravity" is here chosen because it allows us to escape the humanistic connotations of terms such as "power." In this regard, the concept of gravity proposed here includes all of the discursivist and practice-based elements of concepts of power proposed by theorists such as Foucault and Bourdieu, while also helping us to recognize the power that things themselves exercise – by virtue of what they *are*, not by virtue of how we symbolize or represent them – both on us and on each other. My hope is that the term "gravity" is unfamiliar enough to allow us to discern other forms of power not often recognized in theoretical frameworks focused on discursivity and practices.

To understand the onto-cartographical concept of gravity and media, take the example of the Brazil nut or *Bertholletia excelsa*. There has been very little success in domesticating Brazil nuts because they require a very complex sociology of associations or ecosystem in order to reproduce. As a consequence, Brazil nuts must be harvested from the forest rather than grown on farms. The flowers of Brazil nut trees have a very heavy lid that only certain insects can lift (PBS 2008). Only bees of a certain type have the strength to lift this flap and therefore transport Brazil nut pollen from flower to flower (Mori 2008). However, these bees, in their turn, are only attracted to orchids of a certain type that grow in the vicinity of these trees that are crucial to the mating of the bees. Yet this is not all. Brazil nuts themselves are found in a very hard container that holds 8–24 seeds. For a long time biologists were perplexed as to how the tree managed to reproduce because the shell of the seed container was so hard that it was difficult to see how any of the surrounding animals could open it to carry off the seeds. Eventually it was discovered that the agouti, a large rodent like a guinea pig with very sharp teeth and strong jaws, is among those able to open the super-hard shells of the tree's fruit. They then carry them off and bury them elsewhere like squirrels burying nuts in preparation for winter. Bees, orchids, and agouti are all *media* for the Brazil nut tree. They mediate its existence, both affording certain possibilities of motion and becoming such as reproduction, while also constraining their being by making it very difficult for them to grow and reproduce anywhere else. Bees, orchids, and rodents thus exert a sort of gravity upon Brazil nut trees that define their movement and becomings.

The Brazil nut tree grows where it does because it has evolved in such a way that it is caught in a series of gravitational fields involving orchids, bees, and agouti that determine where it can and cannot grow. These fields bring a variety of machines together into a social assemblage. However, that social assemblage isn't limited to the trees, rodents, and orchids, but also brings together humans in particular ways. Brazil nuts bring in about $44 million to South American countries annually (Taylor 1999). As such, they constitute a substantial source of income for indigenous peoples that harvest the nuts. However, because harvesting the nuts requires people to enter the jungles, they are brought into contact with jaguars, poisonous vipers, and a variety of different diseases. Moreover, territorial wars arise between different groups over possession of the valuable trees (ibid.). The trees themselves generate a gravitational field that draws people together in particular ways insofar as they are dependent on the nuts for both food and income, and also create paths along which humans come into contact with other organic machines such as vipers. As climate change has intensified, the trees themselves have become endangered because organisms they rely on to reproduce have become endangered. Should these trees become extinct the entire social assemblage reliant on these ancient giants will itself undergo massive transformations in its organization.

The Brazil nut tree thus functions in a manner analogous to what Lacan called a "quilting point" (see Lacan 1993: 258–70). It creates or quilts together an ecology of machines, drawing together people, tribes, animals, plants, economies, and nations. However, it is also caught in the gravitational fields of other machines that function as its "condition of possibility" (the bees, rodents, and flowers), and that also threaten its continued existence (overharvesting, automobiles, factories, and so on). These trees both condition relations, drawing machines together in various associations, and are conditioned by other machines.

This is how it always is with social assemblages or worlds. Machines generate gravitational fields that generate spatio-temporal paths along which other machines move and become. In other words, machines become *captured* in the *orbit* of other machines. Sometimes this gravitation is *symmetrical*, while at other times it is *asymmetrical*. Moreover, there can be varying degrees of symmetry in gravitational relations. The relation between Brazil nut trees and agouti is a symmetrical relation, though it is one where the tree is more dependent on the agouti than the rodent is on it. Brazil nut trees need the agouti to reproduce themselves, while agouti draw food from the Brazil nuts. Nonetheless, it is likely that were the Brazil nut tree to become extinct the agouti would be able to find food elsewhere.

Analogously, as Marx and Engels noted, the relationship between owners and workers is asymmetrical in favor of the *workers*. Owners rely on the workers to create surplus value through their production. They cannot produce that surplus value themselves. By contrast, the workers merely need the owners to provide the capital to set up factories, purchase machinery, and so on. It is an incorporeal, expressive ideology-machine that leads us to believe capital issues from owners and money rather than workers. Indeed, as David Harvey notes, if we take the Lockean theory of property seriously, there should be a point in which workers are no longer obligated to sacrifice their profit to owners. Under the Lockean theory, something becomes property because of the labor we put into it. The thing that we labor upon, in other words, becomes an extension of our own body. The factory is the owner's property because he invests in it with his capital. However, insofar as factory production produces surplus value or profit, there must come a point where the workers have entirely paid back the owner's investment, thereby entailing that the factory should become their own (Harvey 2010: 248–9). The relation between owner and worker is an "asymmetrically symmetrical" relation. Both worker and owner are dependent upon one another and therefore the gravitational relation between them is symmetrical. However, the relation between them is also asymmetrical in that owners are more dependent on workers than workers are dependent on owners. By contrast, a relation is perfectly symmetrical when two entities are entirely dependent on one another for their continued existence such that one ceasing to exist would lead to the destruction of the other.

A gravitational relation is absolutely asymmetrical when one entity is dependent on another without the other being caught in the gravitational field of that machine in any way whatsoever. Take the relation between prediction markets like IntraTrade. com and presidential candidates. IntraTrade allows you to wager money on the likely future of certain things like which presidential candidate is likely to win an election. Here the relation is asymmetrical because the traders are dependent on the presidential candidates, while the presidential candidates are not dependent on the traders. Presidential candidates would exist regardless of whether or not speculators invested money on the likelihood of each one winning an election. By contrast, the traders could not exist without machines such as presidential candidates upon which to wager.

Based on the foregoing, we thus encounter the central aim of onto-cartography. Onto-cartography seeks to map the gravitational relations between machines arising from the manner in which they mediate one another so as to determine why assemblages take on the patterned organization they possess. It seeks to determine why entities move and become as they do, why certain worlds or assemblages do not degenerate into entropy but rather maintain a particular form of organization over time, what machines produce dominant gravitational fields for other machines in an assemblage, and, above all, how we might intervene in those assemblages that we find destructive and oppressive so as to produce more satisfying and just assemblages. Such a project entails taking stock of the corporeal and incorporeal machines that populate a world, society, or assemblage, and taking account of the symmetrical and asymmetrical relations between entities that structure movement, local manifestations, and becoming in these assemblages.

Gravitational Relations Between Machines: The Objects

Depending on how one machine mediates other machines or is mediated by other machines, we can refer to it as a particular type of object. I refer to a machine as an object whenever it is mediated by another object or mediates other objects. There are roughly six types of gravitational relations a machine can occupy within an assemblage, ecology, world, or society. Machines can be dark objects, bright objects, satellites, dim objects, rogue objects, or black holes. It is crucial to note that no object is *intrinsically* one of these types of object. These characterizations are purely a matter of how a machine exercises gravity or is conditioned by the gravity of other machines. In other words, a machine can pass from being a dim object to being a bright object. One machine can be a black hole for one machine, but a satellite for another machine. Similarly, a dark object can become a rogue object, bright object, dim object, or satellite for other machines. Here the sort of gravitational relations a machine has to other objects determines what type of object it is. Because relations can change, a machine can pass from being one type of object to another. The different types of objects are crucial to the sort of mapping proposed by onto-cartography. They allow us to determine what machines are dominant in a world, symmetrical and asymmetrical gravitational relations between machines, why worlds don't fall into entropic decay, and what possibilities for change lie within a world.

It is important to note that the categorization of a machine as one type of object rather than another type of object is *relative* to the sort of assemblages we're talking about. Not only can a machine pass from being one type of object to another in a given assemblage, but *one and the same* machine can be one type of object in one assemblage and another type of machine in another assemblage. Thus, for example, a virus can be a "bright object" in a particular person's body insofar as the cellular processes of the person's body, their ability to move, their ability to think, and so on are all dominantly impacted by the presence of the virus using their cells to replicate itself. Viewed from the standpoint of the broader social world, however, this same virus can be a rather dim object insofar as it is not broadly distributed among the population of people that inhabit that world and does not significantly impact the machinic interactions or processes of the machines that populate the world. Here, despite the presence of the virus, things continue largely as before. For this reason, it is always important to specify the frame of reference within which a machine is being categorized as a particular type of object.

As we saw in our discussion of the being of machines, machines can be detached from their relations to other machines. In some instances, this will lead to their eventual destruction as in the case of a frog being detached from oxygen. In other cases, this will lead the machine to merely become dormant as in the case of an automobile detached from gasoline or electricity. We also saw that properties are *happenings* that take place within machines, not fixed features of machines. Machines are defined by their powers, not their properties. Properties or qualities can be locally manifested in one of two ways. They either arise from inputs arriving from outside a machine activating certain operations that produce an output as in the case of an apple reflecting red light when interacting with the input of sunlight, or they take place as a result of inputs arising from operations *within* a machine as in the case of a twitch of the muscle due to a random electrical excitation arising from inside the nervous system.

These observations allow us to imagine the *possibility* of dark objects. I emphasize the term "possibility" because if dark objects do exist, they would be so thoroughly unrelated to other machines – most importantly, ourselves – that we would have no idea of their existence whatsoever. These would be objects that exist, that are out there floating about in the void, but that are entirely invisible to all other objects. An absolutely dark object would have to meet two criteria. First, they would have to be so thoroughly unrelated to other machines that they would receive no inputs generating local manifestations. Second, their powers or operations would have to be *dormant* such that they generated no inputs from within themselves. Because such objects would receive no inputs from other machines, nor produce any inputs from within themselves, they would thus undergo no local manifestations. They would be there in the world without appearing or manifesting themselves in any way. A dark object is an object so thoroughly withdrawn (to use Graham Harman's Heideggerian terminology) that it doesn't manifest itself or appear in the world at all.

Like spirits or ghosts, it is therefore possible that any given assemblage is haunted by all sorts of dark objects that do not manifest themselves and that have no effect on the other machines of the assemblage whatsoever. These objects would exist without appearing in any way. Perturbed or provided with just the right input, they would suddenly erupt into the world, affecting the other machines that compose that world in all sorts of ways. Of course, the existence of dark objects is merely an ontological *possibility* following from the thesis that machines are external to their relations and the claim that properties or qualities are activities performed by machines rather than intrinsic features that are always present. We have no way of knowing whether or not dark objects in fact exist because a thing must locally manifest itself in response to a perturbation (input) for us to have knowledge of it.

If, then, we have no way of knowing whether or not dark objects exist, why even suggest the possibility of a machine so withdrawn that it exists and is there without manifesting any qualities or properties whatsoever? Is not the idea of dark objects an outlandish metaphysical concept of the most disreputable sort? Is it not the idea of a being deduced from reason, from a philosophical system, without any empirical justification whatsoever? The concept of dark objects is of value for three reasons. First, we must distinguish between *absolute* and *relative* dark objects. An absolute dark object would be a machine so withdrawn that it doesn't manifest itself to *any* other machine in the entire pluriverse. It is questionable as to whether objects of this sort exist. They might, they might not. There's no way to know. However, we *do* know that there are, in fact, many *relative* dark objects. It will be recalled that a machine can be one type of object in one assemblage and another type of object in another assemblage. Granting this, a machine can be a dark object for one assemblage, while manifesting itself for other things. Examples of such machines would be electromagnetic waves that humans can't perceive such as ultraviolet light or neutrinos that are unable to interact with most forms of matter with which we are familiar due to their neutral electric charge. Another example of a relative dark object would be the Dead Sea Scrolls. For centuries these writings remained hidden in West Bank caves. Discovered by accident, once translated they erupted onto the world of Biblical scholarship and religious belief, calling into question our understanding of the life and teachings of Jesus. Clearly the Dead Sea Scrolls were locally manifested to all sorts of other entities that populated the caves in which they were found, but for religious and social assemblages they were unknown dark objects, waiting to be unleashed upon the world.

Returning to Ian Bogost's concept of alien phenomenology, the concept of dark objects reminds us not to reduce the world to the machines that we happen to encounter in the world. As we seek to understand the behavior and actions of other machines, including other humans, it reminds us that they might be responding to agencies that we ourselves don't register. In this regard, we ought not jump to the conclusion that mysterious behavior indicates irrationality or madness, but ought to hold open the possibility that perhaps agencies are at work that we ourselves do not register.

Second, there's a sense in which every machine contains a little bit of darkness within it. There's something a bit demonic in every machine. Our tendency is to reduce objects to those properties or qualities that happen to manifest themselves to us under specific gravitational conditions. However, as we have seen, machines are defined not by their qualities but by their powers, capacities, or abilities. A machine is what it *can* do, not the *doing* that it happens to do under particular circumstances. The domain of a machine's power is always greater than how it happens to locally manifest itself at any given point in time and under one particular set of circumstances or gravitational relations to other machines. Every machine harbors within it the capacity to locally manifest itself in different ways under different sets of worldly, ecological, or environmental conditions. As Harman likes to say, every object has subterranean volcanic powers waiting to be unleashed upon the world. The concept of dark objects reminds us not to reduce machines to how they locally manifest themselves in a particular world, recognizing instead that as relations between machines change machines can come to behave in very different ways.

Third and finally, the concept of dark objects reminds us to be attentive to what Lucretius called "the swerve" or the *clinamen*, or, in Batesonian terms, to be attentive to the fact that the map – which is itself a machine that acts on other machines – is not the territory. As Lucretius writes:

> I'd have you know
> That while these particles come mostly down,
> Straight down of their own weight through void, at times –
> No one knows when or where – they swerve a little,
> Not much, but just enough for us to say
> They change direction. Were this not the case,
> All things would fall straight down, like drops of rain,
> Through utter void, no birth-shock would emerge
> Out of collision, nothing be created.
>
> (Lucretius 1969: 58)

Whatever the merits of Lucretius' concept of the *clinamen* might be, it at least reminds us to exercise caution in believing that our maps or theories are complete by virtue of the recognition that often the unexpected and surprising happens. Machines swerve by virtue of darkness. That darkness might consist of hitherto unknown powers residing in machines that only manifest themselves when the machine is perturbed in the right way. Alternatively, the swerve might result from a machine that has not before manifested itself in a particular assemblage, but that, under the right circumstances, suddenly erupts in that world like an alien visitation. Like Hamlet to Horatio, the concept of dark objects reminds us that there's more in heaven and earth than what is mapped or currently operational within a particular world.

Where a dark object is a machine that either does not manifest itself to any other entity in the pluriverse or that does not manifest itself in a particular assemblage (thereby producing no gravitational effects), a bright object is a machine that gravitationally overcodes the local manifestations, movements, and becomings of other machines. A prime example of a bright object would be the Sun. As Reza Negarestani has argued, the Sun overcodes everything on the planet Earth (see Negarestani 2008). Contrary to popular belief, the Sun is not bright because it illuminates the daytime sky. Or rather, this is only one dimension of the Sun's brightness. No, the brightness of the Sun consists in the manner in which it captures the Earth and other planets in its orbit, the way in which all life on the planet is dependent on its electromagnetic waves, and the way in which the fuels upon which we rely are derived from sunlight. What is oil, coal, and natural gas if not sunlight transformed into black ooze and gaseous clouds? Within the frame of reference of the Earth, all politics is ultimately, in one way or another, solar politics. The Sun captures all life on Earth in its orbit, in its gravity – a gravity consisting not only of its literal gravity, but also the gravity of the energy upon which life is dependent – serving as a necessary condition under which life, technology, and social assemblages inhabited by humans among other things are able to exist. Indeed, the planet would not have accreted at all were it not for this star. The brightness of the Sun consists in how it organizes the movement of the Earth, the other planets, comets, asteroids, and life.

A bright object is an object that overcodes, not overdetermines, the movements, local manifestations, and becomings of other objects. Between a bright object and other machines, there is an asymmetrical gravitational relation. Bright objects *capture* other

machines in their orbit, organizing or structuring their local manifestations, their movements, and their paths of becoming. Those
machines caught in the orbit of a bright object thereby become *satellites*. The relationship between young children and their parents
is the relationship of a satellite and a bright object. In their frailty
they are dependent in nearly every way on their parents. While the
actions and choices do not *determine* what the child will be – every
parent knows that Skinner was wrong – they do substantially
organize the paths along which the child moves and develops. This
structuration extends to everything ranging from diet, to clothing,
to the entertainment the child is exposed to, to hygiene, to sleep
schedules. Moreover, the child's parents are a field they must navigate. Children are caught in a web of the parents' desires, regrets,
neuroses, beliefs, obsessions, values, and quirks. All of these things
form so many resistances, so many obstacles, that create paths the
child moves along. It is not that the child internalizes these things,
becoming a copy of its parents through *mimesis*, but rather these
things are warps and depressions in the world that the child navigates as it develops.

Rice is yet another example of a bright object. The rate at which
it develops, how it is planted, how it is harvested, the number
of times it can be harvested a year, all contribute strongly to the
organization of people's lives that rely on rice. These properties of
rice influence the sort of labor people engage in, the tools that they
fabricate, their bodily postures, how their bodies develop as a function of rice-heavy diets, the sorts of social relations that develop
between people, and feast and famine as a result of weather events
that affect harvests or diseases that befall plants. Once the technology or practices are developed allowing rice to be planted in water,
new problems emerge. Harvest sizes are increased through these
new planting methods, but the water in which the rice is planted
also becomes a nest for diseases. Now these diseases must be dealt
with. Rice organizes the space-time of these people's lives, especially before the advent of robust international trade and things
like supermarkets. It organizes the rhythm of days, when things
are done, how long they're done, cooking methods, and a variety
of other things besides.

In small towns where jobs are scarce, particular businesses can
function as bright objects. Here, for example, we might think of
the small West Virginia coal-mining towns where "the company"
owned not simply the mine, but the general store, the homes, and

everything else. With alternative jobs far away and people tied to friends and family in regions, "the company" becomes a bright object capturing everyone in its gravity. "Company scrip" is a perfect example of how companies that owned coal-mining towns captured their employees within their gravity. Rather than issuing federal tender, companies would instead issue money owned by them (scrip) that could not be exchanged for federal currency and that could only be redeemed for goods at the company stores. In this way, employees and their families became entirely dependent on the company for all their food, clothing, and shelter, and were without the means to leave the town because scrip couldn't be exchanged for regular currency. One's only option was to work for the company in some form or another, and the necessities of shelter, food, clothing, and energy could only be acquired through the mediation of the company. Everyone became a satellite caught in the orbit of the company.

Perhaps the brightest object of all today is oil. There is nothing on the planet that is not somehow caught in its gravitational pull and transformed into a satellite by it. The transportation we use and our agriculture are all organized along the paths created by oil. Economy fluctuates in response to oil speculation and shifts in the availability of oil. Many of our technologies are dependent on oil through the plastics they use. Nations are brought to war over oil. And, of course, the climate change wrought by the burning of fossil fuels transforms the weather, creating a drought here, tornadoes there, hurricanes here, while also endangering the existence of millions of plants and animals. In one way or another, all life on the planet is currently structured by paths created by oil. It is what allows us to run our technologies, to enter into contact with one another when separated by vast distances, to live in suburbs, and so on.

Bright objects are like stars. They capture a variety of other objects in their orbit, defining their local manifestations and the paths along which they move and become. They transform other machines into satellites. It is not that there is no choice for non-trivial machines caught in the orbit of a bright object. The young child, for example, can choose among the different foods offered to him by his parents or refuse to eat altogether. What he can't choose is the *field* of choices. He will eat peas *or* fish sticks *or* chicken noodle soup *or* strawberries *or* cucumber *or* cereal. The field of choices is pre-delineated by the bright object of the parent.

Likewise with oil as a bright object. The key point is that it is very difficult for satellites to extricate themselves from a bright object. The company that presides over a small coal-mining town might be brutal and oppressive, but the people of the town, being satellites, might find it very difficult to change anything in their circumstances because they lack the means to move away, or the price of severing relations with family and friends would be too high, or they lack the bargaining power to compel the company to adopt more just practices. Often we find ourselves trapped in the orbit of bright objects because there simply are no readily available alternatives. The question therefore is one of *building* alternatives that might generate lines of flight or paths of escape from these orbits.

However, in noting these things we must also take care not to assume that bright objects are necessarily oppressive. As media in which satellites are caught, bright objects can afford as many possibilities of local manifestations, movements, and becomings as they constrain. We see this in the case of the Sun that is among the conditions for the possibility of the infinite diversity of life on the planet Earth. Similarly, unions and revolutionary parties can function as bright objects that create paths opening the way for lines of flight from the despotic grip of other bright objects. Whether or not a bright object is oppressive is something that can only be decided on a case-by-case basis.

In contrast to bright objects and satellites, some objects in assemblages can be classified as dim objects. Dim objects are objects that exist in assemblages or gravitational fields, but that exercise very little gravity of their own. As Badiou might put it, these are objects that only very faintly appear in a world (see Badiou 2006: 153–68). Alternatively, we can equate dim objects with what Rancière calls "the part of no part." Rancière characterizes the part of no part as those members of a collective that are there in a collective, but that have no voice, nor ability to participate in the collective. They are ". . . those who have 'no part in anything'" (Rancière 1999: 9). Examples of dim objects would be slaves, the homeless, the disabled, women prior to suffrage, the mentally ill, people of religions other than the dominant religion of a social assemblage, atheists, the proletariat, non-heterosexuals, illegal immigrants, and so on.

Clearly there are degrees of dimness ranging from a machine being a nearly full-blown satellite to being an almost entirely dark object. Thus, for example, if we compare the disabled and the homeless, it is clear that the disabled appear much more intensely in worlds than the homeless. The disabled have been able to organize, to enact legislation that fights discrimination, to form organizations, and so on. While they are often overlooked and societies around the world continue to be organized around those deemed "able," they have nonetheless been able to organize in ways that have exerted significant gravity on various social assemblages. The homeless, by contrast, radiate almost no gravity on the assemblages within which they dwell. They are there, we see them on street corners daily, but they are generally forgotten and with little voice.

We must take care not to restrict dim objects to human beings. As Jane Bennett remarks with reference to Rancière:

> When asked in public whether he thought that an animal or a plant or a drug or a (nonlinguistic) sound could disrupt the police order, Rancière said no: he did not want to extend the concept of the political that far; nonhumans do not qualify as participants in a demos; the disruption effect must be accompanied by the desire to engage in reasoned discourse. (Bennett 2010: 106)

The "police" is Rancière's name for the dominant structure of a social assemblage. As he defines it, the police is ". . . the logic that . . . counts the lots of the parties, that distributes bodies within the space of their visibility or their invisibility and aligns ways of being, ways of doing, and ways of saying appropriate to each" (Rancière 1999: 28). In short, the police is roughly equivalent to onto-cartography's gravitational fields structured around relations between bright objects and satellites. For Rancière, politics is that moment in which dim objects rise up from their faintness, speak, and challenge the police order in the name of "anyone whatsoever."

As we saw in the last section, the social and the natural cannot be tenably separated in this way. Social assemblages are composed of *both* humans *and* non-humans, and often just non-humans. There is no gravitational field or social assemblage composed solely of humans. This entails that non-humans can be among the dim objects that populate a gravitational field or social assemblage. If this is the case, then the way is opened for what might be called a "geopolitics" or a politics of the earth. As climate change intensifies and we witness the growing impact of technologies on the environment, the need for a geopolitics becomes incredibly pressing. Paradoxically, the rise of the anthropocene, or that age of the planet dominated by humans and the impact of our technologies, has increasingly brought to the fore non-human machines such as animals, plants, microbes, and weather events that were before dim and almost dark objects. For example, events like the 2010 BP oil spill bring into relief entire ecosystems, revealing the manner in which the livelihoods of many and indeed entire economies are imbricated with the non-human.

Dim objects are often the site of politics. Questions of the political often revolve around issues of how it might be possible for dim objects, those parts of no part, to become full-blown actors in social assemblages. At present, within dominant forms of cultural theory and social and political thought, non-human entities are almost entirely invisible. They are the dimmest of the dim objects. To be sure, we find exceptions to this such as the work of the new materialist feminists, the actor-network theorists, eco-theory, Isabelle Stengers, the post-humanists, and so on. By and large, however, the domain of the non-human and the role it plays in social assemblages is off the radar. Not only is this detrimental to our understanding of why human social assemblages take the form they have, but it also leaves us without a viably developed account of the political with respect to climate change. Geopolitics would include all the issues of traditional social and political thought with its emphasis on ideology critique, questions of identity, political economy, and so on, while opening the political onto the domain of the non-human, investigating how non-humans such as microbes, animals, geography, and technologies contribute to how social assemblages come to be organized through the gravity that they exert, while also striving to give voice to non-humans as beings deserving of recognition within human social assemblages.

Perhaps the most terrifying objects of all are black holes. A black hole is an object whose gravitational bending of space-time is so great that nothing can escape from it. For many thousands of years, the Earth was a black hole for the life that dwelled upon it. Until the advent of rocket technology, life was restricted to Earth. Certainly there is nothing particularly terrifying by a black hole such as this, unless we think in the long term and contemplate the extinction of the Sun many millions of years from now. However, black holes such as terminal illnesses, overwhelming drug addictions, imprisonment without recourse to any legal system for political crimes, and so on, are truly terrifying. Today many wonder whether capitalism is a black hole. As Žižek somewhere says, it is easier to imagine the end of the world than the end of capitalism. Given the tendency of capitalism to generate endless war and inequality, to undermine the ability for long-term planning, to bring about environmental devastation, and to continuously go through cycles of instability, the impossibility of moving to a more stable, sustainable, and equitable economic system would be truly demoralizing. Let us hope that black holes are rare.

Finally, there are rogue objects. The concept of rogue objects is modeled on that of rogue planets in astronomy. In 2012 astronomers discovered a rogue planet moving throughout the galaxy, unattached to any particular solar system (Kahn 2012). Like the planet Melancholia in Lars von Trier's 2011 film by the same name, rogue planets wander about galaxies, potentially entering into other solar systems. There's even speculation that there might be rogue stars and black holes (in the astronomical sense). A rogue object is a machine similar to rogue planets. Indeed, rogue planets are themselves varieties of rogue objects. Unattached to the gravitational field of any particular world, they wander in and out of assemblages, appearing as if from nowhere. In this regard, rogue objects are like the Lucretian swerve or *clinamen*. No one can anticipate when or where they'll appear, but they suddenly erupt into worlds, transforming relations between the machines that compose an assemblage.

Sometimes rogue objects appear from elsewhere as in the case of the bubonic plague that migrated from Asia to Europe as a result of trade. Hurricanes, tornadoes, earthquakes, and volcanic eruptions are all rogue objects of this sort. At other times, rogue objects will erupt from *within* worlds or assemblages, like dragons that have slumbered beneath our feet for thousands of years. Rogue objects of this sort are things such as new fashion fads, new forms of art and music, political revolutions, ideas that strike from nowhere, encounters with love, and new technologies that seem to sweep in from nowhere. In these cases, nothing about the gravitational field of the world and its historicity could have predicted that these things would have erupted in the world. Here we might think of eruptions such as the Occupy Wall Street (OWS) movement of 2011, the Arab Spring, or the emergence of a new form of art such as rock and roll. In the case of OWS, for example, American politics was organized around the gravitational field of the two-party system and the way they situated issues. Nothing suggested the possibility of a very different set of politics and questions. To be sure, traces of vectors or tendencies preceding these eruptions can always be found, but nothing about these vectors indicates that they would congeal into something new in this way.

Here it is worth noting that no one has gone further in thinking rogue objects than Alain Badiou (see Badiou 2005). Under the name of "events," Badiou conceptualizes eruptions that nowhere could have been anticipated in the world where they occur. However, while there is much that is inspiring and commendable in Badiou's theory of the event, it is our view that his theory is far too restrictive. Badiou limits events to the domains of love, politics, science, and art. While these are certainly the most interesting examples of sites where rogue objects erupt, there is no reason to suppose that a new fashion or the emergence of a completely unexpected technology is any less a rogue object than a scientific revolution. To be sure, the eruption of a new fashion is trivial when compared to a political revolution, but it is no less a rogue object or "swerve" for all that.

Rogue objects have two essential features. First, they seem to appear out of nowhere. They either arrive in a world from another world, or they result from within a world as a consequence of a series of movement vectors through which machines come together in such a way as to produce something new and unexpected. Second, and more importantly, rogue objects reconfigure gravitational relations between entities within the world in which they appear. When a rogue planet like Melancholia enters our solar system, the gravitational relations between all the planets are modified because of the way its mass curves time-space. As a consequence, Earth might either be pushed closer to the Sun or further away, turning it into a fiery hell or a frigid ball of ice. Similarly, the advent of a new technology such as the Internet transforms a variety of different social relations. People from distant parts of the globe are now brought into contact that would have never otherwise had contact with one another. Ideas spread at an astonishing rate, and new forms of organization become possible. Groups are now able to organize independent of dominant media systems and academic institutions, defining their own missions and trajectories. Economies are transformed as new forms of trade become possible and certain businesses fold as a result of the easy availability of books and films online.

As the foregoing suggests, we must take care not to treat rogue objects as inherently positive. Badiou has a tendency to treat events as necessarily affirmative and emancipatory, treating them as the mark of truth. In certain instances this will certainly be true, as in the case of Occupy Wall Street that has been vital to opening broad-based public discussions of economic inequality and injustice produced as a result of governmental policies, favoritism towards corporations, and the logic of capitalism. However, other rogue objects such as Hurricane Katrina in 2005 or the 9-11 terrorist attack can be incredibly destructive. The valence of rogue objects has to be determined on a case-by-case basis, and a number of rogue objects will be ambivalent. The Internet, for example, has certainly assembled a number of positive relations between people around the globe, but it has also created venues for child predators, contributed to pornography addictions, generated new forms of crime such as identity theft, and made it easier for hate groups to assemble. It is also possible to make the case that it has contributed to a greater sense of alienation due to the way in which it encourages people to replace real-world interactions with online interactions, and that it perhaps contributes to growing illiteracy because of the way hyperlink reading functions and the way in which it is dominated by images and video clips. A rogue object like the Internet cannot univocally be defined as positive or negative. Rather, it produces a variety of effects on other machines.

The six objects allow us to develop a more robust understanding of what onto-cartographical analysis looks like. Onto-cartography seeks to map the symmetrical and asymmetrical gravitational relations or interactions between machines so as to determine why worlds are negentropically configured as they are. This project requires taking inventory of the machines that populate or compose a world and what flows between them as inputs upon which machines carry out their operations. However, in order to engage in such an analysis it is necessary to determine the functional role that the various machines play in assemblages or worlds. One begins in such an analysis by locating the bright objects that structure gravity in a particular assemblage. From there the next step is to determine how these bright objects influence the local manifestations, movements, and becomings of satellites. In addition to this, it is necessary to determine the symmetrical and asymmetrical flows between satellites, as well as the manner in which the *bright objects* are dependent on their satellites. Analysis of the relations between bright objects and satellites allows us to determine the general ecology or gravitational structure of a world. Of special importance is the analysis of the mechanisms by which that field is structured: the role of signs, chemicals, flows of energy, geographical features, weather patterns, institutions, and so on. With a general topography of the gravitational field, we can then begin investigating how it dynamically functions to maintain certain objects as dim objects.

The aim of onto-cartographical analysis is not simply the mapping of worlds. Mappings are undertaken for the sake of intervening in worlds in ways that might render other more satisfying, more just, more sustainable assemblages possible. With good onto-cartographical maps we can begin to determine strategic sites for intervention that will either open the way to producing lines of flight or escape from despotic gravitational relations, or where it might be possible to build new forms of gravity. In this regard, we must always remember that machines are classified as particular objects as a function of their relations to other machines. Their status as this or that type of object is not an *intrinsic* feature of the machine in question. What Deleuze and Guattari say of the game of Go holds true of every machine. The most insignificant machine can pass from being a dim object to toppling a bright object and itself becoming a bright object (Deleuze and Guattari 1987: 352–3). Relations can always shift and with those shifts in relations we encounter new forms of gravity, new possibilities of local manifestation, movement, and becoming. Onto-cartography seeks to compose maps that would enhance our capacity to produce such gravitational transformations.

Subjects, Quasi-Objects and Catalysis

A long philosophical tradition beginning in the seventeenth century trains us to think in terms of subjects and objects. The subject is treated as the seat of experience, thought, agency, will, normativity, and is, quite naturally, equated with us – human beings. Objects are treated as brute clods with their properties, and are thought as governed entirely by mechanical causality. Animals are something in between. Subjects – human subjects, regardless of how transcendentally we conceive the subject – are thought as the pole of agency, while objects are treated as the pole of passivity. Subjects are those beings from which action arises, while objects are the recipients or patients of those actions. Insofar as we happen to be subjects and our most immediate relationship is our relationship to ourselves – to our own experience and cognition – this tradition concludes that philosophical speculation must begin with an analysis of the subject and then proceed to an analysis of the subject's relationship to objects.

It will also be noted that with few exceptions, while this philosophical tradition treats the subject as a seat of action, discussions of the subject present it as being a curiously passive being. While the subject is supposed to be defined by its agency, philosophical analysis instead tends to focus on the analysis of experience and judgment. Rather than investigation of the subject in movement, grappling with other things of the world as when working clay, painting, building a house, hiking, cooking, or gardening, it is instead as if the subject is reduced to a giant eyeball fixed in one place, encountering the world as a spectacle for the gaze. We find the privilege of the gaze that regards the world as a spectacle very early in the history of philosophy. For example, in the opening lines of the *Metaphysics*, Aristotle remarks that:

> All men by nature desire to know. An indication of this is the delight we take in our senses; for even apart from their usefulness they are loved for themselves; *and above all others the sense of sight*. For not only with a view to action, but even when we are not going to do anything, we prefer sight to almost everything else. The reason is that this, most of all the senses, makes us know and brings to light many differences. (Aristotle 1984: 980a25)

This is an extraordinary claim, but one that is repeated many times throughout the philosophical tradition. If, from the standpoint of machine-oriented ontology, Aristotle's privileging of vision as that sense most intimately related to knowledge seems so untenable, then this is because machines are defined by their powers, not by their qualities or local manifestations. Powers, what a machine or object can do, are never discovered by vision, but only by *acting* on machines to trigger operations so as to discover the outputs of which an object is capable when encountering a particular input. As Hume famously remarked, nothing about the brown of bread tells us of its powers to nourish. We need not take machine-oriented ontology's word for this, but can merely look at the role that the experimental method plays in the sciences. It is doing, acting upon things, not looking, that generates knowledge.

Nonetheless, the subsequent philosophical tradition will endlessly privilege vision and treat the domain of passive observation, looking, as the paradigm of knowledge production. We see this in Descartes' famous analysis of the piece of wax in the Second Meditation. We see it in Hume's analysis of impressions as the paradigmatic source of knowledge. While phenomenology does far better in analyzing movement – especially in the work of Merleau-Ponty, but also Husserl in much of his later work – there is still a privilege of the gaze in these analyses. There are probably a variety of reasons for this privilege of the gaze, some pertaining to gender, others pertaining to the class position generally enjoyed by philosophers. As psychoanalytic and feminist thought has taught us, masculine desire tends to be organized around the gaze or vision. Insofar as philosophy has been overwhelmingly dominated by men throughout its history, it is not surprising that this sense would come to be privileged. Elsewhere, Bourdieu suggests that the core assumptions of philosophical thought are intimately tied to the class position generally enjoyed by academics (see Bourdieu 2000). Generally philosophers and academics have been free from the constraints of hands-on labor and gifted with a great deal of leisure time. As a consequence of not working on things directly with their hands, they thus have a tendency to analyze the world in terms of how it's given to *thought* in cognition and vision in experience; for vision, as Heidegger noted in his brilliant analysis of curiosity in *Being and Time* (Heidegger 1962: 214–17), is that sense that comes to the fore when we are not actively engaged. If there is some validity to this critique, we might wonder how many philosophical riddles result from privileging vision and ignoring motion and direct engagement with other machines in the world.

However, the subject/object divide and the treatment of the subject as a largely passive spectator also has other odious consequences. In the domain of epistemology, knowledge becomes modeled on judgment and cognition in addition to specular experience. We come to think of knowledge as a judgment about the truth and falsity of a proposition, and reasoning as the providing of other *discursive* reasons. The paradigmatic example of such a model of knowledge would be Brandom's inferentialist theory of knowledge (see Brandom 1998). The problem here is not that these aren't important components of knowledge, but that they ignore the embodied and engaged agent grappling with other beings in the world through hands-on action. Latour has shown just why such a focus on the discursive significantly distorts our approach to questions of knowledge in works like *Science in Action* (Latour 1987). This denigration of direct engagement with machines extends as far back as Socrates' treatment of the slave boy in the *Meno*. There the command is to transform all knowledge into the signifier – the discursive – ignoring any practical engagement with the world. With the notable exception of thinkers such as Dewey in the experimentalist tradition (Dewey 2008), the focus has over-whelmingly been on judgment and the discursive to the detriment of knowledge-producing *practices* ("linguistic practices" don't count) and learning. Analysis of experiment in philosophy, for example, has received rather thin treatment in epistemological circles outside of philosophy of science.

In social and political thought and cultural studies, the subject/object split presents itself in similar ways. Like traditional epistemology that focuses on judgment and the discursive, cultural theory tends to focus on *meaning* and the signifier, both of which are, again, the cognitive dimension arising from human subjects. Because non-human objects are placed outside the domain of agency, all they can contribute is resistance to agents (humans) and their properties. Beyond that, they become mere *screens* for *human* meanings, intentions, and significations. As Stacy Alaimo so nicely puts it, "[m]atter, the vast stuff of the world and of ourselves, has been subdivided into manageable 'bits' or flattened into a 'blank slate' for human inscription" (Alaimo 2010: 1). *Sans* allowances for non-human entity's resistance to our own motion and will, cultural theory tends to treat beings other than humans as mere carriers or vehicles for our significations, inscriptions, intentions, or meanings. Like Baudrillard's magnificent *System of Objects*, the order of the day thereby becomes the analysis of how what we take non-human machines to be is really a veiled, exter-nalized, and alienated projection of *our own* meaning. In other words, in a gesture similar to Feuerbach's analysis of how our religious beliefs about god are really alienated projections of our own aspirations, we discover that what we took to be properties of objects were really projections of our own. Like Alan Parker's 1987 film *Angel Heart*, we discover that the person we were pur-suing was ourselves all along. Such is the elementary schema of the hermeneutics of suspicion issuing out of variations of Marx's analysis of commodity fetishism, Freud's analysis of the dream work, and Nietzsche's critique of morality.

It is not that these forms of analysis are mistaken. As we saw in our analysis of machines, all machines are structurally open in their own specific ways and transform inputs that pass through them as a function of their operations. Moreover, machines are generally blind to the fact that they do this. They take the outputs that they experience as identical to the inputs that initiated these operations. It thus comes as no surprise that we see the world as an alienated mirror of ourselves. As Donald Harrington depicts in *The Cockroaches of Stay More*, if cockroaches dominated the world, they would see god and all other beings in terms of their own interests and most aspired to attributes (Harington 1989). Similarly, and in a far more interesting way, Flusser and Bec use the world of the fictional vampire squid as a frame through which to evaluate humans (Flusser and Bec 2012). The problem is not that these analyses are mistaken, but rather that they lead to the evaporation of non-human agency. All the agency is placed on the side of humans, while non-humans are reduced either to mere behavior or to being screens for human inscriptions. What we need is a theoretical framework that can both integrate these points about human inscription, while also preserving the agency of non-humans. As we saw in the case of Latour, machines are simultaneously real and discoursed about, and forge social relations. We need a framework that can think these three dimensions simultaneously.

The first step in developing such a framework lies in overcoming human exceptionalism. As I argued in *The Democracy of Objects*, ontology must be flattened (see Bryant 2011: ch. 6). Rather than bifurcating being into two domains – the domain of objects and the domain of subjects, the domain of nature and the domain of culture – we must instead conceive of being as a single flat plane, a single nature, on which humans are beings *among* other beings. While humans are certainly exceptional, for us they are not *ontologically* exceptional. To be sure, they differ in their powers and capacities from other beings, but they are not lords or hierarchs over all other beings. They are beings that dwell among other beings, that act on them and that are acted upon by them. As extended mind theorists such as Andy Clark have argued – but also the new materialist feminists and actor-network theorists such as Latour – mind and culture are not special domains that

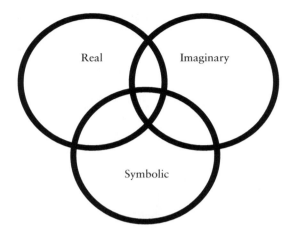

Figure 7.1 Borromean knot

can be separated from the other non-human entities of the world for special investigation. Rather, we are intimately bound up with the other entities of the world, coupled and conditioned by them in all sorts of ways. Above all, we must avoid treating the world as a field given for the contemplative gaze of humans. A world is something within which we act and engage, not something we passively contemplate.

A flat ontology must therefore be conceived along the lines of Lacan's famous Borromean knot (see Figure 7.1). A Borromean knot consists of three inter-linked rings of string fastened together in such a way that if any one ring is severed, the other two fall away. Lacan indexes each of the three rings to one of his three orders: the real, the symbolic, and the imaginary.

With the Borromean knot, Lacan's work undergoes a fundamental transformation. In his earlier work, one of the three orders had always been privileged as dominating and overcoding the others. In his earliest work, the imaginary dominated the real and the symbolic. In the work of his middle period, it was the symbolic that overcoded the real and the imaginary. In his third phase, it was the real that overcoded the symbolic and the imaginary. With the Borromean knot, no order overcodes the others. Rather, they are all now treated as being on equal footing.

This is how we need to think about the order of being. The domain of the real indexes machines. Machines exist in their own right, regardless of whether anyone registers them or discourses about them. The domain of the symbolic refers to the plane of expression, or how beings are discoursed about, signified, imbued with meaning, and so on. Finally, the domain of the imaginary refers to the way in which one machine encounters another under conditions of structural openness and operational closure. Situated within the framework of the Borromean knot, we can *simultaneously* investigate how a machine is ideologically coded as in the case of Baudrillard's analysis of objects in *System of Objects*, how a machine is phenomenologically encountered by another machine, and how a machine is a real, independent being in its own right that produces effects irreducible to how it is signified or phenomenologically given.

The second step in providing such a framework consists in resolving to discern machines in their *movement*. In philosophical reflection we have a tendency to approach beings in terms of fixed and static positions. The subject is here as a spectator on the world. The object is there as a spectacle for the subject's regard and thought. What we must strive to remember in our analyses is that all things, all machines, are perpetually in motion, even when they appear to be still. The absence of motion is always a sort of illusion produced by a particular frame of reference. For example, the table upon which I now write might *appear* to be still, but like all other objects it is falling through the void, undergoing all sorts of local manifestations in response to flows triggering operations, and undergoing all sorts of changes that are either occurring at a scale too small for me to perceive or too slow for me to register. It is only because I and the table are falling at the same rate or because the changes in the table are too slow for me to discern that I encounter the table as without motion.

Motion takes three forms: travel along a path from one point in a world to another, local manifestations, and becomings. Generally we reduce motion to the first instance, equating it with happenings such as a kitten climbing a Christmas tree. However, local manifestations are also forms of motion. We must recall that the properties of a machine are happenings that take place within it, not givens that always abide within the machine. The color of the table upon which I write, the properties of its wood, its persistence through time, and so on are all *activities* on the part of the table arising in response to inputs from other machines in the world around it. The color of the table is a local manifestation that arises in response to the light it interacts with. As the Sun moves across the sky, that color changes and fluctuates. Turn out the lights and the color disappears. The properties of the wood locally manifest themselves in terms of a variety of different environmental conditions ranging from humidity, chemicals in the atmosphere, temperature and air pressure. Changes in these conditions produce changes in how the wood locally manifests itself. If these local manifestations seem like fixed and abiding properties, then that is because the spatio-temporal gravitational field of the table's world is relatively stable. Nonetheless, within that field the activities producing these qualities are ongoing and continuous. If we never really know what a machine is until we act on it and vary its environment, then this is because we are unable to discover the powers that reside in a machine without a variation of inputs. Finally, movement can consist of becomings where the powers or capacities of a machine change as a result of inputs passing through it or arising from within it, as in the case of a caterpillar turning into a butterfly and developing the capacity for flight.

Recollection of the fact that machines are always in motion helps us to avoid reducing objects to their manifested qualities and treating them as fixed and static points presented as a spectacle for the gaze. On the one hand, it reminds us that the properties we encounter in machines are the result of *activities* arising from interactions between a machine and its environment. On the other hand, it reminds us that machines harbor furtive and hidden powers that, under different circumstances, might generate very different local manifestations. As a consequence, we come to recognize that if we wish to understand a machine we must act upon it to see what local manifestations it produces. It is only through interaction with machines that we begin to discover what they can do or the powers that they harbor within them.

Third and finally, we must problematize our understanding of the subject. Our tendency is to treat subjects as a *type* of being. Human beings or rational agents – a type of being – are subjects and everything else is an object. This is a confusion of the highest order. Subject is not a fixed attribute of a particular type of being, but rather is a transitory *role* defined *functionally* in particular situations. One can pass in and out of being a subject, sometimes being a subject, at other times being an object. Moreover, subjects need not be human at all. Functionally, animals, technologies, microbes, rocks, and balls can all be subjects under certain circumstances. If a subject is not a particular type of being but a circumstantial, functional role, then what is it? A subject is a catalytic operator that draws together machines in particular gravitational relations.

Before we discuss the subject, it is necessary to distinguish between subjects and agents. While anything can function or operate as a subject, not everything is an agent. The ontology of agency is extremely complicated, and to my knowledge we still have not progressed beyond Kant's third antinomy that states the contradiction that everything is both caused and that there are causes through freedom (see Kant 1998: A444/B472 – A451/ B479). I will not here attempt to resolve that antinomy, leaving it to intellects more talented than my own, but will merely outline the concept of agency advocated by onto-cartography. In other words, onto-cartography holds that agency or freedom exists, but does not have an ontological account of how this is possible in a universe governed by causality. A machine will be said to be an agent when it meets two criteria. First, a machine is an agent if it is able to initiate action from within itself. Thus a machine is an agent if its movement or action is not simply the result of another machine acting upon it, but rather when the local manifestation or action arises from the agent itself. Therefore, for example, a billiard ball rolling across a table is not an agent because its motion was only initiated by being hit by another billiard ball. The ball cannot initiate action of its own accord. By contrast, a cat is an agent insofar as it is able to leap up from its repose on the couch and saunter over to its food bowl. It is not the agency of another machine acting upon the cat that initiates this action, but rather the action arises from within the cat.

It's important to note two points with respect to this first criterion. On the one hand, the claim here is *not* that agentive action is *uncaused*, but that the cause of agentive action arises from within the machine. It *may* be that agentive action is uncaused in the sense of being a purely free cause originating from nothing but itself, but I have difficulty seeing how such causes can exist without appeals to magic. In this regard, onto-cartography strongly leans towards compatibilist accounts of free will that hold that free will and causality are compatible with one another. In cases of agency, the act is caused by processes originating from within the agent – it is caused by these processes – such that the action does not arise from an outside stimulus.

On the other hand, the claim that agency consists in action

arising from within the machine does not undermine a relationship between the action and an outside stimulus. A particular action might have been *occasioned* by an encounter with a particular stimulus received from another machine; however, this doesn't entail that the action is *caused* by the stimulus or information event. How an agentive machine responds to a stimulus such as an encounter with one of Shakespeare's plays, a bit of information, a discussion with another person, a buffet, and so on, is a function of operations unfolding within the machine. The response is not pre-delineated by the stimulus in the way that how the rock responds to another rock is pre-delineated by the impact coupled to the internal structure of the rock. In other words, interactions between agents and the world seem to be characterized by a *gap* between stimulus and response, where the action arises from how the agent works over the information or stimulus in acting. Whether or not the agent is *conscious* of what it is doing is secondary to whether or not it is an agent. It's unlikely that bacteria have consciousness as they seem to lack a nervous system that would allow them to be aware. Nonetheless, it seems to be that case that the way in which a bacterium moves its flagellum arises from within the bacterium itself, and is not simply a pre-delineated response to a stimulus.

Second, in order for an agent to count as an agent, it seems that they must have the capacity to act *otherwise* than they do in initiating an action or in response to a stimulus. Agents seem to have the capacity to choose whether or not to initiate an action. For example, the cat might choose not to arise from its repose, simply allowing the thought of food to pass through its mind without acting upon it. Likewise, in response to a stimulus, agents seem to have the capacity to choose how they respond or act. A person might choose to throw Shakespeare down in frustration in response to the difficulty of his language, or might choose to trudge on and work to understand him. The stimulus or information passing through the machine does not predetermine the outcome.

These remarks are very schematic and are not intended to give an account of *how* agency is possible or the mechanics of agency. To my knowledge, no one has given a non-controversial account of agency. Rather, my intention here is to merely outline what features seem necessary in order for a machine to count as an agent. Three additional points should be noted. First, it seems reasonable to hold that agency comes in a *variety of degrees*. Bacteria appear to have more agency than rocks insofar as they seem capable of initiating action from within themselves, whereas rocks cannot, while cats seem to have more agency than bacteria in that they are capable of choosing among a broader range of possible actions (or inactions), and perhaps even have the capacity to set goals for themselves as Mark Okrent argues is the case for many more advanced organisms such as dogs, octopuses, dolphins, apes, and so on (see Okrent 2007). For similar reasons, humans and other great apes probably have more agency than other organisms such as octopuses and cats. There are degrees of agency ranging from that found in organisms that aren't markedly different from thermostats such as bacteria, to more complex organisms such as bonobo apes, octopuses, humans, and dolphins. Where we might draw the line as to where agency begins in nature and where it ends is probably impossible to determine insofar as it is likely that there are many gradations between trivial, inanimate machines and non-trivial, agentive machines. For example, it is difficult to determine whether a virus is an agent like a bacterium, or whether it is an inanimate machine like a rock.

Similarly, we shouldn't assume that there are simply grades of agency between different types of machine – bacteria, plants, animals, certain technologies, and so on – there are also grades of agency over the course of a single machine's existence. For example, an adult human has more agency than a newborn infant because it has a greater capacity to set its own goals or aims, rather than simply acting out of random neuronal firings, and it has, over the course of its development, established a greater gap between stimulus and response, allowing it to deliberate over possible actions in response to flows of information.

Likewise, the adult has probably developed the capacity to form what Harry Frankfurt describes as "second-order desires and volitions," or "desires to desire" (Frankfurt 1998) in a way not possessed by the newborn infant. In this context, a desire to desire is a desire to develop a particular desire that one does not currently have. An alcoholic, for example, might have an overwhelming craving for alcohol, but nonetheless have the desire not to have this desire. Such a person does not currently have the desire not to crave alcohol, but nonetheless desires to develop this desire. If second-order desires and volitions are so important, then this is because they play a role in how agents develop. It is through a desire to have a particular desire that one in fact begins to develop such desires. While Frankfurt sees the capacity to form second-order desires as unique to humans (ibid.: 12), onto-cartography remains agnostic as to whether or not other non-human agents such as octopuses and dolphins have this capacity. Given that nature seems to be characterized by analog gradations rather than digital either/or alternatives, it seems unlikely that this capacity is restricted to humans.

Gradations of agency can arise not simply from development, but also from *circumstances* or the world within which an agent finds itself. A person paid in company scrip seems to have less agency than a person paid in federal tender. Similarly, a hawk locked in a cage at a zoo seems to have less agency than an eagle that is free. In these instances, agents are restricted in their capacity to exercise their agency and are therefore restricted in their agency. Much ideology tends to overlook the way in which agents can be restricted or limited in their agency by their circumstances, treating the agent that is so restricted as no different than an agent that is completely free of these restrictions. One of the central aims of onto-cartography is to draw attention to the way in which circumstances can structure the agential possibilities open to machines as a result of the gravity they exercise in forming paths along which the machine moves, locally manifests itself, and becomes.

Second, this concept of agency suggests that there are many more agents in the world than are often recognized. Not only are there agencies ranging from the humble bacterium up through complex organisms like chimpanzees and blue whales, but if the arguments of Part 1 are sound, we must also treat entities such as institutions – corporations, states, revolutionary groups, and so on – as agents, and increasingly it looks as if certain technologies are becoming full-blown agents rather than mere machines in the restricted sense critiqued in the first chapter. But this is not all. It is not simply that we should include larger-scale machines such as institutions and certain technologies within the category of agents, but that we should also recognize that *cyborgs* are distinct agents. The soldier on horseback with stirrups is an agent *distinct* from either the horse, the human, or the stirrups. This entity has an agency distinct from any of the machines that compose it taken alone. Likewise, the person with a gun or with a smart phone is, for similar reasons, an agent distinct from a person separated from these things. In each of these cases, the agent has a range of action that they wouldn't have when separated from these things, and we are unable to say whether the actions come from the person alone, the smart phone, or a sort of conjunction of the two. We here have, if only for a time, a distinct agent. Our tendency is to treat the agency as residing in the human *alone*, ignoring the way in which the associations among the entities that compose the assemblage generate both new capacities for action and lead to decisions that the person alone wouldn't make in the absence of their conjunction with these other machines. In the realm of political thought, this leads us to treat machines as being alike that are quite distinct insofar as they are entirely different assemblages.

Third and finally, the foregoing suggests that we need to revise our concept of *responsibility*. As Dennett notes, questions and concerns about agency often arise in the context of worries about ethical responsibility (Dennett 2003: 1). To say that a being is an agent is to say that it is responsible for its action because that action arose from itself rather than from something else. However, as the example of circumstances, institutions as agents, and cyborgs suggest, there are many instances in which agency is *distributed*. Agency is distributed when action arises from an assemblage of many distinct machines, rather than a single machine. Anyone who has sat on a committee is familiar with distributed agency. The final action taken by the committee generally does not arise from any *particular* member of the committee, but rather tends to be the unholy offspring – or compromise – of all the members. In the case of a cyborg like a person-car assemblage, it is difficult to determine whether the action arose from the driver or the car. There's a good reason for this: the person plus the car is a distinct agent from either the person or car taken alone, leading to distinct forms of action that would not be found in either taken alone. Indeed, the car taken alone would not be an agent at all insofar as it is unable to initiate action from out of itself. Recognition of distributed agency requires us to take greater care in how we allot responsibility, recognizing that a variety of agentive and non-agentive machines contribute to action.

Agents and subjects are distinct from one another. An agent is a being that is able to initiate action from out of itself and to choose among possible courses of action. A subject, by contrast, is a being that *subjects*, or that catalyzes relations between other entities (regardless of whether or not they're agents). Whereas an agent must be capable of initiating action and choosing, more or less, between possibilities in order to be an agent, a subject is a functional role that can be served by any entity regardless of whether or not it is an agent. In other words, whether or not something functions as an agent is a transitory and functional role, not an intrinsic feature of a being. No one has gone further than Serres in thinking the subject as a transitory catalytic operator. In his discussion of quasi-objects, he makes the astonishing claim that "[t]he ball is played, and the teams place themselves in relation to it, not vice versa. As a quasi object, the ball is the true subject of the game" (Serres and Latour 1995: 108). Subjects are quasi-objects in this sense. A subject or quasi-object is a dynamic quilting point that draws other machines together in a world. As the ball in a soccer game bounces and moves about the field, the players reconfigure themselves and are brought into different arrangements with one another. Similarly, their statuses change. As Serres elsewhere puts it, "[t]his quasi-object, designates him" (Serres 2007: 226). A player intercepts the ball from a player from the opposing team. Where before he pursued the other player or played defense, he now becomes the pursued. Speaking in the context of rugby, Serres remarks that the player that captures the ball is

> . . . now, a subject, that is to say, exposed to being thrown down, exposed to falling, to being placed beneath the compact mass of the others; then you take the relay, you are substituted for "I" and become it; later on, it is he who gives it to you, his work done, his danger finished, his part of the collective construction. (Ibid.: 227)

Like Deleuze's dark precursor (Deleuze 1995: 119), the ball as quasi-object weaves together divergent beings and assigns them roles or positions. The ball subjects, as it were, other beings to its own agency. As a consequence, we cannot determine whether the agency arises from the subject (the ball) or its objects (the players). Rather, the assembly of the beings is a result of both.

As the example of the ball indicates, there is no necessity to restrict the category of subject to human beings. Sometimes footballs are subjects. At other times, humans are subjects. At yet other times it will be a technology or falling rocks in an avalanche that are subject. And at yet other times, revolutionary collectives will be subjects. Moreover, a machine's status as subject is not an intrinsic feature of the machine. When the ball is thrown in the garage after a game, it ceases to be a subject. A machine's status as subject is purely occasional and functional, determined by the role it plays under particular circumstances. Any machine can, for a time, function as a subject and can just as easily cease to be a subject.

Quasi-objects or subjects quilt other beings together in assemblages or assembles them. As such, Serres remarks that "... quasi-objects [are] astonishing constructor[s] of intersubjectivity" (Serres 2007: 227). Serres is careful to note that collectives or assemblages are not simple sums of individuals. "The 'we' is not a sum of 'I's, but a novelty produced by legacies, concessions, withdrawals, resignations, of the 'I.' The 'we' is less a set of 'I's than the set of the sets of its transmissions" (ibid.: 228). Those transmissions are effectuated by the subject or quasi-object that circulates among a set of machines, weaving them together in ever changing configurations. However, in point of fact, it is not simply the production of intersubjectivity that is at work here. Intersubjectivity or relations between humans are only one form that the dynamic quilting wrought by subjects can take. The quilting forged by subjects can take place in any machinic assemblage, regardless of whether or not humans are present. Wherever some machine takes on the role of assembling other machines in a collective we are before a subject or quasi-object.

Subjects or quasi-objects thus have five features. First, subjects or quasi-objects do not define a particular *type* of being (humans or rational agents), but a functional role that a machine plays in an assemblage under particular conditions. As a consequence, second, anything can function as a subject or a quasi-object, whether human or non-human, a person, a ball, an institution, a sign, a signifier, or a collective group. Moreover, humans and rational agents can therefore be objects for subjects. Third, with the possible exception of black holes, they are transitory. "Being a subject" is a functional role that a machine plays in an assemblage under certain conditions, not abiding and permanent traits of a machine. Machines pass in and out of being subjects. Fourth, subjects are machines that function as *catalysts*. They are catalysts that assemble other machines into relations with one another in assemblages. As the ball moves about the soccer field, the players perpetually reconfigure themselves in different relations and take on different roles with respect to the ball. Fifth and finally, quasi-objects or subjects are *dynamic* quilting points. They are not fixed buttons that hold down a series of intersecting threads in a fabric, but rather are moving points that constantly reconfigure relations and states among the machines they call to assemble. This dynamism takes one of three forms (and often all three at once). It can take the form of simple travel. As the subject moves about, the other machines it assembles move about in response to it. It can take the form of new local manifestations. As the quasi-object acts, entities can locally manifest new qualities in response to the subject and the relations they enter into with one another. Finally, the subject or quasi-object can initiate new becomings. In response to the way in which they're assembled by the subject, other machines can undergo becomings in which they develop powers or capacities that they did not have before.

Quasi-objects or subjects thus have a wavelike pattern that Karen Barad, drawing on quantum mechanics, refers to as a "diffraction pattern" (see Barad 2007: 29–30). Like pebbles thrown in a pond that radiate concentric circles within the water, subjects or quasi-objects radiate turbulence that entangle other machines with one another and sets them in motion. Subjects do not proceed by identity and sameness, but rather produce difference. We must, however, exercise caution. It is unusual for a network or assemblage to contain just *one* subject as in the case of a soccer game. Rather, worlds and assemblages tend to be inhabited by a variety of different subjects, each contributing to the assembly of other machines in their own ways. As a result, we must be attentive to the way in which the waves emanating from quasi-objects or subjects intersect with one another, interfere with one another, and produce differences in and through these entanglements.

For onto-cartography, the question is thus not "how does the subject relate *to* the world?" but rather "how do subjects or quasi-objects relate machines *to one another* in a world?" In other words, among the tasks of onto-cartography is the mapping of subjects and how they assemble other machines in relations or interactions with one another. If such a mapping is crucial to the project of onto-cartography, then this is because subjects play a key role – though not the sole role – in the movements, becomings, and local manifestations that take place within worlds. Mapping the dynamic quilting points operated by subjects thus amounts to mapping the fluctuations of movement that take place within assemblages or networks.

Happenings and Events

As we have seen, with the possible exception of certain incorporeal machines such as those found in mathematics, everything that takes place in machines and among assemblages of machines is a happening. On the one hand, individual machines are perpetual happenings in three ways. First, in their struggles with entropy, machines must engage in perpetual operations lest they disintegrate and are destroyed. Every machine is perpetually falling apart and must engage in subsequent operations to maintain its organization. Second, the local manifestations of machines are *activities* arising from inputs that are received from flows issuing from within or without. The way in which a machine manifests itself is not something that the machine is, but something that happens. Third and finally, machines have an indefinite duration of existence from their point of birth where they come into existence from out of other machines to their point of death where they lose their battle with entropy and disintegrate. On the other hand, relations between machines within assemblages or worlds are perpetual happenings. Relations between machines in worlds are not abstract relations such as being to the left of something or shorter than something, but rather are interactions between machines produced through flows traveling along paths. Worlds, as fuzzy assemblages, only hold together so long as the machines that populate these worlds interact with one another through these flows. In the absence of these interactive flows, worlds fall apart and either disintegrate into entropy or take on new forms of organization.

Nonetheless, while everything in machines and worlds is a happening, it would be a mistake to suggest that the pluriverse consists of nothing but events. Following Badiou – without sharing his particular theory – we ought to reserve the concept of event for something a bit more significant than a mere happening. Things happen all the time, but the concept of event seems to signify a break, a transformation, a bifurcation. Accordingly, within the framework of onto-cartography, we will define an event as the emergence of a quasi-object or subject that systematically catalyzes *becomings* in the machines that populate a world or an assemblage.

Before proceeding, it is necessary to say a few words as to how this concept of the event differs from Badiou's. In the first place, unlike Badiou's theory of the event, events do not summon subjects who then bear fidelity to them through truth procedures; rather they *are* a particular form the subject or quasi-objects take within assemblages. Events differ from other quasi-objects or subjects in that they induce becoming in the other machines that populate the assemblage, rather than simply assembling them together or effectuating their local manifestations. Second, where Badiou's theory of the event is restricted to the realm of humans – it is humans that engage in truth-procedures pertaining to science, love, politics, and art in response to an event – the onto-cartographical conception of events places no particular emphasis on humans. To be sure, events can take place in assemblages or worlds involving humans, but they also take place in domains that don't involve humans. As a consequence, third, within the framework of onto-cartography, events have no particular ethical or political privilege. Some events are positive, others are negative, most are simply ambivalent. Unlike Badiou, onto-cartography sees no particular reason to grant events a political and ethical privilege. None of this is to suggest that we reject Badiou's particular theory of truth-procedures, as it seems to us that he presents an exemplary phenomenology of committed engagement to political truths, amorous encounters, revolutionary scientific wagers, and artistic revolutions. What Badiou indexes under his conception of events, truth-procedures, and subjects strike us as describing something real and tremendously significant. Onto-cartography rejects none of this. Rather, all that is contested is the thesis that events should be restricted to the human. Perhaps a different word is in order to distinguish Badiou's conception of event and that advocated by onto-cartography so as to preserve both without confusion, yet it is difficult to see what other term would adequately describe those ruptures that set everything else in becoming.

Within the framework of onto-cartography, then, an event is the emergence of a quasi-object that systematically leads other machines to become. It will be recalled that local manifestations and becomings differ from one another in that in the former we only encounter the exercise of a power in the production of a quality without that power or capacity changing, while in the latter a machine acquires or loses capacities or powers. A machine becomes when it gains or loses powers. Thus, for example, when garlic is sautéed in a frying pan it undergoes a becoming. It loses powers that it had in its raw state, while taking on new powers that lead it to interact with other machines or ingredients that it would not have had before. Sautéed garlic has powers that raw garlic does not, and vice versa. In the case of raw garlic, for example, you can plant a clove and it will grow a plant. Sautéed garlic does not have this power. Of course, it doesn't follow that every acquisition of a new power is the loss of another power. When a child learns, they gain new powers while retaining many of their old ones. In the case of local manifestations, there's a certain reversibility of powers that isn't found in becomings. The qualities of a simple local manifestation can come and go, while the power that allows the machine to undergo this local manifestation remains the same. By contrast, in a becoming an entirely new power is acquired.

Nonetheless, a becoming alone does not, for onto-cartography, constitute an event. Becomings happen all the time, while events are fairly rare. It is scale, not the presence of becomings, that constitutes an event. Events are marked by the fact that they set nearly all of the beings inhabiting an assemblage into becoming, leading them to develop new powers. Like ordinary quasi-objects or subjects, events assemble other entities together in new networks, but they differ from run-of-the-mill quasi-objects in that they generate extensive becomings in the machines they assemble. Perhaps the quintessential example of an event in this sense would be the Cambrian explosion that occurred about 530 million years ago. With the Cambrian explosion there was a proliferation of new species and bodily structures, while the extinction of many other species. There is a variety of different theories as to just why the Cambrian explosion occurred. Some evolutionary biologists speculate that millions of years of photosynthesis saturated the oceans and the environments with oxygen to such a degree that the conditions were set for energy expenditures allowing new body morphologies to develop. Others suggest that increases in calcium concentrations in the oceans rendered the formation of exoskeletons and bones feasible for organisms. Yet others suggest that the Earth underwent a dramatic climate change, becoming a giant snowball, thereby killing off massive numbers of species and opening the way for new niches. There is a variety of other explanations as well. Whatever theory turns out to be true, oxygen saturation, calcium concentration, snowball earth, or some other agency would be the evental operator or quasi-object that initiated a set of becomings leading to the formation of a variety of new powers and machines. Other examples of events would be the Industrial Revolution, the invention of the printing press, the advent of the Internet, climate change, and the French Revolution. In each instance we have transformations in relations between entities, practices, and forms of life, as well as the development (and loss) of powers and capacities. The Industrial Revolution, for example, led to a deskilling of labor due to the assembly line. Events are thus like supernovas that send ripples of gravity throughout the rest of an assemblage causing it to undergo diffuse and prolific transformations.

In light of the foregoing, it is important to note that events – or rather their effects – do not happen all at once. Despite what the name "Cambrian explosion" suggests, the new proliferation of life that we name with this term did not occur immediately, but over the course of millions of years. Organisms still had to pass through the process of random mutation and natural selection for these becomings to take place, and these are processes that take tens of thousands of years. Thus if we treat increased oxygen saturation in the oceans and atmosphere as the catalytic operator that initiated this process, that catalytic operator was only a condition that initiated this process, not something that effectuated it all at once. The case is similar with the Industrial Revolution. The invention of the steam engine as the subject of the Industrial Revolution did not itself immediately transform everything. Rather, it had to gradually work its way throughout the field of existing technologies, social relations, city structures, and the natural environment (coal mining and the impact of coal burning on the environment), slowly reconfiguring all of these things. Events unfold over the course of a duration, and are seldom as dramatic as 9/11. Rather, they are often furtive and quiet, winding their way through assemblages until one day we wake up and notice that everything is different. Events are a process, not a strict localization in space-time. They spread throughout an assemblage or world in waves like tsunamis from afar approaching a distant coast.

It is incredibly difficult to individuate events because of their wavelike nature and their relation to scale, and I will not attempt to provide a principle that would allow us to do so here.[1] Machines often exist within the field of events without even registering them, because of the slow, processual way in which they unfold. This is the case, for example, with the advent of the anthropocene, where the world has yet to fully register the impact of the dominance of humans on the planet. A greater difficulty lies in the issue of scale.

Events can happen at a variety of different levels of scale and can be embedded within one another. Thus, for example, a parent contracting a terminal illness can be an event for a family insofar as it leads to becomings and transformations for all the people inhabiting this assemblage. Here the quasi-object presiding over the becomings that unfold in the assemblage is not the parent, but the terminal illness. However, this event is largely restricted to the family, not the broader social field. Moreover, it is an event that is embedded in larger events such as the information revolution and the anthropocene. As with so many things, we must specify the assemblage in question to determine the way in which it counts as an event.

Following Badiou, what we seek in the domain of revolutionary politics are events. It is not merely the reconfiguration of relations through the agency of quasi-objects or subjects that revolutionary politics seeks, but rather evental interventions that set all machines inhabiting an assemblage in becoming. If this is so, then it is because, in fact, quasi-objects are always modifying relations between machines in social assemblages. As the stock market fluctuates, for example, one man becomes rich and another poor. The stock market and money themselves remain as the primary conjunctive agency. By contrast, revolutionary interventions seek to fundamentally transform the relations composing a social assemblage, how things are produced, how things are distributed, how roles are allocated, and how people interact with one another. Events of this kind can occur at a variety of different levels of scale. For example, in a small coal-mining town owned by a company, the abolition of scrip and payment in federal currency can lead to transformations in all the workers, opening entirely different possibilities of action, subjectivization, and the undermining of the power of the company. Such an abolition constitutes a small-scale event. On the other hand, revolutions such as the French Revolution lead to society-wide becomings and transformations. The political question is always that of what ought to be added or subtracted to set the assemblage in becoming, allowing a new society to come into existence.

The concept of events is important to the project of onto-cartography because it draws our attention to the *vectors* along which a world is becoming or unfolding. Onto-cartography does not simply map how machines are coupled to one another forming worlds, but also seeks to determine how these worlds are becoming or unfolding. What is the direction, as it were, in which a particular world or assemblage is developing? What are the vectors of becoming that animate a world? Identification of the events that haunt a world play a central role in the identification of these vectors.

Note

1. I owe these thoughts to a discussion with medievalist Karl Steel.

8

Earth, Maps, and Practices

Geophilosophy: A Revised Concept of Nature

Onto-cartography is a geophilosophy. I borrow the term "geophilosophy" from Deleuze and Guattari (see Deleuze and Guattari 1996: ch. 4), but here develop the concept in accord with the requirements of onto-cartography. What I wish to retain from the concept is the idea of a philosophy necessarily of the earth and restricted to the material world. Geophilosophy has connotations of the earth and territory. At the level of theory or ontological commitments, geophilosophy contends that there are only worlds and that worlds are composed entirely of machines and couplings between machines which are themselves machines. Even incorporeal machines require corporeal bodies to travel throughout the world. The medium through which incorporeal machines take on a corporeal body will have a profound effect on thought and social relations. For example, a society based on orality will be different than one based on writing. Cognition will be different as a result of these two media as well. Thus geophilosophy is committed to the tradition of materialism descended from Democritus, and advocates a strict immanence of being against all transcendence. In the final analysis, there are only material or earthly beings. Whatever matter might turn out to be – discovery of the being of matter is still an ongoing project – the matter that makes up earth is never a formless stuff awaiting formation from the outside, but rather has a form or structure internal to it or constitutive of its being.

Here language might be misleading, so it's important to proceed with care. By "corporeal" I just mean "physical," "material," or "embodied." Whatever matter might turn out to be – energy, indestructible particles, patterns, etc. – *all* machines are corporeal, embodied, or material. This entails that onto-cartography is

233

committed to the thesis that entities such as souls as conceived by Plato, forms, angels, gods, and so on don't exist. However, here it's necessary to distinguish between "part materialism" and, for lack of a better term, "emergence materialism." "Part materialists" hold that only fundamental parts – whatever they might turn out to be (Lucretian atoms, bosons, strings, etc.) – are the only things that truly exist. Here we might think of Peter van Inwagen's materialism (Inwagen 1990). For him, when a baseball breaks a window, it is not *ontologically* true that there is either a window or a baseball, because only fundamental parts truly exist. Rather, all we have here is an interaction of elementary particles. By contrast, emergence materialists hold that there are emergent entities such as trees, stars, and baseballs that, while they cannot exist without the parts of which they are composed, are nonetheless absolutely real and distinct entities by virtue of the relations between these parts and the powers that emerge or come into being as a result of these compositions. In other words, material beings exist at a variety of different levels of scale ranging from the smallest units of matter, to entities such as atoms, molecules, rabbits, corporations, nations, stars, galaxies, and galactic clusters (see DeLanda 2011). Here we must remember that relations are themselves material entities. For example, corporations do not simply consist of "elementary" units such as the people that work for the corporation, but also require *communication* between those elements in order for the corporation to exist and continue as a corporation. Indeed, where that communication ceases, the entity falls into entropy or disintegrates. Those communications, however, require material media to relate these entities such as soundwaves, written documents, telephone wires and the electric pulses that pass along them, and so on. Here a corporation is not markedly different from an atom. Atoms are made up of more elementary particles, but those more basic particles must materially interact – through electric charges, for example – for that atom to be constituted as the atom it is. In this regard, whether or not an entity is *solid* is irrelevant to whether it is material. Any physicist will say that atoms are composed mostly of empty space. Likewise with tables. It is only a *perceptual* bias that leads us to conclude that tables are corporeal beings whereas corporations are not, because in the case of tables we don't discern the void and dynamic processes that compose it, whereas in the case of corporations it seems as if "nothing" is there.

The issue becomes confusing when we turn to *incorporeal* entities (here better terminology might be required). Initially we might take "incorporeality" to signify "without a body or materiality." However, within the framework of onto-cartography, there are *only* material beings. This entails, paradoxically, that incorporeal entities are *corporeal*. Why, then, introduce the category of incorporeality at all? Incorporeality refers not to immaterial beings, but rather to *iterable* beings. Take the example of Beethoven's 9th Symphony or Kim Stanley Robinson's *Red Mars*. These entities have the characteristic of being *repeatable*. Thousands of copies of *Red Mars* can be printed and exist all over the world. Likewise, Beethoven's 9th can be performed on multiple occasions. Each performance of the symphony and each copy of the novel is still *that* entity. However, this is very different from the claim that these entities are without a body or materiality. Copies, iterations, repetitions can only exist in material media. They require brains in which to be inscribed, performances to take place, paper on which to be written, computer databases in which to be stored, and so on. These are all material media for the iterable.

This is part of what makes materialism unique within the history of philosophy. Where most philosophy predetermines the being of being through a concept, materialism's central concept – matter – is always hypothetical and in question. We begin with hypotheses as to what matter might be, yet this concept is perpetually revised and developed through encounters with new phenomena in the world. Thus, for example, the materialisms of the eighteenth century suggested a mechanistic model of the universe as articulated by thinkers such as La Mettrie and Laplace, yet deeper investigation into the nature of life, atomic particles, as well as dynamic systems called for significant revisions in our understanding of matter. The concepts of materialism are in a perpetual state of motion and development. Materialism is minimally committed to the thesis that whatever else things might be, they are physical and they must physically interact in some way in order to be related.

Graham Harman has rejected materialism on the grounds that it erases or undermines objects by reducing them to their material parts. As he put it during a question-and-answer session at a round-table hosted by the CUNY graduate center, "the New York stock exchange is something more than glass, steel, and concrete" (Bennett et al. 2011). This is entirely true, for machines such as the New York stock exchange also involve relations between a variety of different entities, both within the building itself and ranging throughout the world to different practices of production, distribution, consumption, money, meaning, and so on. However, such a criticism of materialism would only be devastating if (1) it were true that materialism reduces machines to their *parts*, ignoring relations among these parts, and (2) materialism rejected the phenomenon of emergence. Yet materialism need do neither. This is true even of materialisms such as Lucretius' that argue that being is composed of fundamental and indivisible elements that he calls atoms. Lucretius perpetually compares atomism to the alphabet. As he writes:

> At certain times of year earth needs the rain
> For happy harvest, and both beasts and men
> Need nature's bounty for their lives' increase,
> A mutual dependence, of the sort
> That words need letters for. Do not believe
> In any world without its A B C's.
>
> (Lucretius 1969: 25)

The atoms make up the "letters" of being; however, these letters must be *combined* in the right way to produce entities. In other words, it is the *relations between* elements that constitute things. As we have seen, Lucretius is careful to distinguish between those properties that belong to the elements or atoms themselves – their shape – and those qualities that are *emergent* from *relations* between elements. Thus, for example, he cautions us against believing that atoms have the color of the object they compose. Properties such as color, Lucretius argues, arise not from the object being composed of colored atoms, but are rather emergent properties arising from how the atoms are combined. While Lucretius got the details wrong, in making this claim he is not claiming that color is *unreal* – quite the contrary – but that local manifestations such as color arise from relations. In other words, he argues that something *new* emerges when atoms are arranged in particular ways. It is difficult to see how this might constitute an undermining of objects. Rather, all that materialism requires is that whatever else a thing might be, it must be physical and relations between elements must also be physical and obey the constraints of information transmission through a medium.

Geophilosophy is an ontology of immanence. The terms "immanence" and "transcendence" require special comment as these terms are used in a variety of ways throughout the philosophical tradition, especially with the advent of phenomenology. Within a phenomenological framework, immanence and transcendence refer to whether or not something is *in* the *mind*. A dream, for example, is something that is only in the mind, while the mind of another person or the tree across the way is *transcendent to* consciousness. Here, then, immanence and transcendence refer to what is within and without. The question then becomes that of how the mind goes beyond its own immanence to relate to a transcendent being.

Onto-cartography does not deploy the concepts of immanence and transcendence in this way. As Deleuze writes, "[a]bsolute immanence is in itself: it is not in anything, nor can it be attributed *to* something; it does not depend on an object or belong to a subject" (Deleuze 2006: 385). Here immanence does not refer to whether or not something is inside or outside of a subject, but rather to whether or not it issues from the earth. An ontology is an ontology of immanence if it is committed solely to the existence of earthly worlds, rejecting any transcendent beings. Transcendent machines would be entities such as God, Platonic forms, eternal essences, the transcendental subject, and so on. In each of these cases, we get a verticality that conditions all other beings without itself being conditioned by them. A machine is treated as transcendent when it organizes all other machines without itself being affected by them.

Alternatively, ontologies premised on transcendence are ontologies of sovereignty. One entity is treated as sovereign over the others and is treated as that which structures everything else and as that from which everything else issues. Like the sovereign conceived as a being that organizes all social relations, the sovereign term of ontologies of transcendence is conceived as structuring, ordering, and legislating all other things. In short, one term overcodes all the others. Similarly, Laplace's demon which surveys the position and velocity of every particle and therefore is able to predict all subsequent events would be an example of a transcendence. In this regard, there can be variants of materialist ontology that are nonetheless premised on transcendence. We can call these ontologies "vertical ontologies," as opposed to the horizontal ontologies of immanence.

As with anything, there are degrees of transcendence within

Table 8.1 Ontologies of immanence and transcendence

	Type of ontology	Relations between machines	Examples
Transcendence	Vertical ontology	One machine overcodes the others, unilaterally conditioning them; sovereignty	• The God of ontotheology • Transcendental idealism • Humanism • Platonic forms • Linguistic idealism
Immanence	Flat/horizontal ontology	Overdetermination, bilateral conditioning between machines, mediation; anarchy	• The way in which organism and environment interact in development • The way in which writing modifies content and content modifies writing • The way in which a tool modifies a user and a user uses a tool

vertical ontologies. At one extreme, there are those ontologies that place God at the top of being, and treat him as creating everything, organizing all events, and legislating all things. Similarly, Platonic forms are conceived as structuring all other things, without themselves being affected by the things that they structures. Less extreme versions of verticality would consist in seeing humans as the pinnacle of creation, as lords of all other things, or would consist in treating language or culture as structuring all other things.

We can schematize these different ontological orientations as follows (see Table 8.1). Within flat or horizontal ontologies of immanence we have a single flat plane of machines in which machines affect and are affected by one another. There is no *outside* to these planes or plateaus of immanence. To be sure, there can be other worlds that are outside one world, but these other worlds do not stand above or beyond the being of the earth. They do not overcode worlds. By contrast, in vertical ontology one machine surveys all the others and conditions them without itself being conditioned by them.

In vertical ontologies we have relations of *overcoding* and the unilateral determination of other machines through the agency of one privileged machine. By contrast, in flat or horizontal ontologies, we have relations of overdetermination where machines bilaterally affect and are affected by one another.

The flat, horizontal, or the immanent ontology of geophilosophy is suspicious of all verticalities. To be sure, different machines exercise different degrees of power on other machines. The Sun, for example, exercises more influence over the Earth than the Earth exercises over the Sun. The owner of a business exercises disproportionate power over his employees. He does this through his ability to hire and fire, how he distributes wages, and how the legal system is largely structured in his favor. As we have seen, bright objects play a central role in structuring the local manifestations, becomings, and the movements of other machines that take on the status of satellites in relation to these objects. Machines become caught in the orbit of other machines in ways that severely restrict their movements, how they manifest themselves, and the trajectory of their becomings. Why, then, isn't this a transcendence or verticality with respect to other machines?

The difference lies in how conditioning is thought. Does a machine like God *unilaterally* condition other beings without itself being mediated by them, or are relations between machines conceived bilaterally such that they affect and are affected by one another? Spinoza's ontology, for example, would be an ontology of immanence because God and nature are conceived as one and the same thing. Here God is not a sovereign that organizes and legislates over all other beings, but is synonymous with those beings. By contrast, Descartes' and Leibniz's ontologies would be vertical ontologies because God stands above being, organizing it, creating it, and legislating it. Similarly, we can ask whether a privileged or sovereign machine is conceived as exercising its will or causal force all at once and in a single stroke, or whether it must pass through many mediations that modify its initial aim or intention? Are machines treated as mere vehicles or carriers for the agency of another machine, or do they contribute something of their own when the action of another machine travels through them? In the first instance we have a vertical ontology of transcendence, while in the latter we have an ontology of immanence. If the latter is an ontology of immanence, then this is because the agency of machines is nonetheless mediated through its interactions with other machines in ways that limit and modify its own agency. Causality is distributed rather than unilateral.

The difference between vertical and flat ontology can be illustrated with reference to the nature/nurture debate in biology and the social sciences. Discussions of development are dominated by gene-centrist preformativism. This is especially true of discussions of biology in the popular press and theoretical orientations in the social sciences such as evolutionary psychology and sociology. As Susan Oyama has argued, gene-centric approaches see the genome of the organism as *already* containing *all* the *information* for the developed organism or phenotype (see Oyama 2000). The genotype of an organism refers to the genes upon which it is based, while the phenotype of an organism refers to its morphology, observable traits, behavior and so on.

Nature/nurture debates revolve around questions of how the phenotype of an organism arises. Is it the genes alone? Is it the genes and the environment? Or is it something else besides? Within a gene-centric approach the development of the organism is merely a matter of *unfolding* the information already contained in the genes in the production of proteins that will eventually become the developed phenotype or organism. Here the genome already contains all the information for what the developed organism will become. The biologist Gilbert Gottlieb represents the basic schema for this model of development as follows (Gottlieb 2001: 47):

$$DNA \rightarrow RNA \rightarrow Protein$$

Based on the information already contained within the DNA or genes, RNA is first transcribed and then translated into proteins. It is through these proteins that the DNA is expressed. For example, a person's hair color might be what is expressed (local manifestation), while a gene or complex of genes codes for this hair color (virtual proper being). The color of a person's hair is already a foregone conclusion once the egg is fertilized because the genome already codes for it. While this is not the preformism of earlier biologists that conceived the fertilized egg as containing a miniature model of the fully developed organism that merely has to grow to adulthood, it is nonetheless a preformism in the sense that the DNA contains all the information necessary for the adult organism to be built. In short, the DNA is treated as being a master plan or blueprint for the adult organism. This is the significance of the arrows in the diagram above. Those arrows only move in one direction, from DNA to protein or from genotype to phenotype. Here the arrows indicate a unilateral direction of causality from genes to phenotype.

While this sort of gene-centrism is unusual in academic biology, it is common in discussions of genetics in the press and in evolutionary psychology and sociology. In evolutionary psychology, for example, human behavior is explained in terms of genetic inheritances from our primate ancestors. Within this framework, we do what we do not because of how we've been socially conditioned, environmental factors, or our beliefs, but because of how our genotype determines our behaviors. Social factors might influence how these demands of genes are satisfied, but in the end it is still the genes that ultimately explain human behavior. Thus, for example, based on observations of chimpanzees and other primates, an evolutionary sociologist might argue that we are genetically determined to engage in warfare as a consequence of our pursuit of mates. The real aim of warfare would therefore be reproduction and reproductive fitness. However, this genetic compulsion could be satisfied in a variety of ways. It could take the form of literal warfare, competition in the arts and business, sport, and so on. While this genetic compulsion can be satisfied in a variety of ways – the evolutionary sociologist would argue – it is nonetheless our genetic inheritance that explains all these activities. Culture does not modify that genetic demand.

In the context of academic biology, biologists generally adopt some model of "interactivism." Here the thesis is that the phenotype or developed organism results from the interaction of the genotype and the environment. As the biologist Lewontin expresses this thesis, ". . . organisms [are treated as] the *objects* of forces whose *subjects* [are] the internal heritable factors and the external environment . . ." (Lewontin 2001: 59). In other words, the organism is treated as an effect of these genetic and environmental factors. While these interactionist models are an advance over the unilateralism of gene-centric models, they still preserve – as Oyama et al. (2001: 2) argue – the basic nature/nurture dichotomy. The project now becomes one of determining what *percent* of the phenotype arises from the genes, and what percent arises from the environment. The point here is that the genotype is still seen as a *distinct* causal factor that *autonomously* contributes to the formation of the phenotype in contrast to environmental factors. The environment contributes sports competitions as a way of pursuing mates, while genes still determine the ultimate goal. We're still left within a framework that tells us some causal factors arise from genes (nature) and others from the environment (nurture).

Gene-centric models of the development of phenotypes are an excellent example of a materialist vertical ontology. In the model DNA → RNA → Protein – what Gottlieb calls "the central dogma" (Gottlieb 2001: 46) – DNA functions as a transcendent term, a master plan or blueprint that conditions everything else. It affects without itself being affected. Everything transpires through *feedforward* mechanisms without feedback. To be sure, this is not the sort of verticality or transcendence we find in, for example, Plato's theory of the forms. There the forms are so transcendent, so vertical, that they condition all beings in the world without themselves ever being conditioned in any way. By contrast, DNA can be affected by other entities in the world through natural selection as well as "random" mutations wrought by ambient chemicals in the environment, highly charged solar particles, transcription errors, and so on. Nonetheless, the genotype of the organism functions as a transcendent term providing the plan or blueprint for all subsequent development. The organism is pre-formed by its genetic code. What is denied is the possibility that through environmental influences genes could take on a function different from the historical context in which they arose, or that they can be actualized and activated in different ways. In other words, strong gene-centric models such as those found in evolutionary sociology are a bit like claiming that a fuel-injected engine is really a perfume bottle because the spray technology used in fuel-injected engines arose out of the technology developed for perfume bottles.

Among the developmental systems theorists (DST), we find a very different account of development that is in accord with the flat or horizontal ontology advocated by geophilosophy. It is not that the developmental systems theorists reject the thesis that DNA plays an important role in the development of the phenotype, but rather that they instead – and on well supported empirical grounds – call for *parity* in explanations of the phenotype. As Susan Oyama articulates it, parity reasoning consists in exploring "... the emergence of form and function in the interaction of heterogeneous internal and external causal influences on various scales, [where] causal interdependencies ... lack ... absolute distinctions between causes and effects" (Oyama 2001: 184). In other words, DST approaches adopt a holistic, epigenetic account of development, in which DNA, RNA, proteins, the organism itself, and the organism's environment all interact to produce the phenotype. As Gottleib schematizes this model, we get a dynamic set of interactions presiding over local manifestations where a variety of agencies, including genes, play a role (Gottlieb 2001: 46):

$$(DNA \leftrightarrow RNA \leftrightarrow Protein) \leftrightarrow \text{structural maturation} \leftrightarrow \text{function, activity, or experience}$$

The key point here is that the arrows are *bidirectional*. Where, in the gene-centric model, we only get *feedforward* relations where agencies such as the genes remain the same and determine everything else down the developmental chain, in the DST framework events that take place at the level of, for example, structural maturation can *feed back* on DNA, RNA, and protein processes *modifying* them and how they unfold. In other words, DNA is no longer unilaterally determinative of the phenotype, but is one causal factor among others. More fundamentally, DNA is no longer a master plan or blueprint that contains all the information for the construction of the organism, but is instead one causal factor among others that can be affected by other factors and that can be actualized in a variety of different ways under different circumstances. To understand why the organism locally manifests itself in the way that it does, we have to investigate the *entire* developmental system.

Initially it is difficult to appreciate the novelty of DST because interactivism has accustomed us to the claim that the phenotype is partially the result of the environment and partially the result of genes. However, within interactivism genes are still treated as determinative agencies that constitute a blueprint and that remain *unchanged* by other processes taking place within the organism and the environment. The radicality of DST lies in arguing that other processes taking place in the organism and environment can feed back on DNA, activating it in different ways. In this model, DNA is no longer a blueprint that already contains all the information necessary for the construction of the organism or phenotype, but is rather a set of *potentials* that can be activated in a variety of *different* ways in response to features of the environment and other processes taking place in the organism at the level of proteins and RNA. A classic example of this would be the development of ants. Whether an ant becomes a worker ant, a warrior, or a queen is not *genetically* encoded in the ant – indeed, every ant genetically can become each type of ant – rather, ants become one type of ant as a result of chemicals it is exposed to while developing. The biologist Richard Lewontin gives another nice example of this with respect to crops:

> In applied biology, especially in plant and animal breeding, the understanding that there is a unique interaction between genotype and environment in development has been of fundamental practical importance for nearly one hundred years. The standard method of breeding crops for, say, increase in yield, is to grow the various varieties under test in several years and in several locations in the region of production. The variety chosen for release is not necessarily the one with the highest average yield over environments because uniformity of result over years and locations is given strong weight . . . In contrast, nearly every developmental geneticist working on morphogenesis in laboratory model organisms ignores completely the effect of interaction of genes and environments. (Lewontin 2001: 55–6)

Assuming that the genotype is a blueprint or master plan that pre-delineates what the organism will become, the laboratory geneticist ignores environmental factors in the production of the phenotype. This impression is reinforced because the laboratory biologist indeed gets similar results for one and the same genotype because *the laboratory environment remains the same.* By contrast, the agricultural and applied biologist is cognizant of the way in which environment impacts the actualization of the genome. Crops possessing one and the same genotype can develop into different phenotypes due to weather conditions from one year to the next when instances of the genotype are planted due to differences in soil conditions, differences in altitude, differences in local plant and animal life, and so on. While the genotype certainly contributes causal influences, it can itself be affected by other factors and is more a *sketch* than a determinative model.

Developmental systems theorists thus recommend a holistic approach to our investigation of organisms and explanation of why they develop the phenotype they do. The organism cannot be studied in isolation nor can the DNA, but rather the entire *developmental system* must be investigated with an eye towards the interactions between all of its elements. Like a Markov chain, states in the previous stage of development and in the current state modify how DNA and RNA will unfold at the next moment. These processes are characterized by a high degree of contingency that can unfold in a variety of different directions depending on circumstances.

A complete schema of developmental systems for organic life would therefore be as follows:

Genetic activity (DNA ↔ RNA ↔ Protein) ↔
structural maturation ↔ function, activity, or experience ↔
organism ↔ environment

Once again, we see arrows pointing in both directions at all levels, indicating feedback relations between each of these domains. What we take to be a cause (DNA) can, in fact, be an effect of how the environment has activated it, which, once activated in this way, then feeds back on the DNA and then forward in the developmental system, e.g., pheromones in a larva's environment activate that genetic sequence for producing a warrior ant and once activated this sequence feeds forward assembling proteins to produce this sort of ant. In development, causality is massively distributed or overdetermined. Nothing is an effect of just one agency. None of this is to suggest that all agencies contribute equally in all situations, nor that things can develop in any way possible. The different agencies constrain one another in their interactions, reliably producing more or less the same form in multiple instances of developmental processes because the environment remains largely stable. The point is that the form a phenotype takes is not the result of just one particular agency.

In the diagram above it will be noted that two additional agencies have been included in the developmental process: the organism itself and the environment. Insofar as the schema models the development of the organism, it is curious to see the organism included as one agency among others in the production of the phenotype. As Lewontin points out, our tendency is to see the organism as an *effect* of its genes and the environment, without contributing anything of its own. However, as Lewontin argues, the organism *itself* plays a role in its *own* construction (ibid.: 59–66). It does this in two ways. First, we can't speak of an environment as a simple "container" that is just indifferently "there" for all organisms because organisms determine their own environments. As we saw in our discussion of selective openness of machines, organisms aren't open to every feature of the world about them, but are only selectively open to particular flows. As Lewontin observes

> [w]hile stones are part of a thrush's environment, tree bark is a part of a woodpecker's, and the undersides of leaves part of a warbler's. It is the life activities of these birds that determine which parts of the world, physically accessible to all of them, are actually parts of their environments. Moreover, as organisms evolve, their environments, perforce, change. (Ibid.: 64)

There is a strong sense in which organisms select their own environments. In selecting their environments, they thus select which features of other machines can exercise selective pressure upon them. Changes in the composition of bark might very well affect the subsequent evolutionary development of woodpeckers, while having little to no effect on warblers. Consequently, the organism is not simply a passive effect of its environment, but actively engages with its environment in ways that contribute to how it is constructed.

Second, as Lewontin and philosopher of biology Kim Sterelny argue (see Sterelny 2003), organisms actively construct their own *niches*. The upshot of this is that developing organisms do not simply inherit genes from those that came before them, but also inherit constructed environments. We already saw this in the case of ant nests, where the placement of a larva in a particular place in the nest plays a key role in the sort of ant it will become as a consequence of the chemicals it is exposed to. Another example would be the dams that beavers build. Sterelny talks about how trees construct their niches through the way in which their roots aerate soil, enhancing chances for their offspring to grow, and pointing out the way in which pine needles make it more difficult for other plants to grow thereby allowing the tree to draw on more soil nutrients (Sterelny 2001: 332). Likewise, Andy Clark discusses the way in which language, the practices we pass on, and the cities and homes we construct impact the development of the body and mind (see Clark 2011: chs 3–4). These constructed niches – especially resulting from theories of diet and crops raised – can rebound on the development of the body impacting how the phenotype is formed. In other words, niche construction is not just a construction of an environment, but also a construction of the phenotype.

However, we must exercise caution with respect to DST on two fronts. First, based on the foregoing, we might conclude that machines are inextricably linked to their environment, such that their environment is a part of their being. Yet there is quite a difference between claiming that environments influence how organisms develop and claiming that organisms are inextricably linked to their environments. Part of the significance of DST lies in recognizing that when organisms are situated in *different* environments they will develop their phenotypes in different ways. One and the same genome of corn will grow in one way in this environment and another in that environment. This wouldn't be possible unless the relations or interactions an organism maintains with one environment can be *severed* and the organism can enter into a new environment. Once again, machines are independent of their relations.

Second, and more importantly, we must avoid thinking the relationship between development and the phenotype as a relation between process and "destination." We think the phenotype as a destination when we conceive of it as an *end-point* that an organism eventually reaches, so that development ends. We see hints of this way of thinking in the work of Brian Massumi. As Massumi writes:

> Nature itself, the world of process, "is a complex of passing events" [. . .] The world is not an aggregate of objects. To see it that way is to have participated in an abstraction reductive of the complexity of nature as passage. To "not believe in things" is to believe that objects are derivatives of process and that their emergence is the passing result of specific modes of abstractive activity. This means that objects' reality does not exhaust the range of the real. The reality of the world exceeds that of objects, for the simple reason that where objects are, there has also been their becoming. [. . .] The being of an object is an abstraction from its becoming. The world is not a grab-bag of things. It's an always-in-germ. To perceive the world in an object frame is to neglect the wider range of its germinal reality. (Massumi 2011: 6)

Massumi is led to reject the existence of things (machines) because he sees things as the absence or cessation of motion, while seeing being itself as composed of nothing but motion. As a consequence, he's led to the conclusion that being consists entirely of events. Massumi's conception of being is here remarkably similar to that of Aristotle's concept of φύσις, where beings are drawn toward a final state where development ceases. Such an end-point of motion is what he calls a "thing."

While we readily agree with Massumi's thesis that the phenotype of an entity is a "freeze-frame" of its being at a particular point in time (Massumi 2002: 3), we see no reason to conclude from this that things (machines) do not exist. As we saw in our discussion of machines, machines *are* processes. At each point in their existence they must engage in operations to stave off entropy so as to continue existing. In this regard, development is not a vector along which a machine moves towards the final destination of the phenotype or local manifestation. Put differently, it is not that a machine *first* develops and *then* produces a phenotype or local manifestation. Rather, the entire existence of a machine across time is a development. There is no point where development ceases, save the destruction of the machine. The phenotype of a machine, its local manifestation, is thus how it happens to locally manifest itself at a particular point in time and space as a result of preceding processes. If this point is so important, then it is because it reminds us that machines can always undergo new local manifestations and becomings as a result of processes taking place within them and new interactions with other machines.

DST provides us with a model for thinking being in terms of immanence as required by geophilosophy. While developmental systems will differ from machine to machine – and will clearly differ between inorganic machines, organic machines, and social machines – causality involved in becomings and local manifestations will nonetheless be distributed or overdetermined for all machines. This has important consequences for how we think about the humanities and social and political thought. As Latour has argued, modernity has been premised on a strong distinction and partition between the realm of nature and the realm of culture (Latour 1993: ch. 2). Culture or society is conceived as the domain of freedom where we construct our cultural world and invent ourselves. Nature is seen as the domain of mechanistic causation. Society is composed of norms, beliefs, language, and meanings, while nature is composed of material things and causal interactions.

Modernity holds that these two domains must be rigorously kept apart and purified. If the social and political enters the domain of natural science, we will get not truth but rather impure political machinations. For example, we'll be led to reject the theory of evolution not on the grounds of whether or not it is the most adequate explanation for the formation of species, but rather on the grounds of whether or not we see it as embodying bourgeois, neoliberal ideology or whether it contradicts our religious beliefs. By contrast, if we treat society or culture as a part of the natural or material world we are, at best, left without an account of ethical responsibility and emancipation because all natural phenomena are mechanistically determined. At worst, naturalistic conceptions of the social risk providing justifications for misogyny, patriarchy, racism, and eugenics.

The second worry arises from the persistence of a pre-Darwinian concept of nature. Within this framework, the being of machines is conceived in terms of fixed essences or natures. Human beings have a particular nature, women have a particular nature, people of various "races" have a nature, sexuality has a particular nature and function, and so on. These categories or essences function not just descriptively, but normatively. They are what Ian Hacking calls "interactive kinds." As he articulates it

> [t]he "woman refugee" (as a kind of classification) can be called an *interactive kind* because it interacts with things of that kind, namely people, including individual women refugees, who can become aware of how they are classified and modify their behavior accordingly. Quarks in contrast do not form an interactive kind; the idea of the quark does not interact with quarks. Quarks are not aware that they are quarks and are not altered simply by being classified as quarks. (Hacking 1999: 32)

In the case of interactive kinds, the category itself both affects the entity subsumed under it – a point that Hacking does not make – and the person that falls under the category can adopt an attitude towards the category. In other words, interactive kinds are characterized by a sort of self-referentiality. On the one hand, the person can end up acting in ways that exemplify the category, as if performing a role pre-delineated by the kind. For example, a person categorized as an alcoholic by a healthcare professional might read up on alcoholism and *begin* behaving and thinking about themselves in ways that accord with alcholism. "I think and feel this way because I am an alchoholic." "I must do x because this is what alcoholics do." Here alcoholism becomes a sort of role that they begin to *enact*. The category doesn't simply describe something that was *already* there in the person, but rather functions as a script that the person animates. The category changes them, rather than describing them due to the way they adopt an attitude towards the category. We see this especially in the case of nationalisms. "Americans *do* x, y, and z." If the person is to genuinely be an American, then they must *do* these things. Thus the category presents itself as being a natural kind, as something that objectively described, as being what people *are*, while covertly functioning as a set of norms that the person *enacts* or performs.

On the other hand, interactive kinds can play a significant role in structuring the social destiny of individuals regardless of whether or not they themselves adopt a stance with respect to the category. The Rwandan genocide of 1994 is a particularly dramatic example of this. Under colonial rule, the Belgians concluded that there was a racial (natural) difference between the Hutu majority and the Tutsi minority. The Tutsi were said to be racially superior, while the Hutu were said to be inferior. Based on this race essentialism, the two tribes were given identity cards that granted rights and, in the case of the Hutu, severely limited what they could and could not do. When the Hutu later gained power, they set about eradicating the Tutsi, killing more than 500,000 people. A Tutsi might not have accepted the racial ideology of the Belgians, he might have believed in equality between Hutu and Tutsi, or he might have even been unaware of this history and these racial distinctions (as in the case of very young children), yet would still be killed for falling under this classification. Here we have an example of the plane of expression, the order of the signifier, presiding over the destiny of human life regardless of whether or not they are aware of it. The *signifier*, the *categorization*, here functions as the gravitational force that sorts people.

In these instances, the signifier or category presents itself as what people *are*, while carrying with it a set of normative imperatives as to how people should relate, what they are entitled to do, whether or not they should live or die, whether or not they can marry, and so on. The force of these arguments arises from treating these categories as essences or *natural* kinds. Women, for instance, are said to have such and such natural cognitive capacities, to be naturally dominated by emotion, and to be naturally nurturing, and on these grounds it's argued that they should be excluded from certain jobs and that their proper place is in the home raising children and attending to the needs of men. The categorization functions as a normative justification for assigning women particular roles and excluding them from other things. When they attempt to do other things, they are told, implicitly or explicitly, that they're going against nature. Strangely we are told that nature is what it is *and* that it is something we have to obey. Nature is simultaneously conceived in causal terms and in teleological terms, so that we can betray what nature tells us to be by refusing to act according to this teleology.

This way of understanding the role that nature plays in the social arises from sorting beings into eternal essences and conceiving those essences simultaneously as causes that make people what they are and as teleological goals they must obey through their own performances. However, if nature is genuinely what *is*, then the dictum articulated in Love & Rockets in their 1987 song "No New Tale to Tell" follows:

You cannot go against nature
Because when you do
Go against nature
It's part of nature too.

Darwin showed us that species aren't eternal essences that precede individuals, but that they are statistical generalities that arise from random mutations, natural selection, and heredity among individuals. Individuals and difference precede sameness and similarity, and resemblances are always statistical generalizations ranging over populations where all individuals differ. As Leibniz puts it, ". . . there are never two beings in nature that are perfectly alike . . ." (Leibniz 1991: 69). Likewise, as the developmental systems theorists show us, there is not one agency – the genes – that presides over the development of the phenotype or individuals, but rather the entire developmental *system* that produces the phenotype. This includes the environment or constructed niches, and among the elements that make up those constructed niches for humans are categories, signifiers, and signs. Categories, elements of the plane of expression, do not simply describe but also contribute to the formation of form.

DST therefore allows onto-cartography to abandon the nature/

culture divide. From a geophilosophical standpoint, being consists of nature *alone*. Culture and society are not something *other* than nature, but, like Amazonian rain forests or coral reefs, are a particular formation of nature. Historically the nature/culture divide has been justified on the grounds that culture is historical and *contingent*, while nature is characterized by necessity and eternity. The forms of nature, the argument runs, are eternal and unchanging, while the formations of culture came about as a result of history and *can and could be otherwise*. Within this framework, the critical gesture is to show that what we take to be natural – gendered sexual orientations, for example – are really historical or social constructions that could have been otherwise and that we have the power to change. If something is treated as natural, then it cannot be changed.

My aim here is not to reject this critical gesture, but rather to contest the conception of nature upon which it is based. This is premised on a deleterious pre-Darwinian concept of nature that should be abandoned. Nature is not characterized by necessity, eternity, and inevitability, but rather by contingency, history, and creativity. This move is first authorized by Darwin insofar as he shows that species – and by extension, ecosystems – are not eternal, but are the result of a contingent *history*. As Stephen J. Gould argues, were we to rewind evolution and allow it to play again, the outcome would be different, with many species we know today never evolving, and others that we can scarcely imagine going on to evolve (see Gould 1989). Life is contingent and historical. From this vantage, it becomes difficult to rigorously distinguish the historicity of life from social and cultural historicity. This historicity of "nature" is not restricted to life, but goes all the way down to atoms. As astrophysicists teach us, the various elements are created in the forge of stars and the laws of physics might have been different had the universe cooled at a different rate immediately following the Big Bang.

More importantly, evolutionary thought develops an account that allows us to dispense with the teleology of nature. The hawk has keen eyesight not *for the sake* of capturing its prey. In other words, a purpose or goal is not the *cause* of a hawk's keen eyesight. Rather, the hawk's extraordinary vision arose from random mutation, natural selection, and inheritance, *enabling* him to capture prey. The acquisition of keen eyesight was chance driven, not goal driven. This rejection of teleology is crucial from the standpoint of how arguments from nature function in the social and cultural world. If it is true that there is no teleology in evolution, then we can no longer talk about what human beings *ought* to be by "nature." Everything is nature, including the deviations and differences. Moreover, there are no genetic essences unilaterally and ineluctably calling the shots.

From this standpoint, we are able to integrate the critical gestures of those who advocate the nature/culture divide, without treating nature as something that is somehow outside of or beyond culture. Nature is historical and contingent all the way down. Culture is not something outside of nature, but rather is a more quickly changing historicity characterized by self-referentiality. It is certainly true that the rate of change in an ecosystem such as a society is far faster – especially with the acquisition of writing – than change in something like the Amazonian ecosystem. The reason for this is that social ecosystems are self-referential in the sense that societies involving humans are able to more pervasively construct their own niches and pass on accumulated cultural memory. However, this does not change the fact that non-human ecosystems are historical and that human ecosystems are natural.

But why go to all the trouble of arguing that culture is a part of nature? Why make the perverse move of geophilosophy? The necessity of this move is twofold. First, cultural studies and social and political thought has reached an impasse as a result of the nature/culture distinction. Focusing on norms, signifiers, beliefs, meanings, and ideologies, it is unable to explain why social formations take the form they do and why they persist as they do even in the face of compelling critiques that *demonstrate* that kinds parading as "natural" essences are really socially constructed interactive kinds. As theorists such as Bruno Latour and Jared Diamond have argued, we can't fully understand why social ecologies take the form they do without taking into account the role played by non-human agencies in constructing these assemblages. Diamond is particularly valuable in this context. "Why," he asks, "did wealth and power become distributed as they now are, rather than in some other way" (Diamond 2005: 15)? Why didn't wealth and power come to be concentrated among the aborigines, the Native Americans, or the Africans? Modernity, premised on the nature/culture distinction, presents us with two possible and unpalatable possibilities. We can explain this distribution by adopting the standpoint of "nature" and argue that Eurasians are biologically superior, and were therefore able to use their greater intelligence to accumulate wealth and power and subdue other people. By contrast, if we deny that these sorts of biological differences exist – as reams of empirical data should lead us to do – then we're left with a cultural explanation. Something about those cultures where wealth and power came to be concentrated must have been superior to these other cultures. In other words, we replace biological racism with cultural racism. Moreover, we're given no real account of how these superior cultures arose.

Diamond takes another approach. Working on the empirically well grounded thesis that people are of more or less equal intelligence around the world and throughout history, and that as a result of their intelligence make maximal use of the resources in their environment (ibid.: 22), he instead looks at what geography contributed to the formation of various societies. Through an analysis of climate conditions in different parts of the world, the number of plants and animals available for domestication in different regions, soil conditions, the availability of mineral resources, and disease epidemiologies, Diamond is able to show that those cultures where there was a greater concentration of resources were able to develop more quickly and therefore subdue other cultures. Europeans, for example, had more domesticatable animals for food and labor than the peoples of the Americas. This led to an acceleration in the development of diseases due to living in close proximity to other animals, as well as the formation of immunities to these diseases. When they went to the Americas they brought these diseases with them, exposing the indigenous population to microbes to which they had never developed immunities. As a result, hundreds of thousands of indigenous Americans were killed off by diseases such as smallpox, allowing the Europeans to subdue local populations and divest them of their land and resources. It wasn't a biological or cultural superiority that allowed them to do this, but rather, in part, the presence of more domesticatable animals in Europe that set up the conditions for this to be possible.

Similarly, geographical location such as longitude play a role in what crops can be grown and how much yield there will be, which in turn plays a role in how large populations can become and how much social differentiation can take place. Thus, for instance, cultures located at high northern latitudes exist in environments with less botanical diversity because of the cold, wintery environment.

This entails that there will be less available food, which, in its turn, has two consequences: more time will have to be spent collectively pursuing food as a result, and due to scarcity, populations will have great difficulty growing beyond a certain size. Consequently, it will become more difficult for social stratification to develop between those who produce food and whatnot, and those who devote themselves to intellectual pursuits such as invention, the scientific exploration of nature, and so on. Here we have an intersection of the spatial network constituted by non-human entities playing a significant role in the temporal structuration of human assemblages.

This is the basic thesis of onto-cartography and geophilosophy. If we are to understand why assemblages take the form they take, we must investigate how corporeal and incorporeal, human and non-human, inorganic, organic, and social machines intersect and interact with one another. The categories informing contemporary cultural theory inhibit this sort of analysis by partitioning nature and culture, thereby restricting social explanation to the domain of meaning. In arguing that culture is itself a formation of nature, that it is continuous with nature rather than separate, geophilosophy hopes to contribute to overcoming this impediment so as to better understand why social ecologies take the form they take and, above all, to multiply our sites of intervention to produce change. Once we understand that non-humans contribute significantly to the form social ecologies take, we also understand that change need not only be produced by changing beliefs and debunking ideologies, but that significant change can also be produced by introducing and subtracting various non-human machines that capture human lives in their gravity.

On the other hand, geophilosophy argues that culture is a formation of nature for ecological reasons. As Timothy Morton has argued, the nature/culture divide leads us to conceive nature as something *outside* of, *beyond*, and independent of culture (Morton 2007). Nature is thought as the wild, untouched by humans. It is the place *to which* we go when hiking or fishing. In this way, we fail to see how social assemblages are intertwined with nature as both a material milieu necessary for continuing to exist, as well as how our social activity affects the broader natural world. When, for example, I eat a Big Mac, I think I am involved in a purely cultural affair that has nothing to do with nature. In analyzing the Big Mac, the cultural theorist might discuss how what I'm really eating is "signifiers," examining how this sandwich is a marker of national identity, class, symbolic position, and so on. What is not examined is how the Big Mac is related to the clearing of Amazonian rain forests for bovine grazing, and all of the material outputs produced in transporting the meat, processing it, cooking it and consuming it. The Big Mac is thought of as something unrelated to these issues of relevance to climate change and ecology.

On these grounds, Morton claims that we should abandon the concept of nature altogether. As he writes:

> *Ecology Without Nature* argues that the very idea of "nature" which so many hold dear will have to wither away in an "ecological" state of human society. Strange as it may sound, the idea of nature is getting in the way of properly ecological forms of culture, philosophy, politics, and art. (Ibid.: 1)

While I share Morton's rejection of the notion that nature is a place outside of culture to which we might go on weekends, geophilosophy sees abandonment of the concept of nature as inadvisable. While Morton is not guilty of such things, such a move risks leading to the view that culture is all there is, that there is only society, and therefore is in danger of reinforcing vertical ontologies premised on human exceptionalism or anthropocentrism.

Instead, geophilosophy proposes that there is only nature, that culture is itself a formation of nature, and that there are no transcendent or vertical terms outside of nature. Geophilosophy advocates an ontology of nature without exception. This requires us to rethink both the concept of culture/society and the concept of nature. The concept of society must be thought ecologically as a part of nature and as continuous with nature, such that social assemblages aren't simply composed of humans and meanings, but rather of a variety of non-human machines. Nature must be thought as historical, riddled with contingency, and creative, without transcendent terms or eternal essences such as unchanging species that overcode everything else.

The Three Dimensions of Geophilosophy

Geophilosophy is composed of three interrelated practices: cartography, deconstruction, and terraformation. These practices are undertaken not simply for the sake of understanding worlds, but more fundamentally for the sake of producing more just, equitable, and sustainable worlds. Moreover, we should not think of these practices in temporal terms, or as discrete and separated. While one practice might, under certain conditions, be undertaken without the others, more commonly they are intertwined and take place simultaneously. Thus, for example, cartography and deconstruction might take place simultaneously, or terraformation might also involve deconstruction. The aim of geophilosophy is to provide us with the means to constructively intervene in worlds so as to produce better ecologies or assemblages.

Cartography: The Four Maps

Throughout the foregoing book we have seen what constitutes a cartography. A cartography – or more properly, an onto-cartography – is a mapping of assemblages of machines or worlds, the machines that flow between them, and how machines exercise gravity over other machines, structuring their movements, local manifestations, and becomings in space-time. These assemblages include incorporeal expressive machines such as signifiers, as well as organic, inorganic, and social machines. The rationale behind onto-cartography, the reason it is so necessary, lies in the fact that we cannot effectively intervene in situations without knowing the lay of the land or how machines are put together, the gravity they exercise, and what flows between them. Physicians and veterinarians cannot heal people and animals without knowing physiology and anatomy, and generals cannot conquer opposing armies without knowing about troop movements, supply lines, factories that produce munitions, and so on. The first step in producing any sort of change or new assemblages lies in having a good map.

Perhaps the first and most important principle of onto-cartography lies in the dictum: "avoid abstractions!" Big umbrella terms such as "capitalism," "patriarchy," "heterosexism," "religion," "society," "racism," "ontotheology," "culture," and so on do more to obscure than explain. We end up introducing verticalities into our thought and come to believe that these transcendent or sovereign terms are the things that we must overcome. The problem is that these big terms end up generating political pessimism. Like a ghost, we see capitalism, for example, as being everywhere and nowhere. Capitalism becomes the sovereign agency from which all other things issue, while being in no specific place. You can't fight a ghost. As a result, we end up falling into a state of theoretical pessimism or revolutionary quietism. In the first instance, because we see capitalism as overcoding everything so that it is simultaneously everywhere and nowhere, we fall into a pessimistic position because we can't imagine a place where we might act on this sovereign entity that would change it. We thus conclude that there's nothing that can be done.

The oxymoron "revolutionary quietism" is the converse of theoretical pessimism. The revolutionary quietist ends up rejecting any and all interventions because they don't topple capitalism (or whatever sovereign term we choose) *as such*. The revolutionary quietist perpetually says "this move leaves sovereign transcendent agency partially intact, therefore we're wasting energy by doing it." What the revolutionary quietist dreams of is a move that would abolish the sovereign agency completely and in a single stroke, and he therefore rejects anything that falls short of those ideals on the grounds that they leave that overcoding term intact. Ironically, they therefore end up perpetuating the very thing they're fighting against. This position arises from failing to recognize the mediated nature of action and that events unfold over a duration as multiplicities.

The problem isn't that things such as patriarchy, capitalism, society, racism, and so on aren't real, but rather that they don't explain. Rather, they are the very things to be *explained*. These terms are all shorthand for *assemblages*. They are generic terms for extremely complex relations between machines in worlds. It is those *assemblages*, the machines that compose those assemblages, that cause things, not these terms. Onto-cartography aspires to get at the organization of these assemblages. It aims at the concrete. Its question is "how is this assemblage put together, what are the interactions between machines, how does it resist entropy?" rather than "how do we overcome capitalism or 'patriarchy' or 'racism' or 'ontotheology'?" It has stopped believing in ghosts and treats these terms as things to be explained by assemblages of machines forming a world, rather than by master-terms. Working on the premise that these things exist in and through assemblages, cartography strives to map those assemblages to determine privileged and strategic points of intervention that would lead to change or destroy these things.

Onto-cartography seeks to produce good maps of assemblages and draws inspiration from exemplary cartographers such as the

Marx of *Capital*, Foucault, the historian Braudel, the Latour of *The Pasteurization of France*, and so on. Based on the foregoing, we can imagine four different types of map. The first type of map – topographical maps – is a sort of snapshot of worlds or assemblages at a particular point in time. The composition of topographical maps is similar, if not identical, to the methods used by ecologists to investigate ecologies. The topographer aims to identify the entities that compose the ecology, the hierarchical relations between them, the feedback loops throughout the assemblage, and so on. The first step in composing a topographical map thus consists in identifying the machines that populate an ecology, assemblage, or world (these three terms are synonymous).

We have to take care not to overly simplify the assemblages we wish to map because often the central actors of these assemblages will be surprising. Take the example of an assemblage or ecology such as empire (another big master-term) in the contemporary world. A crude topographical map might conclude that this assemblage is composed solely of people, governments, international organizations, laws, corporations, money, and militaries. All of these machines are indeed inhabitants of contemporary empire; the problem is that such an inventory fails to raise the question of the *material* conditions under which contemporary empire is possible. In referring to material conditions, I am not speaking of *practices* as the Marxists, critical theorists, and post-structuralists would have it, but of genuine material or physical agencies. What material machines, what *technologies*, had to come into existence in order for something like contemporary empire to come into existence? As James Gleick suggests, the world had to develop a *nervous system* (see Gleick 2012). Contemporary empire is above all an ecology that conquers time and space. Within empire, economic and political events that take place in Greece can *immediately* affect economic and political events in Great Britain, Japan, and the United States. In prior periods, news of these events would have taken days, weeks, and months to reach other locations because of their distance from one another in space. Contemporary empire, by contrast, is distinguished by the speed at which information can be conveyed across great distances, allowing for unprecedented coordination of action and responses to events from elsewhere. The material conditions under which this is possible are to be found in fiber optic cables, satellites, radio waves, cell phone towers, computers, Internet servers, highways, airports, automobiles, ocean shipping routes, clocks, container ships, binary computer codes, and a host of other things besides. Without these technologies and the way in which they are assembled in the world, contemporary empire would not be possible. These technologies and the way in which they are related is the condition for the possibility of an ecology that overcomes time and space in the manner characteristic of contemporary empire. A good topographical map of empire would thus devote significant attention to these elements from the plane of content and how they function and contribute to the structuration of the world.

Composing a topographical map first consists in identifying the machines that compose the ecology to be investigated. In the case of assemblages populated by humans, these machines will include incorporeal semiotic machines (laws, norms, identities, ideologies, etc.), and corporeal inorganic, organic, social, and technological machines. The next step will consist in identifying the hierarchical relations between machines, or the structure of gravity that organizes the ecology. The question here is one of determining the mechanisms by which an ecology or assemblage resists the decay of entropy. Three things are to be analyzed in this connection. First, it is necessary to identify the bright objects and their satellites. What entities capture other entities in their orbit and how? Good topographical analysis will often lead to surprising conclusions. We might think, for example, that people at a particular point in history live and labor as they do because they are in the grips of a certain ideology or set of beliefs, only to discover that in fact the *clock* functions as a far brighter object in organizing their movements and social relations than the incorporeal machines of ideology. With the invention of the clock and its proliferation throughout social assemblages, a revolution takes place in how people live their lives, labor, and relate to one another. Now days can be organized into precise units, times of meeting can be set, durations of labor can be defined, and activities between people diversely located throughout space can be coordinated. The clock functions as a bright object that striates the movements and actions of people into collective units. Those who refuse to organize their actions in the way rendered possible by the clock suffer sanctions from everyone else.[1] In short, when mapping relations between bright objects and satellites, we must take care to suspend our anthropocentric tendencies – our tendency to see people, beliefs, meanings, and institutions as the sole organizers of gravitational relations in social assemblages – so as to discern the role played by non-human agencies.

Second, a good topographical map will investigate how machines are linked together. As we saw in Part 1, there is no such thing as action at a distance. In order for two or more machines to interact, they must either directly contact one another, or there must be some sort of material flow that passes between them – in the form of energy, matter, or information – that allows them to interact. Put differently, there is no relation between two entities without a *medium* of interaction. Thus, as Andrew Blum suggests, when, in 2007, Senator Ted Stevens was mocked for describing the Internet as a series of "tubes," he was in fact right (Blum 2012: 5). While the Internet is not literally composed of tubes, there is nonetheless no information transfer without fiber optic cables, satellites, computers, phone lines, cell phone towers, and so on. Machines at a distance can only relate to one another through the agency of a medium that relates them. This is true even of incorporeal entities which always require a corporeal body in order to affect other machines in the world.

Understanding these flows and how they create paths is crucial to understanding the gravitational structure of assemblages. We saw this in the case of contemporary empire versus prior social ecologies. Economies are able to function as they do today because of the paths that have been built between geographically distant machines through technology. Without these intermediaries, we would not have the sort of economy we today have. This is the problem with strong holisms that claim that *everything* is related to *everything* else. They have the right intuition in recognizing that relations are important, but go too far in suggesting that everything is related to everything else. Such a thesis leads us to ignore how things are actually related or not related, and the consequences the absence and presence of relations has for understanding the structuration of particular ecologies.

Third, it is necessary to map the sources of energy upon which machines rely in order to engage in their operations and the work they do in carrying out their operations. As we saw in Part 1, no machine can sustain its existence without drawing on some source of energy to continue its operations. Those operations, in their turn, require work in the sense that thermodynamics uses the term. Fatigue is a real feature of all machines. A good topographical map will map, among other things, the sources of energy from which the machines composing an assemblage draw the energy required for their operations. If the mapping of energetic relations is so important to onto-cartographical analysis, then this is because energy dependencies are one of the primary ways in which machines in assemblages exercise their gravity on other machines.

While ideology is a real gravitational mechanism in social ecologies involving human beings, energy dependencies very likely exercise far more power in leading people to tolerate oppressive social assemblages. Once again, the example of company scrip nicely illustrates this point. It is not so much an ideology that leads people to tolerate the oppressive conditions of employment by "the company," but rather the fact that they are paid in company scrip that cannot be exchanged for federal tender and that can only be redeemed at the company store. What does this have to do with energy? People need to eat and require fuel to heat their homes and for transportation. If these things can only be acquired through the company as a result of scrip, they are reduced to the status of satellites and are trapped within its orbit. They can't go elsewhere for better and more free opportunities because they lack the tender that would allow them to satisfy the energetic demands required for their operations. While an ideological critique might have some value here in helping people to see that payment in terms of scrip is not just, abolishing the bright object of scrip would be a far more effective strategy. Cultural studies and critical theory has a strong tendency towards dematerializing social relations, treating them as arising from beliefs, ideologies, signs, norms, and laws alone. Geophilosophy reminds us that social assemblages always require energy to maintain themselves and that intervention in energetic relations and dependencies is one way in which we can change oppressive social orders.

Fourth and finally, a good topographical map will also map the *material outputs* of operations carried out by machines. Machines draw on inputs or flows from other machines to produce not only themselves, but also products. There is no corporeal machine that doesn't produce some sort of material output in the course of its operations that then travels throughout the world affecting it in new ways. We see this clearly in the case of labor producing commodities and surplus value, in people writing books, in conversations that generate new thoughts, in classrooms that produce workers through socializing them and transforming them into particular types of epistemic and practical agents, and so on.

However, with the exception of ecotheory, we have a tendency to ignore the dimension of *waste* produced in all operations. Like long division for odd numbers where there's a remainder, the operations of corporeal bodies produce waste that becomes machines acting in the world in their own way. There is the heat and energy that dissipates into the environment when technologies and organic bodies operate. There is the waste that results from metabolism and digestion. There is the trash that is produced through consumption and building. There is the garbage that arises from producing goods and commodities. A good topographical map will map the outputs of various machines, how they create niches for other machines – for example, the microbes and insects that feed off the waste of poultry farms – and how these outputs contribute to structuring the gravity and problems an assemblage or ecology encounters.

The second sort of map belonging to cartography is a genetic map. Genetic maps chart the *genesis* or history of how particular worlds came to be. Marx, Braudel, Freud, Darwin, and DeLanda (see DeLanda 2000) are all exemplary genetic cartographers. Here I will limit myself to outlining why genetic maps are so important to the cartographical dimension of geophilosophy. Genetic maps serve two critical functions. First, they perform a sort of *epoché* on the present. The topography of contemporary worlds can be difficult to chart because they are familiar and obvious to us. We might not recognize the role that machines like clocks and satellites play in the organization of our world, for example, because they make up the ubiquitous stuff of everyday life, thereby becoming invisible in our investigations. As a consequence, we might be led to explain social assemblages purely in terms of the plane of expression – signs, signifiers, beliefs, ideologies, laws, and norms – ignoring the role that non-human agencies play in the formation of social ecologies. Good historical or genetic analyses such as Landes' *Revolution in Time*, for example, acquaint us with social ecologies where the clock was not present and how. As a result, they show us how these ecologies were organized very differently (see Landes 1983). Through the recollection of past assemblages and how they were organized, the world in which we live is defamiliarized and we are better able to discern those machinic agencies that contribute to the gravitational organization of our world. Historical or genetic analysis gives us the eyes to see the present and thus serve a crucial function in the drawing of topographical maps.

Second, genetic maps reveal the *contingency* and *historicity* of the *present*. Genetic analysis reveals that things have been *otherwise*, and that therefore they are not a product of "nature" in the *pre-Darwinian* sense. In this regard, genetic analyses serve an important critical function. For example, when we read ethnographic analyses such as *A Society Without Fathers or Husbands*, as well as other ethnographic works, we learn that the nuclear family is not the only kinship structure (Hua 2008). There, Hua explores the kinship structures of the Na, a people that live in the Himalayas, where brothers and sisters live with one another their entire lives, and where there is no marriage and where no monogamy is required. In encountering peoples that live this way, a critique is carried out of social explanations such as those we find among evolutionary psychologists and sociologists. Due to an inattention to history and ethnography, evolutionary sociologists have a strong tendency to essentialize contemporary ways of doing things, treating the nuclear family or capitalist competition as ahistorical universals, ignoring the fact that throughout history and the world, people have done things in very different ways. Genetic analysis reveals the contingency of how *we* do things, that others have done them differently, and thereby opens the way to more sophisticated analyses of social assemblages.

Above all, however, in revealing the contingency of how social assemblages are organized, genetic analysis reveals that things do not *have* to be this way and that they can be *otherwise*. Genetic analysis is not simply an analysis of history or how other people have done things, but is directed towards the *future*. Through genetic analysis we are able to de-"naturalize" (in the pre-Darwinian sense) contemporary social practices. Where the economist, for example, might see competition and debt as essential features of *all* economic activity throughout history and therefore lead us to conclude that there is no alternative to capitalism, genetic analysis can reveal that things have been otherwise at different times and among different cultures. In this way, genetic cartography opens a space for imagining other ways of doing things. In short, genetic analysis frees us from the iron constraints of the present by defamiliarizing it and revealing its contingency. As such, the way is opened to producing another world.

The converse of genetic maps are *vector maps*. Every assemblage, ecology, or world is becoming or unfolding in certain directions as a consequence of interactions among machines and especially the way in which bright objects and quasi-objects influence the movements, local manifestations, and becomings of other machines. Assemblages or worlds are not static beings, but rather unfold in particular directions. Vector maps chart the trajectories along which worlds are unfolding. The climatologist James Hansen is an excellent example of a vector cartographer. Through the examination of the contemporary topography of the world in terms of population, the emission of greenhouse gases, and so on, he plots what climate is likely to be in the future. The work of Marx in *Capital* is another outstanding example of work in vector cartography. Through the examination of the dynamics of capital in the present, he was able to chart the future it was tending toward. Elsewhere, the literature and science fiction of Philip K. Dick developed vector maps of where society is likely to go as a result of surveillance and information technology. The case is similar with R. S. Bakker's novel *Neuropath* (Bakker 2009) and Peter Watts' novel *Blindsight* (Watts 2008), where both novels explore what our future selves might be like as a result of neurology and increasingly pervasive interfaces between technology and brain.

Vector maps are mappings of the future based on gravitational tendencies operating in the present. They are maps – always fallible – that allow us to anticipate the future. This anticipatory function of vector maps is crucial to onto-cartography because it helps us to determine what we need to respond to in the present. A topographical map alone can leave us without any sense of what it is necessary to address in and through our practices. We end up simply responding to the happenings of the day, to the demands of the immediate moment, without knowing the crucial things to which we *ought* to respond. This was a common refrain in Marx's critiques of leftist politics. On the one hand, he contended that because activists had a poor topological map of what organizes contemporary social relations, they often ended up calling for things that simply reinforce the existing gravitational structure of capitalism. For example, teachers unaware of how standardized testing and assessment feed into an entire capitalistic system designed to benefit testing companies and so on, might fight for more efficient and precise testing methods that might preserve some of their educational ideals, thereby leaving that entire network of capitalistic relations intact. They assume that the issue is one of *educational excellence*, rather than one of capitalistic exploitation. On the other hand, he contended that without good vector cartographies of where capitalism is going, we're unable to determine where we need to intervene in the present. Thus, for example, if we don't understand that there's an intrinsic tendency for capitalism to depress wages, benefits, and taxes so as to maximize profit, if we don't understand that this is a general vector along which capitalism ineluctably unfolds over time, we might conclude that wage cuts really are just about foreign competition and not strategies businesses devise to increase profit. We might therefore see the appropriate response to declining wages as consisting of raising tariffs on foreign trade – which certainly can't hurt – rather than workers organizing to prevent such cuts. By giving us a glimpse of the future, no matter how imperfect, vector maps help us to determine where we ought to intervene and what ought to concern us.

Finally, there are *modal maps* or maps of *possible* futures. Initially modal maps and vector maps might appear to be the same, but in reality they are quite different. A vector map charts the likely future of a world, assemblage, or ecology based on tendencies unfolding in the present. Given these tendencies, a vector map says, this is the likely future. Modal maps, by contrast, map futures that *could* exist if we were to intervene in ecologies in particular ways. Where a vector map charts a picture of the future that will likely occur if an assemblage is left to its own devices, modal maps chart how we might actively produce a particular future were we to add or subtract certain machines populating an ecology. As such, modal maps are the domain of activists, militants, and generals. They are a sort of synthesis of topographical maps and vector maps. Envisioning a particular future that they find desirable, the modal cartographer asks "how would we have to change the existing assemblage to produce this world?" For example, the environmental activist might note that the world is unfolding along a particular vector that will, in the future, lead to the extinction of thousands of organisms, world hunger because of changes in agricultural conditions, more destructive weather events, and tremendous economic and political instability as people fight over resources. A modal map would consist of acting on the topography of the present, the arrangement of machines in the present, to produce a possible future that would avoid this fate. This would entail understanding how machines are interrelated in the topography of the contemporary world, feedback relations that sustain this organization of the world, dependencies among machines that lead this world to persist, and a map of what machines would have to be added and subtracted to change the vectors of this world. To understand modal maps it is necessary to understand the two other dimensions of geophilosophy.

Deconstruction

Deconstruction is that dimension of geographical practice that involves *severing* relations between incorporeal and corporeal machines that sustain particular ecological patterns through the gravity these interactions enact. With the term "deconstruction" I want to preserve both the loose concept of deconstruction as it functions in cultural studies and critical theory, while also proposing a far more literal concept of deconstruction. In other words, there will be one dimension of deconstructive practice devoted to the plane of expression or incorporeal signifying machines, and another dimension of deconstruction that pertains to the plane of content or relations between corporeal machines in the world.

Generally deconstruction has been restricted to the plane of expression, referring to a set of operations that act on signifying assemblages, challenging their "naturalness" (in the pre-Darwinian sense), internal cohesiveness, and internal necessity. Other names for critical theory would be "the hermeneutics of suspicion" or "critical theory." While deconstruction had a fairly precise meaning in the work of Derrida and his followers, in popular culture it has come to signify any form of cultural critique that challenges the legitimacy and force of various signifying assemblages or expressive formations. Thus, for example, Derridean deconstruction, Žižekian ideology critique, psychoanalysis, historicist critique, queer and feminist theory, Marxist economic critique, pre-Habermasian Frankfurt school critical theory, and a variety of other forms of critical theory would fall under the title of deconstruction.

An excellent example of deconstruction in this sense would be Judith Butler's *Gender Trouble* (see Butler 2006). Butler challenges the naturalness of our sexual identities and orientations, showing instead how they are the result of *performative practices*. Rather than being born as a man or a woman that necessarily desires the opposite sex, we instead *perform* masculinity, femininity, and heterosexuality. These performances are based on *scripts* that we inherit from the broader culture in which we're brought up. Butler's analysis of sexual identity and desire thus *dematerializes* these things. Rather than being intrinsic qualities or properties of our being, we discover that they instead result from how incorporeal semiotic-machines act upon us and how we enact these machines in our own practices through our performances. Insofar as culture is the domain of history and contingency – though we've learned this is true of nature as a whole – this deconstruction allows us to recognize the contingency of our sexual identities and to begin imagining and enacting other possibilities.

Another example of expressive deconstruction can be found in Althusser's analysis of ideology. In his famous essay "Ideology and Ideological State Apparatus," Althusser attempts to show how institutions such as the church, media, and schools function to reproduce the dominant modes of production and class relations under capitalism (see Althusser 2001). Where we take the church to be devoted to spiritual edification, the schools to be devoted to distributing knowledge and training, and the media to be about entertainment and information, Althusser strives to demonstrate that these institutions have very different aims: the production of obedient and capable workers necessary to engage in the processes required for the production of surplus value. Here the deconstruction consists in showing that venerated and celebrated institutions that we thought had one particular aim in fact have another aim that is oppressive and that reproduces a social order that, were we clearly aware of it, we might very well not support. Through such a deconstruction, Althusser contributes to the conditions for the possibility of emancipation by helping to separate us from the oppressive operations of these institutions so as to form new institutions that might be more just, free, and equitable.

I have not remotely done these examples the justice they deserve, but only present them here to provide a sense of how geophilosophy thinks about deconstruction at the level of the plane of expression. A deconstruction at the level of the plane of expression shows either that an expressive machine we believed to have one aim instead has another, or that something we took to be natural and necessary is, in fact, historical and contingent. In revealing the contingency behind expressive-machines, these deconstructions thus open a path for the creation of new social assemblages. Insofar as incorporeal, expressive, semiotic-machines exercise gravity upon assemblages inhabited by humans, geo-

philosophy retains the various techniques of expressive deconstruction as crucial elements in onto-cartographical analysis and
practice. Severing the efficacy of various semiotic-machines is
part of the way in which social assemblages are changed. These
various deconstructive techniques have to, of course, be modified
in light of the findings of onto-cartography and developmental
systems theory – especially with respect to the deconstruction of
the nature/culture divide effected by geophilosophy – but they are
nonetheless generally sound. What needs to be changed in these
techniques is the implicit assumption common in much cultural
critique that expressive-machines unilaterally determine and structure corporeal entities. Instead, we need to explore the dynamic
interplay between the expressive or semiotic and the corporeal.

In addition to the practice of expressive deconstruction, geophilosophy also proposes *corporeal* or *material* deconstructions.
A material deconstruction consists of severing a relation of
dependency between two or more corporeal machines so as to
open freedom of movement, local manifestation, or becoming for
a machine. Where expressive deconstructions operate on signs,
texts, beliefs, and ideologies, material deconstructions operate on
relations between bodily things. The premise of material deconstruction is that one reason machines locally manifest themselves
and move as they do is that they are caught in the gravity of other
machines. In other words, it's not just ideologies and mistaken
beliefs that lead us to tolerate intolerable social relations, but also
our relations to material things.

There are two ways in which a machine can exercise power
over another machine. First, one machine can structure the possible movements of another machine simply by being an obstacle
to that machine. Because the machine presents an obstacle to
the other machine, the second machine's movement is channeled
along certain paths and it is unable to enter into contact – at least
without great labor and difficulty – with other machines. Halls,
speed bumps, rivers, deserts, mountain ranges, roads, train routes,
and oceans are all entities that can modulate the movement and
paths of other entities, forcing them to move in this direction
rather than that, to relate to these entities rather than those entities. The layout of the space or territory itself therefore plays a
catalytic role in how social assemblages come to be organized and
what entities belong to those social assemblages.

Second, a machine can become trapped in the gravity of another machine insofar as it relies on flows from that machine for the energy necessary to sustain itself. We've seen this in the case of company scrip, where the miner might find life under the company oppressive but is without any alternative because there are no other job opportunities in their region and they're paid in a tender that can only be redeemed through the company. The situation is similar in the case of dependence upon fossil fuels. A person might be convinced of the reality of climate change, understand how it is related to the burning of fossil fuels, yet nonetheless live in circumstances that prevent them from doing things that would contribute to preventing it. Perhaps they do not make enough money to afford things such as solar panels and hybrid cars, thereby locking them into dependence on fossil fuels for transportation and to run their home. Perhaps they're in the construction industry and need a large vehicle to haul their equipment. Perhaps they live in an area where they can't buy locally grown foods and therefore are dependent upon foods that have been shipped from far away and that have been grown using environmentally destructive techniques. Perhaps their job is far away and they must therefore drive rather than bike to get to work. In circumstances such as this, it is not a lack of belief in climate change that motivates the person's actions, it is not indifference, but rather necessity generated by material circumstances. They are more or less forced by circumstances to depend on fossil fuels, even though they would prefer not to. In these cases, what is required is a transformation of the material world, not the deconstruction of a signifying assemblage or constellation.

A material deconstruction intervenes in the obstructions and energy dependencies constituting a territory, severing relations in ways that open a path for new forms of movement, local manifestation, and becoming. In other words, a material deconstruction literally deconstructs the way in which a particular assemblage is put together, undermining the gravitational force one entity or set of entities exercises over another. Such deconstructions can range from the somewhat trivial – though that's a matter of perspective – to the profound. Thus, for example, we might imagine a remote town in a mountain valley that is largely cut off from other towns and therefore from opportunities. Here the difficult to pass mountain functions as the obstruction that organizes the economic and social life of the people that live there. Something as simple as building a tunnel that allows for ease of travel between the town and other towns could open up all sorts of possibilities of movement for the people in the town. What we get here is a sort of deconstruction of the gravity the mountain exercises over the people of the town.

Another example of a material deconstruction would be the practice of "rolling jubilee" that has recently been adopted by participants in Occupy Wall Street.[2] Rolling jubilee is a deconstructive strategy for intervening in debt. Student loan debt, mortgage debt, credit card debt, and so on, exercise a tremendous gravity on the life of a person as well as the ability of collectives to change and challenge the social assemblage within which they dwell. The person in massive debt quite literally becomes the equivalent of a battery for other institutions, not unlike the people trapped within the Wachowski brother's Matrix. As interest accrues, significant portions of their income must perpetually go to the creditor, often with no end in sight. In many instances, the debtor has to take on additional jobs to meet monthly payments on their debt. For all intents and purposes, they become indentured to their creditors.

The gravity of debt thereby comes to structure their entire life and has effects well beyond their own individual life. Their time is swallowed by the necessity of working enough to make the funds to pay their monthly payments. This, in turn, places tremendous pressure on relationships and leads to the neglect of children. The disappearance of time also makes it difficult for people to pursue forms of training and education that might improve their economic circumstances. Likewise, insofar as they are locked into perpetual labor to pay their bills, their mobility is decreased. It becomes difficult to simply pick up and move elsewhere as they must work in order to pay their debts and are therefore attached to the jobs they currently have. Debt therefore has significant political effects as well. Having become attached to their job out of the necessity of paying their creditors, the debtor becomes reluctant to engage in collective movements to contest unfair labor practices and becomes more willing to accept cuts in wages and benefits. The job must be protected at all costs and any action that might threaten the job must be avoided as unemployment would be catastrophic for the debtor and their family.

Debt therefore functions as a gravitational mechanism, a bright object that organizes the life of the individual as well as the structure of the social assemblage. Debt functions to organize the social assemblage by diminishing the spatial mobility of people, by diminishing activism against unfair labor practices, thereby keeping the unequal structure of capitalism intact, by undermining the ability of people to cultivate themselves educationally due to the absence of time, and by perpetually funneling money to the creditors. We and the social assemblage all become locked in the gravitational web of debt, indentured to a life of perpetually working to acquire money to pay our creditors. Depending on the size of the debt and the interest rates of our loans, we find that we are never able to escape this gravity.

Rolling jubilee is a materialist deconstructive practice that strategically targets the gravity exercised by debt. Participants in rolling jubilee buy the debt of others from creditors for pennies on the dollar. Usually creditors purchase debt from other creditors with the intention of collecting that debt themselves and making a profit on its interest. One creditor sells rights to its debtor at a cheaper price on the grounds that it will still make some profit from the debt, even though it doesn't get the full amount of money it could have gotten had it retained rights to payment. The other creditor buys the debt on the grounds that it will be able to make money on the debt payments and interest that remain. What makes rolling jubilee unique is that it purchases debt not with the intention of collecting on it, but rather with the intention of *forgiving* it. In other words, rolling jubilee asks for no return on its purchase. The hope is that the debtors that have their debt forgiven will invest in buying the debt of others so as to continue this process of forgiveness.

Rolling jubilee thus severs or deconstructs a person's capture in a certain energetic gravitational relation. It literally severs them from functioning as an energy source for creditors. Through this deconstruction, all sorts of possibilities are open. At the individual level, the person no longer needs to work as much, it becomes possible to pursue training and education to enhance their opportunities, more time can be spent with family and loved ones, a good deal of destructive stress dissipates, and people are no longer as trapped in particular geographical locations. At the collective level, it becomes more possible to organize and contest unfair labor practices so as to pursue more equitable labor conditions. The deconstruction of debt doesn't *guarantee* that this will happen, but it does contribute to enhancing the *possibility* that it *can* happen. A deconstruction of this sort accomplishes something like this through sensitivity to the material gravity that organizes the lives and actions of people. Rather than comprehending reluctance to challenge capital as arising from being duped by ideological beliefs that see these inequalities and oppressive conditions as just and natural, it instead examines the gravitational fields that trap people in certain paths.

Based on the foregoing, we get a better sense of what a modal map might be. At the level of expressive and material deconstruction, a modal map hypothesizes that if these relations are *severed*, then it will be possible to produce this kind of future. Recognizing, at the level of topography, that movement, local manifestation, and becoming in a particular world or assemblage are structured by these networks of relations, deconstructive strategy intervenes by severing certain relations at the level of expressive and corporeal machines so as to render alternatives possible. This is only possible, however, where relations can be severed. At the ontological level this requires machines to be independent of relations. Machines are indeed related to one another, but they must be able to break with those relations for change to occur. However, we must exercise caution with our material deconstructions, as often the severing of relations can lead to unintended consequences. We can see this in the case of the introduction of cane toads into Northern Australia. In 1932 Australian farmers introduced cane toads into their ecosystem to prey on insects that were ravaging their sugar cane fields. In other words, they sought to deconstruct the relation between the sugar cane plants and insects. They were wildly successful in accomplishing this aim, but the problem was that lacking any natural predators, the cane toads quickly came to dominate the Australian ecosystem, destroying local wildlife and fauna. In short, the cure turned out to be worse than the sickness. In devising a modal map to be produced through deconstruction, it is important to take contingencies into account as much as desired outcomes. This requires a knowledge of the topography of the system into which we're intervening, the nature of the machines that populate that topography, and how they're likely to react to these deconstructions.

Terraformation

Terraformation, or the building of worlds, is the third dimension of geophilosophy. Just as relations between machines can be severed to open new paths of movement and becoming, new machines can be *added* to existing worlds to create new paths of movement and becoming. Often deconstruction and terraformation will go hand and hand, taking place at one and the same time. Thus, for example, we might think of what takes place when building a house. First there is the deconstruction of the plot of land effected through clearing trees and other brush, leveling the ground, and so on, and then there is the terraformation of actually building the foundation, the house, etc. The deconstruction is a necessary component of the terraformation.

One of the drawbacks of contemporary critical theory is that it has a tendency to focus on deconstruction alone. From the Marxists, for example, we get a compelling and sound critique of all that is wrong, destructive, and oppressive about capitalism, but little to no picture of an alternative. We're given little in the way of a picture of how we can do otherwise. This is a bit like giving an account of how a disease ravages our body, without formulating any treatment for that sickness. Such knowledge is necessary for eventually treating the disease, but in and of itself it does us little good. Absent any discussion of how we might go about constructing an alternative, people remain trapped in the gravitational structure of capitalism. The situation is similar to that of the episode entitled "Gnomes" in the second season of the television show *South Park*. There we are introduced to a group of gnomes that go about collecting underwear from people's homes. When the boys finally enter their lair, they discover that the gnomes are engaged in this strange activity as a part of a business plan:

> Phase 1: Collect Underpants
> Phase 2: ?
> Phase 3: Profit!

This is how it is with much critical and deconstructive theory:

> Phase 1: Radical Critique
> Phase 2: ?
> Phase 3: Revolutionary Society!

Because we have no picture of phase 2 or terraformation, these critiques therefore end up producing very little change. People might very well recognize the soundness of the critique, but remain trapped in the gravitational web of the agencies critiqued. Lacking any alternative, they resign themselves to these conditions and go on as before. In a circumstance such as this, it is not because they are duped by ideology that they tolerate such assemblages, but because they still have to work, eat, take care of their families, and so on, and there is no other discernible way of doing these things. One of the aims of geophilosophy is to encourage more work and thought devoted to terraformation.

Like deconstruction, terraformation can take place at the level of both expression and content. At the level of expression, terraformation consists of the production or construction of new signifying assemblages that weren't previously there in the social assemblage. This can consist of the invention of new conceptual assemblages for understanding the world, new norms and goals for life, and so on. Occupy Wall Street is often criticized for having accomplished very little of note, but at the level of expression they accomplished quite a bit. Prior to OWS, discussions of income inequality were almost entirely absent in the United States. The massive gap between that segment of the population that earns the most money and controls the majority of the wealth and everyone else simply was not an issue in mainstream politics. Through the construction of a signifying universe accessible to people without a deep background in economics and critical theory, OWS brought national attention to this issue, allowing us to discern how this wealth gap and the operations through which it is maintained and deepened affect every aspect of our lives and politics. The terraformation of this signifying universe, in its turn, opens the way for the construction of alternatives. In short, OWS *added* something to the plane of expression that wasn't brightly there before.

At the level of content, terraformation consists in adding new corporeal entities and forging relations between corporeal machines so as to open new paths of movement and becoming. Like deconstruction, terraformative interventions can range from the small to the large. At the small end of the spectrum we might imagine a young elementary student having difficulty learning at school. Further investigation might reveal that the child isn't suffering from a learning disability or something like attention deficit disorder, but rather is nearsighted. The simple introduction of a new medium, eyeglasses, opens an entirely new world for the child . . . a world the child didn't even know existed. With the *addition* of this machine, the child is now able to follow the class, what is transpiring on the board, and new possibilities of learning are open to him. Here a change at the level of content opens the possibility of a change at the level of how the child relates to expressive-machines (the material taught at school).

This is a trivial example – though not for the child – of a terraformation. What would constitute a profound and far reaching transformation? We will recall that many people tolerate capitalism not because they believe that it is natural, just, or that if they just work hard enough they too will someday become millionaires, but because they have no *alternative*. Rather, they must support themselves and their families, and as a consequence they must submit to wage labor and the jobs that are available. One way of changing this would be to produce an alternative that allows people to meet these needs. It is precisely this that "local economic transaction systems" (LETS) – discussed by Kojin Karatani (see Karatani 2003: 23–5) and first proposed by Michael Linton – strive to do. LETS is an economic system in which people earn credit for services done for others that can then be redeemed for services from others.[3] Thus, for example, I might earn x number of credits for trimming the hedges of another person. I can then use these credits to purchase food from a local farmer that participates in my local LETS system.

LETS thus differs from a barter system in that I earn credits for my labor that can be redeemed for other services and commodities. Where in a barter system I might trade the corn that I've grown for some fabric and then have to await an encounter with someone else in search of fabric to engage in other exchanges, in the LETS system I earn credits that can be exchanged for services and commodities in the community of equivalent value. Initially LETS might appear identical to wage-labor in that I earn credits for the goods and services I give to others. However, the crucial difference is that under LETS no surplus value is produced in the process of exchange, nor is interest accrued from sitting on your credits. As Karatani puts it, ". . . it is so organized that the sum total of the gains and losses of everyone is zero" (Karatani 2003: 23). The goods, services, and credits are equivalent in value to one another without profit being derived from the exchange. As a consequence, there is no incentive to hoard credits to profit from interest, nor are workers deprived of that which is rightfully theirs. Finally, LETS differs from a scrip system in that credits earned for goods and services can be exchanged for federal tender, allowing persons to depart from the economy if they so desire, and credits aren't awarded by a single machine such as the company, but rather by those who purchase your goods and services.

As John Croft points out, LETS allows people to actualize the wealth of their community in ways that bypass traditional economy (Croft n.d.). Suppose, for example, that money is scarce in a local community due to an economic depression and that there is high unemployment. People in the community continue to need goods and services, a great deal of wealth remains in the community, and there are many skilled workers within the community, yet there isn't enough money to access this wealth in the form of skills, services, and goods. LETS is a way of bypassing this problem. Services and goods, along with the number of credits they're worth, are listed on a billboard online – as are the number of credits each person that participates in the system has – and those with the skills to provide those services and goods contact those in need of them. Unlike a capitalist system where jobs are predominantly provided by a business, corporation, or owner, exchange relations take place between individuals in the LETS system. In this way, LETS allows the wealth of a community to be accessed even during periods of economic turmoil and instability where money is scarce. Within such an economic system, the skills of people can continue to be utilized, and people can continue to provide for their educational, legal, clothing, energy, and feeding needs.

In a related vein, where capitalist systems tend to divest communities of their wealth because money flows up to the owners and outside of the community, LETS helps to keep wealth within communities and functions to actually build communities. On the one hand, community relations are forged and strengthened because economic transactions take place directly between individuals. On the other hand, because one must join a LETS collective in order to participate in this economy, and because the sum of gains and losses in such a system is zero, wealth does not pass out of the community but instead circulates about the community.

These brief remarks have not done LETS nearly the justice it deserves, so I strongly encourage readers to do further research on their own. LETS is a perfect example of terraformation. I am not suggesting that it is a perfect system, nor that it solves all the woes of capitalism, but merely evoke it as an example of what terraformation on a large scale looks like. Terraforming practices do not seek to challenge existing assemblages organized around particular forms of gravity head on as in the case of a slave rebellion against slave owners or a political revolution that seeks to overturn the existing regime. Rather, terraformation attempts to construct an alternative assemblage that allows people to sidestep the gravitational forces of the existing assemblage altogether. Rather than fighting the existing assemblage, one simply flees it and sets up camp elsewhere. As we see in the case of LETS, this flight need not entail movement from one node to another in space. Rather it can be a flight in place, right there within the same geographical region of the other assemblage.

Like deconstruction, terraformation requires a good cartography of assemblages or worlds. If you don't understand the way in which worlds are put together, you cannot know what needs to be deconstructed. If you don't understand the gravitational structure of an existing assemblage, you are unable to determine what other types of assemblages should be constructed. Both deconstruction and terraformation will always involve cartography. However, cartography will not always involve deconstruction or terraformation. For example, clearly terraformation is not an appropriate response to a social assemblage characterized by slavery. Slaves cannot simply opt out of such assemblages precisely because they are slaves; at least they can't do so without great risk and sacrifice to themselves. The only way to overcome slavery is to shatter the signifying assemblages that justify it at the level of law and belief, and to shatter the material system that supports it. Likewise, deconstruction will not always be the appropriate response to changing relations, as we see in the case of the nearsighted child with learning problems.

More often than not, transformative practices will involve a combination of both deconstruction and terraformation. For example, addressing climate change will require deconstruction of both beliefs and ideologies that render us blind to the environmental impact of our ways of living, as well as the deconstruction of our dependence on certain technologies and fossil fuels. It will also require the terraformation of new technologies, new modes of travel, new agricultural practices, new forms of energy, new ways of relating to ecosystems, and the building of new sets of ideals and views about what constitutes "the good life" at the level of expressive machines. Likewise, short of awaiting a massive economic catastrophe such as that which motivated the Russian Revolution of 1917 by plunging people into such squalor that they had no alternative, it's unlikely that critique alone will substantially affect capitalism. Until we begin to *build* alternatives that allow people to support themselves and their families, until we begin to present something other than a critique, until we begin to show what a real alternative world would look like, it's unlikely that many will act on critiques of capitalism.

Conclusion

The three dimensions of geophilosophy can be summed up as in Table 8.2.

The aim of onto-cartography is threefold. First, onto-cartography proceeds from the premise that Continental social and political theory – with a few notable and important exceptions – has been dominated by a focus on the discursive and first-person experience of subjects. As the foregoing hopefully makes clear, onto-cartography wishes to preserve these modes of analysis and believes that they are valid so far as they go. However, onto-cartography holds that these forms of analysis – largely products of the linguistic turn and phenomenology – give us a very limited understanding of how power functions because they do not take into account the role played by non-human machines in structuring our social relations. Problems that arise from how non-humans channel our movements, becomings, and local manifestations become invisible

Table 8.2 Summary of the three dimensions of geophilosophy

	Practice	Aim	Product
Cartography	Mapping	Understanding the gravitational organization of worlds	Topographical, genetic, vector, and modal maps
Deconstruction	Severing relations/ subtraction	Toppling gravity to free movement, becoming, and local manifestations; creation of "lines of flight"	Destruction of machines at the level of expression and content (undermining existing ecologies)
Terraformation	Forging relations/ addition	Building new assemblages that are more satisfying, just, and sustainable; creation of new fields of life, materiality, and affectivity	Construction of machines and assemblages at the level of expression and content (building new ecologies)

because we treat the discursive as that which solely structures social relations. One of the central aims of onto-cartography is to draw attention to these non-humans, how they structure our social relations, and how they intersect with signifying assemblages on the plane of expression. In this way, onto-cartography seeks not to diminish our points of social and political intervention, but to multiply them. The point is not to abandon modes of critique such as we find in Judith Butler, but to also recognize, as Jane Bennett has it, that things too exercise power or gravity. When we understand how things exercise their power in particular assemblages, we can begin intervening in those machines as one strategy for producing change.

Second, onto-cartography aims to comprehend social assemblages as ecologies and processes, rather than as a domain distinct from nature. There are two motivations for this move. On the one hand, when we understand that social assemblages – indeed all machines and ecologies – are processes that function in such a way as to stave off entropy, we also understand being in terms of *operations* and operations as requiring work– in the thermodynamic sense, but also in the sense of labor – and energy. Rather than asking "what is it?" we should instead ask "what does it do?" And in asking "what does it do?" we are led to ask upon what does a particular machine operate, how does it transform that flow, and what is the output of that operation in terms of waste, material products, local manifestations, and becomings?

However, understanding machines and assemblages in terms of operations also reminds us that all machines and assemblages require *work* and *energy*. Work is the capacity to carry out operations either within a machine or upon another machine such as a flow. Energy is what is required to carry out work. It is astonishing that the concepts of work and energy are almost entirely absent from the history of philosophy. It's as if, for the philosopher, being consisted entirely of objects, concepts, and minds, and that the philosopher seeks to demonstrate how being is built out of these three things. If the absence of these concepts is so detrimental from the standpoint of social and political philosophy, then this is because energy– whether or not it is available, whether or not one has it – is one of the primary mechanisms by which power (in the political sense) or gravity exercises itself within social assemblages. We speak as if it were merely signifying assemblages – beliefs and ideologies – that organized social machines, ignoring completely the role that exhaustion and wakefulness produced through work and leisure organize social relations. We have scarcely begun to think of work and energy – both in the domain of individual lives and in broader social and natural ecosystems – but one of the central aims of onto-cartography is to bring these things to the forefront of social and political thought. Given the persistence and growth of economic inequality, as well as the growing climate crisis, more than ever do we need to develop a "thermopolitics" and "thermoethics" (thermodynamics + politics). Such inquiries will also require uncomfortable self-reflexive deconstructive analyses at the level of the plane of expression, raising questions of just why theorists so persistently overlook work and energy in their social and political thought.

On the other hand, in understanding social assemblages as ecologies rather than as domains distinct and separated from nature, onto-cartography hopes to draw attention to the way in which social agency is both distributed and dependent on non-humans belonging to the broader natural world. Contrary to Timothy Morton's "ecology without nature," what we need more than ever is social and political thought as a thought of nature. While Morton's intuitions are in the right place, it is not that we need to abandon the concept of nature, but that we need to transform the concept of nature in light of discoveries from the last 300 years and that we need to abolish the nature/culture distinction. This distinction is destructive for two reasons. First, as a result of the nature/culture distinction, we're led to see social relations as arising solely from signs, ideologies, beliefs, norms, discourses, economy, laws, ideologies, and signifiers, thereby ignoring the role that geography, natural events like plagues, hurricanes, floods, and so on, relations to local fauna and animals, ocean currents, weather patterns, seasons, available resources, technologies, etc., play in the form that social relations take. Recognizing societies or cultures as ecologies and as embedded in the larger natural world helps us to discern the role played by these other machines. It's not that there are no discursive contributions to social relations, but that they're only part of the story. Second, treating social assemblages as an ecology reminds us that thermodynamically we draw from non-humans for the energy that sustains our social relations – as in the case of plant and animal agriculture, as well as fossil fuels – and that we release all sorts of waste into the world around us. The nature/culture divide encourages us to forget these flows between domains, while treating social assemblages as ecologies reminds us to count both that which flows into social assemblages allowing them to persist, while also counting that which flows out of them affecting both us and the broader natural world. As climate change intensifies, it is crucial to remember that whenever we eat a Big Mac we're also drawing energy from the broader natural world of which we're an instance and introducing waste into that world upon which we depend.

Third and finally, onto-cartography is motivated by a plea for the *concrete*. As discussed in the last section, there's a tendency for theory to traffic in abstractions: "capitalism," "patriarchy," "racism," "environment," "sovereignty," "colonialism," etc. As Hegel taught us in the "sense-certainty" section of the *Phenomenology of Spirit*, we necessarily traffic in abstraction by virtue of the nature of language. The signifier or sign /dog/ will never fully capture individual dogs or the variety of dogs. It will always reduce dogs to a grouping based on a set of resemblances that betray their diversity and individuality. In this regard, terms like "capitalism" and "racism" are shorthand for very complex assemblages. However, as Lukács has taught us, we also have a tendency to *reify* these things (see Lukács 2002). In other words, we forget that these things are shorthand for very complex assemblages and instead end up treating them as *agencies* that issue social relations through some sort of occult magic. As we saw earlier, we thus end up in a position of either practical pessimism or revolutionary quietism. The practical pessimist recognizes that she is unable to fight ghosts or abstract entities that are everywhere and nowhere and therefore elects to give up altogether. The revolutionary quietist is someone that claims that unless we can overturn the entire ghost in a single stroke, no *process* or *sequence* of interventions is worthwhile. The revolutionary quietist dreams of being a Shaolin warrior monk who, through a single gesture, can bring about the death of his enemy. As a result of the dream of a single death blow, they refuse any other intervention.

Onto-cartography's call to attend to the concrete is a call to attend to how the assemblages or worlds underlying these reified terms are actually put together. The premise is that understanding how assemblages are put together at the level of expression and content will allow us to discern the structure of gravity, how power functions, why oppressive and destructive assemblages resist entropy, and thereby devise strategies to transform these assemblages through deconstruction and terraformation. We can't act on *capitalism*, but we can act on this or that relation between machines, and can produce this or that assemblage of machines. The cry of onto-cartography is "attend to the machines and relations between machines in worlds," while the prohibition of onto-cartography is "forget abstract machines or disempowering machines." Clearly it is not Deleuze and Guattari's "abstract machines" that onto-cartography here has in mind, but rather disempowering reifications that are so vague as to provide us with no points of intervention in worlds.

Based on the foregoing, we can imagine two interrelated forms of politics: normative politics and cartographical politics. Normative politics and ethics outline those goals and aims that ought to animate our political and ethical interventions. Here we must remember that political and ethical evaluations are themselves incorporeal, expressive machines. An ethics is a machine that proposes certain operations and that selects certain machines in the present for the sake of produce certain futures. It is a modal map. A politics is a machine that proposes a plan for producing that future. The thing that we must remember as geophilosophers is that ethical and political machines do not fall from the sky like what Dennett calls "skyhooks," but that they arise from the earth, the world, and the circumstances in which we find ourselves. Within Continental social, political, and ethical theory we have plenty of ethical machines. We know that inequality is wrong, that sexism is wrong, that racism is wrong, that capitalism is destructive and oppressive, that non-sustainable energy and consumption practices are disastrous. In short, our situation has presented us with the problems that – if we attend to the vector maps that follow from contemporary practices – ought to generate the norms which we should obey. In this regard, denunciations, at this point, are of limited value. We know them, we've heard them. What we need are modal maps that would allow us to transform these normative machines into actualities in the world.

Cartographical politics, by contrast, consists of a *mapping* of how gravity is structured. Cartographical politics seldom tells us what we *ought* to do, but instead gives us a map of how and why gravity is structured in an assemblage as it is. Marx and Foucault are the two exemplary cartographical political theorists. Through their analyses, both showed us how the gravity of social assemblages are organized. Cartographical politics is not a discourse about the norms that ought to direct our activity, nor a discourse about what we ought to do, but is instead a mapping of how power or gravity functions in particular social assemblages or worlds. In the case of Marx's *Capital*, for example, we're not told what to do, nor what is right and wrong. Rather, we're presented with a genetic map of how capitalism came to be, a topographical map of how capitalism systematically produces inequality and divides the world into workers and owners, and a vector map of where capitalism is likely heading due to the antagonisms that inhabit it. Marx shows how technologies, resources, factories, money, and labor interact with one another to produce certain gravitational fields and local manifestations. Armed with these maps, it thereby becomes possible to devise strategic interventions to break this gravity. The case is similar with Foucault in *Discipline & Punish*. Through careful historical analysis, Foucault shows us how we internalize power, becoming our own jailors, and how an entire set of practices and architectural structures functions to produce this sort of subjectivity.

Through their maps, Marx and Foucault reveal the *contingency* of social ecologies. Rather than treating these ecologies as the way the world naturally is, they instead show that they came to be through a set of genetic processes. Marx, for example, shows that not only have different conditions and relations of production – different social ecologies – existed throughout history, but that they have also generated different forms of subjectivity or agency. The subjectivity of the peasant farmer, the skilled tradesman, and the factory worker are, according to Marx, different. In showing this, Marx shows both that how we produce and trade today is not an ahistorical and universal feature of all production, but a particular historical configuration, and that how we experience ourselves and exist is similarly historical. The case is the same with Foucault. As he shows in *The Use of Pleasure*, there have been a variety of different types of "selves" or subjects arising from different practices throughout history (Foucault 1990: 25–32). Both provide careful mappings of the assemblages that produce these subjectivities. In revealing that both these assemblages and forms of subjectivity are contingent, they also reveal that other ways of living and arranging social ecologies are possible and open a space where we can begin to imagine these other ecologies and strive to produce them.

What we have to remember in this context, however, is the *spec-*

ificity, the concreteness, of Marx and Foucault's maps. These are maps of particular social ecologies under particular historical conditions. And just as you can't transfer the findings of an ecological map of the Amazonian rains forests to the great sequoia forests of California, you can't transfer Foucault's analysis of power in *Discipline & Punish* to just any geographical location or point in history. It is not just their findings that we should take from Marx and Foucault, but also their *techniques*. The paradoxical danger of cartographical analyses is that they can blind us to the new forms social ecologies are taking. We forget that the map is not the territory and that, in any event, territories change. We thereby end up striving to intervene in the territory based on our maps in ways that just aren't responsive to how gravity is organized within this geography or under these conditions.

However, while thinkers such as Marx and Foucault have made valuable contributions to onto-cartography, these styles of thought are not yet onto-cartographical enough. These discourses still remain too mired in human exceptionalism, as is reflected by their modes of explanation and their political aims. In the case of Marx, for example, the central political aim is human emancipation. This comes out with special clarity in the case of *Economic and Philosophic Manuscripts of 1844*, where humans are unique in that they both form themselves and the world about them, and where the aim is to overcome how we are alienated in our labor (Marx 1978: 66–125). The problem is not that human emancipation is not a laudable goal, but rather that this characterization both forgets the teachings of developmental systems theory where we are also formed by all sorts of non-human agencies, and forgets the broader ecology of our world that also requires political engagement. While John Bellamy Foster has made a compelling case for a deep and rich ecological thought in Marx's work, this way of thinking has not been deeply represented in mainstream and dominant strains of Marxist thought (see Foster 2000). Indeed, much subsequent Marxist thought, arising out of the pre-Habermasian Frankfurt school and Althusserian French Marxism, came even to largely ignore Marx's rich meditations on the formative role played by technologies and entities such as factories, instead presenting cultural explanations of social relations in terms of ideology. The case is similar with Foucault, where discussions of the role played by technology and non-humans in the formation of social ecologies is severely underdetermined.

What we need is a post-humanist framework that is able to synthesize the findings of the linguistic turn, Marxist thought, Foucaultian thought, media theorists such as McLuhan, Kittler, and Ong, as well as the post-humanist thought of the ecologists, the new materialists, the actor-network theorists, and the work of thinkers such as Diamond and Braudel. It is only within a framework that is capable of thinking overdetermination in and through the intersection and interaction of a variety of different types of machines functioning as media for one another that we can begin to develop maps adequate to the political and ethical demands that face us today. Moreover, insofar as climate change threatens us with a danger unprecedented in human history, we need to overcome the bias of human exceptionalism we find in our social and political thought, so as to take into account the manner in which human social assemblages are embedded in a broader ecology. It is this framework that onto-cartography attempts to provide.

Notes

1. I owe this observation to a discussion with Noah Horowitz in 2002.
2. For more on rolling jubilee, see Rolling Jubilee at <http://rollingjubilee.org/>.
3. For more on LETS, see. John Croft, "A FAQ on LETS," at <http://www.gdrc.org/icm/lets-faq.html>.

References

Alaimo, Stacy (2010) *Bodily Natures: Science, Environment, and the Material Self*. Bloomington: Indiana University Press.

Althusser, Louis (2001) "Ideology and Ideological State Apparatus (Notes Towards an Investigation)," in *Lenin and Philosophy and Other Essays*, trans. Ben Brewster. New York: Monthly Review Press, pp. 85–132.

Aristotle (1984) *Metaphysics*, in *The Complete Works of Aristotle: Volume Two*, ed. Jonathan Barnes. Princeton: Princeton University Press.

Badiou, Alain (2005) *Being and Event*, trans. Oliver Feltham. New York: Continuum.

Badiou, Alain (2006) "Being and Appearing," in *Briefings on Existence: A Short Treatise on Transitory Ontology*, trans. Norman Madarasz. Albany: State University of New York Press.

Badiou, Alain (2008) "What is Love?" in *Conditions*, trans. Steven Corcoran. New York: Continuum, pp. 179–98.

Badiou, Alain (2009) *Logics of Worlds: Being and Event II*, trans. Alberto Toscano. New York: Continuum.

Bakker, R. Scott (2009) *Neuropath*. New York: Tor Books.

Barad, Karen (2007) *Meeting the Universe Halfway: Quantum Physics and the Entanglement of Matter and Meaning*. Durham, NC: Duke University Press.

Bateson, Gregory (2000a) "The Cybernetics of 'Self': A Theory of Alcoholism," in *Steps to an Ecology of Mind*. Chicago: University of Chicago Press.

Bateson, Gregory (2000b) "Form, Substance, and Difference," in *Steps to an Ecology of Mind*, Chicago: University of Chicago Press.

Baudrillard, Jean (1981) *For a Critique of the Political Economy of the Sign*, trans. Charles Levin. New York: Telos Press.

Baudrillard, Jean (2006) *System of Objects*. New York: Verso.

Bennett, Jane (2010) *Vibrant Matter: A Political Ecology of Things*. Durham, NC: Duke University Press.

Bennett, Jane, Bryant, Levi R., and Harman, Graham (2011) "Speculative Realism: A Round-Table with Jane Bennett, Levi R. Bryant, and Graham Harman," hosted by the CUNY Graduate Center <http://vimeo.com/30101429>.

Berger, Peter L. and Luckmann, Thomas (1967) *The Social Construction of Reality: A Treatise in the Sociology of Knowledge*. New York: Anchor Books.

Bergson, Henri (2010) "Introduction to Metaphysics," in *The Creative Mind: An Introduction to Metaphysics*. New York: Dover Publications, pp. 133–69.

Bhaskar, Roy (2008) *A Realist Theory of Science*. New York: Routledge.

Blum, Andrew (2012) *Tubes: A Journey to the Center of the Internet*. New York: HarperCollins.

Bogost, Ian (2006) *Unit Operations: An Approach to Videogame Criticism*. Cambridge, MA: MIT Press.

Bogost, Ian (2012) *Alien Phenomenology, or What It's Like to Be a Thing*. Minneapolis: University of Minnesota Press.

Bourdieu, Pierre (2000) *Pascalian Meditations*, trans. Richard Nice. Stanford: Stanford University Press.

Bourdieu, Pierre (2002) *Distinction: A Social Critique of the Judgement of Taste*, trans. Richard Nice. Cambridge, MA: Harvard University Press.

Brandom, Richard (1998) *Making it Explicit: Reasoning, Representing, and Discursive Commitment*. Cambridge, MA: Harvard University Press.

Braudel, Fernand (1981) *The Structures of Everyday Life: Civilization & Capitalism, 15th – 18th Century*, Vol. 1, trans. Siân Reynolds. New York: Harper & Row.

Bryant, Levi R. (2011) *The Democracy of Objects*. Ann Arbor: Open Humanities Press.

Butler, Judith (2006) *Gender Trouble: Feminism and the Subversion of Identity*. New York: Routledge.

Casey, Edward S. (1999) *The Fate of Place: A Philosophical History*. Berkeley: University of California Press.

Casey, Edward S. (2009) *Getting Back into Place, Second Edition: Toward a Renewed Understanding of the Place World*. Bloomington: Indiana University Press.

Clark, Andy (1998) *Being-There: Putting Brain, Body, and World Together Again*. Cambridge, MA: MIT Press.

Clark, Andy (2003) *Natural-Born Cyborgs: Minds, Technologies, and the Future of Human Intelligence.* Oxford: Oxford University Press.

Clark, Andy (2011) *Supersizing the Mind: Embodiment, Action, and Cognitive Extension.* Oxford: Oxford University Press.

Clark, Andy and Chalmers, David (2011) "The Extended Mind," in *Supersizing the Mind: Embodiment, Action, and Cognitive Extension,* Oxford: Oxford University Press, pp. 220–32.

Croft, John (n.d.) "A FAQ on LETS," available at <http://www.gdrc.org/icm/lets-faq.html>.

DeLanda, Manuel (2000) *A Thousand Years of Nonlinear History.* Cambridge, MA: MIT Press.

DeLanda, Manuel (2005) *Intensive Science and Virtual Philosophy.* New York: Continuum.

DeLanda, Manuel (2011) "Emergence, Causality and Realism," in Levi R. Bryant, Nick Srnicek, and Graham Harman (eds) *The Speculative Turn: Continental Materialism and Realism.* Melbourne: Re.Press, pp. 381–92.

Deleuze, Foucault (1988) *Foucault,* trans. Sean Hand. Minneapolis: University of Minnesota Press.

Deleuze, Gilles (1986) *Cinema 1: The Movement-Image,* trans. Hugh Tomlinson and Barbara Habberjam. Minneapolis: University of Minnesota Press.

Deleuze, Gilles (1990) *The Logic of Sense,* trans. Mark Lester and Charles Stivale. New York: Columbia University Press.

Deleuze, Gilles (1995) *Difference and Repetition,* trans. Paul Patton. New York: Columbia University Press.

Deleuze, Gilles (2006) "Immanence: A Life," in *Two Regimes of Madness: Texts and Interviews 1975–1995,* ed. David Lapoujade. New York: Semiotext(e).

Deleuze, Gilles and Guattari, Félix (1983) *Anti-Oedipus: Capitalism and Schizophrenia,* trans. Robert Hurley, Mark Seem, and Helen R. Lane. Minneapolis: University of Minnesota Press.

Deleuze, Gilles and Guattari, Félix (1986) *Kafka: Toward a Minor Literature,* trans. Dana Polan. Minneapolis: University of Minnesota Press.

Deleuze, Gilles and Guattari, Félix (1987) *A Thousand Plateaus: Capitalism and Schizophrenia,* trans. Brian Massumi. Minneapolis: University of Minnesota Press.

Deleuze, Gilles and Guattari, Félix (1996) *What Is Philosophy?,* trans. Hugh Tomlinson and Graham Burchell. New York: Columbia University Press.

Dennett, Daniel C. (1995) *Darwin's Dangerous Idea: Evolution and the Meanings of Life*. New York: Simon & Schuster.

Dennett, Daniel C. (2003) *Freedom Evolves*. New York: Penguin Books.

Dewey, John (2008) *The Later Works of John Dewey, Volume 12, 1925–1953: 1938, Logic: The Theory of Inquiry (Collected Works of John Dewey 1882–1953)*. Edwardsville: Southern Illinois University Press.

Diamond, Jared (2005) *Guns, Germs, and Steel: The Fates of Human Societies*. New York: W. W. Norton.

Elder-Vass, David (2010) *The Causal Power of Social Structures: Emergence, Structure and Agency*. Cambridge: Cambridge University Press.

Flusser, Vilém and Bec, Louis (2012) *Vampyrotheuthis Infernalis: A Treatise, with a Report by the Institute Scientifique de Recherche Paranaturalistic*, trans. Valentine A. Pakis. Minneapolis: University of Minnesota Press.

Foester, Heinz von (1971) "Perception of the Future and the Future of Perception," available at <http://ada.evergreen.edu/~arunc/texts.old/readings.htm>.

Foster, John Bellamy (2000) *Marx's Ecology: Materialism and Nature*. New York: Monthly Review Press.

Foucault, Michel (1990) *The Use of Pleasure: History of Sexuality: Volume 2*, trans. Robert Hurley. New York: Vintage Books.

Foucault, Michel (1994) *The Order of Things: An Archaeology of the Human Sciences*. New York: Vintage.

Foucault, Michel (1995) *Discipline & Punish: The Birth of the Prison*. New York: Vintage.

Frankfurt, Harry G. (1998) "Freedom of Will and the Concept of a Person," in *The Importance of What We Care About*. Cambridge: Cambridge University Press, pp. 11–25.

Freud, Sigmund (2001a) *Civilization and Its Discontents*, in *The Standard Edition of the Complete Psychological Works of Sigmund Freud*, Vol. 21, trans. James Strachey. New York: Vintage.

Freud, Sigmund (2001b) *The Interpretation of Dreams*, in *The Standard Edition of the Complete Psychological Works of Sigmund Freud*, Vol. 4, trans. James Strachey. New York: Vintage Books.

Freud, Sigmund (2001c) "A Note Upon the 'Mystic Writing-Pad,'" in *The Standard Edition of the Complete Psychological Works of Sigmund Freud*, Vol. 19, trans. James Strachey. New York: Vintage, pp. 227–32.

Gleick, James (2012) *The Information: A History, A Theory, A Flood.* New York: Vintage Books.

Gottlieb, Gilbert (2001) "A Developental Psychobiological Systems View: Early Formulation and Current Status," in Susan Oyama, Paul E. Griffiths, and Russell D. Gray (eds), *Cycles of Contingency: Developmental Systems and Evolution.* Cambridge, MA: MIT Press.

Gould, Stephen Jay (1989) *Wonderful Life: The Burgess Shale and the Nature of History,* New York: W. W. Norton.

Grandin, Temple (2005) *Animals in Translation: Using the Mysteries of Autism to Decode Animal Behavior.* New York: A Harvest Book.

Greenblatt, Stephen (2012) *The Swerve: How the World Became Modern.* New York: W. W. Norton.

Hacking, Ian (1999) *The Social Construction of What?* Cambridge, MA: Harvard University Press.

Haraway, Donna J. (1991) "A Cyborg Manifesto: Science, Technology, and Socialist-Feminism in the Late Twentieth Century," in *Simians, Cyborgs, and Women: The Reinvention of Nature.* New York: Routledge.

Harington, Donald (1989) *The Cockroaches of Stay More.* Las Vegas: Toby Press.

Harman, Graham (2002) *Tool-Being: Heidegger and the Metaphysics of Objects.* Chicago: Open Court.

Harman, Graham (2005) *Guerrilla Metaphysics: Phenomenology and the Carpentry of Things.* Chicago: Open Court.

Harman, Graham (2010) "Time, Space, Essence, and Eidos: A New Theory of Causation," *Cosmos and History,* 6 (1): 1–17.

Harman, Graham (2011) *The Quadruple Object.* Washington, DC: Zero Books.

Harvey, David (2010) *A Companion to Marx's Capital.* New York: Verso.

Hegel, G. W. F. (1969) *Hegel's Science of Logic,* trans. A. V. Miller. Atlantic Highlands: Humanities Press International.

Hegel, G. W. F. (1977) *Hegel's Phenomenology of Spirit,* trans. A. V. Miller. Oxford: Oxford University Press.

Heidegger, Martin (1962) *Being and Time,* trans. John Macquarrie and Edward Robinson. San Francisco: HarperCollins.

Hjelmslev, Louis (1969) *Prolegomena to a Theory of Language,* trans. Francis J. Whitfield. Madison, WI: University of Wisconsin Press.

Hoy, David Couzens (2009) *The Time of Our Lives: A Critical History of Temporality.* Cambridge, MA: MIT Press.

Hua, Cai (2008) *A Society Without Fathers or Husbands: The Na of China*. New York: Zone Books.

Hume, David (1999) *An Enquiry Concerning Human Understanding*, ed. Tom L. Beauchamp. Oxford: Oxford University Press.

Inwagen, Peter van (1990) *Material Beings*. Ithaca: Cornell University Press.

Kafka, Franz (1974) *Amerika*, trans. Willa and Edwin Muir. New York: Schocken Books.

Kahn, Amina (2012) "Giant Rogue Planet, Without a Home Star, May Roam Nearby Heavens," *Los Angeles Times*, November 14, available at <http://articles.latimes.com/2012/nov/14/science/la-sci-sn-giant-rogue-planet-lost-space-star-20121113>.

Kant, Immanuel (1998) *Critique of Pure Reason*, trans. Paul Guyer and Allen W. Wood. Cambridge: Cambridge University Press.

Karatani, Kojin (2003) *Transcritique: On Kant and Marx*, trans. Sabu Kohso. Cambridge, MA: MIT Press.

Kelly, Kevin (2011) *What Technology Wants*. New York: Penguin Books.

Lacan, Jacques (1993) *The Psychoses (1955–1956): The Seminar of Jacques Lacan – Book III*, trans. Russell Grigg. New York: W. W. Norton.

Lacan, Jacques (1998) *Encore: The Limits of Love and Knowledge (1972–1973)*, trans. Bruce Fink. New York: W. W. Norton.

Lacan, Jacques (2006) "The Instance of the Letter in the Unconscious or Reason Since Freud," *Écrits: The First Complete Edition in English*, trans. Bruce Fink. New York: W. W. Norton.

Landes, David S. (1983) *Revolution in Time: Clocks and the Making of the Modern World*. Cambridge, MA: Harvard University Press.

Latour, Bruno (1987) *Science in Action: How to Follow Scientists and Engineers Throughout Society*. Cambridge, MA: Harvard University Press.

Latour, Bruno (1988) *Irreductions*, in *The Pasteurization of France*, trans. Alan Sheridan and John Law. Cambridge, MA: Harvard University Press.

Latour, Bruno (1993) *We Have Never Been Modern*, trans. Catherine Porter. Cambridge, MA: Harvard University Press.

Latour, Bruno (2004) *Politics of Nature: How to Bring the Sciences into Democracy*. Cambridge, MA: Harvard University Press.

Latour, Bruno (2005) *Reassembling the Social: An Introduction to Actor-Network-Theory*. Oxford: Oxford University Press.

Lautman, Albert (2011) *Mathematics, Ideas, and the Physical Real*, trans. Simon B. Duffy. New York: Continuum.

Leibniz, G. W. (1991) *The Principles of Philosophy, or, the Monadology (1714)*, in *Discourse on Metaphysics and Other Essays*, trans. Daniel Garber and Roger Ariew. Indianapolis: Hackett.

Lewontin, Richard C. (2001) "Gene, Organism and Environment," in Susan Oyama, Paul E. Griffiths, and Russell D. Gray (eds), *Cycles of Contingency: Developmental Systems and Evolution*. Cambridge, MA: MIT Press.

Lovejoy, Arthur O. (1936) *Great Chain of Being*. Cambridge, MA: Harvard University Press.

Lucretius (1969) *The Way Things Are: The De Rerum Natura of Titus Lucretius Carus*, trans. Rolfe Humphries. Bloomington: Indiana University Press.

Luhmann, Niklas (1995) *Social Systems, The De Rerum Natura of Titus Lucretius Carus*, trans. Humphries John Bednarz, Jr. and Dirk Baeker. Stanford: Stanford University Press.

Luhmann, Niklas (2000) *The Reality of the Mass Media, The De Rerum Natura of Titus Lucretius Carus*, trans. Humphries Kathleen Cross. Stanford: Stanford University Press.

Luhmann, Niklas (2002a) "The Cognitive Program of Constructivism and the Reality that Remains Unknown," in *Theories of Distinction: Redescribing the Descriptions of Modernity*, ed. William Rasch. Stanford: Stanford University Press, pp. 128–52.

Luhmann, Niklas (2002b) "Deconstruction as Second-Order Observing," in *Theories of Distinction: Redescribing the Descriptions of Modernity*, ed. William Rasch. Stanford: Stanford University Press, pp. 94–112.

Luhmann, Niklas (2002c) "What is Communication?" in *Theories of Distinction: Redescribing the Descriptions of Modernity*, ed. William Rasch. Stanford: Stanford University Press, pp. 155–68.

Lukács, Georg (2002) *History and Class Consciousness: Studies in Marxist Dialectics*, trans. Rodney Livingstone. Cambridge, MA: MIT Press.

Malabou, Catherine (2008) *What Should We Do With Our Brain?*, trans. Sebastian Rand. New York: Fordham University Press.

Marx, Karl (1978) "Economic and Philosophic Manuscripts of 1844," in *The Marx-Engels Reader: Second Edition*, ed. Robert C. Tucker. New York: W. W. Norton.

Marx, Karl (1990) *Capital: Volume 1*. New York: Penguin Classics.

Massey, Doreen (2005) *For Space*. Los Angeles: Sage.

Massumi, Brian (2002) *Parables for the Virtual: Movement, Affect, Sensation*. Durham, NC: Duke University Press.

Massumi, Brian (2011) *Semblance and Event: Activist Philosophy and the Occurrent Arts*, Cambridge, MA: MIT Press.

Maturana, Humberto R. and Varela, Francisco J. (1998) *The Tree of Knowledge: The Biological Roots of Human Understanding.* Boston: Shambhala.

McLuhan, Marshall (1994) *Understanding Media: The Extensions of Man.* Cambridge, MA: MIT Press.

McLuhan, Marshall and McLuhan, Eric (1998) *Laws of Media: The New Science.* Toronto: University of Toronto Press.

Metzinger, Thomas (2009) *The Ego Tunnel: The Science of Mind and the Myth of the Self.* New York: Basic Books.

Miéville, China (2010) *The City & The City.* New York: Del Ray.

Miller, Adam (2013) *Speculative Grace: Bruno Latour and Object-Oriented Theology.* New York: Fordham University Press.

Minard, Anne (2008) "'Weird Beastie' Shrimp Have Super-Vision," *National Geographic News*, May 19, available at <http://news.nationalgeographic.com/news/2008/05/080519-shrimp-colors.html>.

Mineault, Patrick J. (2011) "What's the Maximal Frame Rate Humans Can Perceive," at *XCORR Computational Neuroscience*, November 20, available at <http://xcorr.net/2011/11/20/whats-the-maximal-frame-rate-humans-can-perceive/>.

Molnar, Georg (2006) *Powers: A Study in Metaphysics.* Oxford: Oxford University Press.

Mori, Scott (2008) "Brazil Nut (*Bertholletia excelsa*)," *The Encyclopedia of Earth*, August 23, available at <http://www.eoearth.org/article/Brazil_nut_%28Bertholletia_excelsa%29>.

Morton, Timothy (2007) *Ecology Without Nature: Rethinking Environmental Aesthetics.* Cambridge, MA: Harvard University Press.

Morton, Timothy (2010) *The Ecological Thought.* Cambridge, MA: Harvard University Press.

Nagel, Thomas (1974) "What Is It Like to Be a Bat?" *Philosophical Review*, 83 (4): 435–50.

Negarestani, Reza (2008) *Cyclonopedia: Complicity With Anonymous Materials.* Melbourne: Re.Press.

Okrent, Mark (2007) *Rational Animals: The Teleological Roots of Intentionality.* Athens, OH: Ohio University Press.

Ong, Walter J. (2002) *Orality & Literacy.* New York: Routledge.

Oyama, Susan (2000) *The Ontogeny of Information: Developmental Systems and Evolution.* Durham, NC: Duke University Press.

Oyama, Susan (2001) "Terms in Tension: What Do You Do When All the Good Words Are Taken?" in Susan Oyama, Paul E. Griffiths, and

Russell D. Gray (eds),*Cycles of Contingency: Developmental Systems and Evolution*. Cambridge, MA: MIT Press.

Oyama, Susan, Griffiths, Paul E., and Gray, Russell D. (eds) (2001) *Cycles of Contingency: Developmental Systems and Evolution*. Cambridge, MA: MIT Press.

PBS (2008) "Deep Jungle: Monsters of the Forest – The Amazing Brazil Nut Tree," in *Nature*, available at <http://www.pbs.org/wnet/nature/episodes/deep-jungle-monsters-of-the-forest/the-amazing-brazil-nut-tree/3365/>.

Peirce, John R. (1980) *An Introduction to Information Theory: Symbols, Signals, and Noise*. New York: Dover.

Plato (1989) *Republic*, in *Plato: Collected Dialogues*, ed. Edith Hamilton and Huntington Cairns. Princeton: Princeton University Press.

Pogge, Richard W. (2009) "Real-World Relativity: The GPS Navigation System," April 27, available at <http://www.astronomy.ohio-state.edu/~pogge/Ast162/Unit5/gps.html>.

Pollan, Michael (2002) *The Botany of Desire: A Plant's Eye View of the World*. New York: Random House.

Rancière, Jacques (1999) *Disagreement: Politics and Philosophy*, trans. Julie Rose. Minneapolis: University of Minnesota Press.

Robinson, Kim Stanley (1993) *Red Mars (Mars Trilogy)*. New York: Spectra Books.

Sartre, Jean-Paul (1956) *Being and Nothing: An Essay on Phenomenological Ontology*, trans. Hazel E. Barnes. New York: Philosophical Library.

Sartre, Jean-Paul (2004) *Critique of Dialectical Reason: Volume One*, trans. Alan Sheridan-Smith. New York: Verso.

Science Daily (2008) "Mother's Diet Influences Infant Sex: High Energy Intake Linked to Conception of Sons," April 23, available at <http://www.sciencedaily.com/releases/2008/04/080422194553.htm>.

Serres, Michel (2000) *The Birth of Physics*, trans. Jack Hawkes. Manchester: Clinamen Press.

Serres, Michel (2007) *The Parasite*, trans. Lawrence R. Schehr. Minneapolis: University of Minnesota Press.

Serres, Michel and Latour, Bruno (1995) *Conversations on Science, Culture, and Time*, trans. Roxanne Lapidus. Ann Arbor: University of Michigan Press.

Simondon, Gilbert (1995) *L'individuation à la lumière des notions de forme et d'information*. Paris: PUF.

Spinoza, Benedict de (2002) *Ethics*, in *Spinoza: Complete Works*, ed. Michael L. Morgan. Indianapolis: Hackett.

Srnicek, Nick (2012) "Navigating Neoliberalism: Political Aesthetics After the Crisis," The Matter of Contradiction Conference, Limousin, France, September 8, available at <http://vimeo.com/52434614>.

Sterelny, Kim (2001) "Niche Construction, Developmental Systems, and the Extended Replicator," in Susan Oyama, Paul E. Griffiths, and Russell D. Gray (eds), Cycles of Contingency: Developmental Systems and Evolution. Cambridge, MA: MIT Press.

Sterelny, Kim (2003) Thought in a Hostile World: The Evolution of Human Cognition. Malden, MA: Blackwell.

Taylor, David (1999) "Tasty Brazil Nuts Stun Harvesters and Scientists," in Smithsonian Magazine, April, available at <http://www.smithsonianmag.com/science-nature/object_apr99.html>.

Uexküll, Jakob von, (2010) A Foray Into the Worlds of Animals and Humans, with A Theory of Meaning. Minneapolis: University of Minnesota Press.

Vernant, Jean-Pierre (1982) The Origins of Greek Thought. Ithaca: Cornell University Press.

Watts, Peter (2008) Blindsight. New York: Tor Books.

Whitehead, Alfred North (1978) Process and Reality. New York: Free Press.

Wollstonecraft, Mary (2009) A Vindication of the Rights of Women and a Vindication of the Rights of Men. Oxford: Oxford University Press.

Žižek, Slavoj (1997) The Plague of Fantasies. New York: Verso.

Žižek, Slavoj (1989) The Sublime Object of Ideology. New York: Verso Books.

Žižek, Slavoj (2006) The Parallax View. Cambridge, MA: MIT Press.

Index